P9-APK-938

VOLUME 551

MONTGOMERY COLLEGE
ROCKVILLE CAMPUS LIBRARY
ROCKVILLE, MARYLAND
MAY 1997

THE ANNALS

of The American Academy *of* Political
and Social Science

ALAN W. HESTON, *Editor*
NEIL A. WEINER, *Assistant Editor*

GLOBALIZATION AND THE
CHANGING U.S. CITY

Special Editor of this Volume

DAVID WILSON
University of Illinois
Urbana–Champaign

WITHDRAWN FROM LIBRARY

 SAGE Periodicals Press   *THOUSAND OAKS   LONDON   NEW DELHI*

MAY 2 8 1997

The American Academy of Political and Social Science

3937 Chestnut Street   Philadelphia, Pennsylvania 19104

Board of Directors

ELMER B. STAATS	LYNN A. CURTIS
MARVIN E. WOLFGANG	MARY ANN MEYERS
RICHARD D. LAMBERT	SARA MILLER McCUNE
LLOYD N. CUTLER	KATHLEEN HALL JAMIESON
HENRY W. SAWYER, III	IRA A. LIPMAN
ANTHONY J. SCIRICA	ELIJAH ANDERSON
FREDERICK HELDRING	

Officers

President
MARVIN E. WOLFGANG

Vice President
RICHARD D. LAMBERT, First Vice President

Secretary   Treasurer   Counsel
ANTHONY J. SCIRICA   ELMER B. STAATS   HENRY W. SAWYER, III

Business Manager
MARY E. PARKER

Editors, THE ANNALS

ALAN W. HESTON, Editor   RICHARD D. LAMBERT, Editor Emeritus
ERICA GINSBURG, Managing Editor   NEIL A. WEINER, Assistant Editor

Origin and Purpose. The Academy was organized December 14, 1889, to promote the progress of political and social science, especially through publications and meetings. The Academy does not take sides in controverted questions, but seeks to gather and present reliable information to assist the public in forming an intelligent and accurate judgment.

Meetings. The Academy occasionally holds a meeting in the spring extending over two days.

Publications. THE ANNALS is the bimonthly publication of The Academy. Each issue contains articles on some prominent social or political problem, written at the invitation of the editors. Also, monographs are published from time to time, numbers of which are distributed to pertinent professional organizations. These volumes constitute important reference works on the topics with which they deal, and they are extensively cited by authorities throughout the United States and abroad. The papers presented at the meetings of The Academy are included in THE ANNALS.

Membership. Each member of The Academy receives THE ANNALS and may attend the meetings of The Academy. Membership is open only to individuals. Annual dues: $51.00 for the regular paperbound edition (clothbound, $74.00). Add $12.00 per year for membership outside the U.S.A. Members may also purchase single issues of THE ANNALS for $15.00 each (clothbound, $19.00). Add $2.00 for shipping and handling on all prepaid orders.

Subscriptions. THE ANNALS (ISSN 0002-7162) is published six times annually—in January, March, May, July, September, and November. Institutions may subscribe to THE ANNALS at the annual rate: $220.00 (clothbound, $260.00). Add $12.00 per year for subscriptions outside the U.S.A. Institutional rates for single issues: $39.00 each (clothbound, $45.00).

Periodical postage paid at Thousand Oaks, California, and additional offices.

Single issues of THE ANNALS may be obtained by individuals who are not members of The Academy for $19.00 each (clothbound, $29.00). Add $2.00 for shipping and handling on all prepaid orders. Single issues of THE ANNALS have proven to be excellent supplementary texts for classroom use. Direct inquiries regarding adoptions to THE ANNALS c/o Sage Publications (address below).

All correspondence concerning membership in The Academy, dues renewals, inquiries about membership status, and/or purchase of single issues of THE ANNALS should be sent to THE ANNALS c/o Sage Publications, Inc., 2455 Teller Road, Thousand Oaks, CA 91320. Telephone: (805) 499-0721; FAX/Order line: (805) 499-0871. Please note that orders under $30 must be prepaid. Sage affiliates in London and India will assist institutional subscribers abroad with regard to orders, claims, and inquiries for both subscriptions and single issues.

Printed on recycled, acid-free paper

THE ANNALS

© 1997 *by* The American Academy *of* Political *and* Social Science

All rights reserved. No part of this volume may be reproduced or utilized in any form or by any means, electronic or mechanical, including photocopying, recording or by any information storage and retrieval system, without permission in writing from the publisher. All inquiries for reproduction or permission should be sent to Sage Publications, 2455 Teller Road, Thousand Oaks, CA 91320.

Editorial Office: 3937 Chestnut Street, Philadelphia, PA 19104.

For information about membership* (individuals only) and subscriptions (institutions), address:

SAGE PUBLICATIONS, INC.
2455 Teller Road
Thousand Oaks, CA 91320

From India and South Asia,
write to:
SAGE PUBLICATIONS INDIA Pvt. Ltd
P.O. Box 4215
New Delhi 110 048
INDIA

From the UK, Europe, the Middle
East and Africa, write to:
SAGE PUBLICATIONS LTD
6 Bonhill Street
London EC2A 4PU
UNITED KINGDOM

SAGE Production Staff: KELLY GUNTHER, ERIC LAW, DORIS HUS, and ROSE TYLAK
*Please note that members of The Academy receive THE ANNALS with their membership.
Library of Congress Catalog Card Number 96-69574
International Standard Serial Number ISSN 0002-7162
International Standard Book Number ISBN 0-7619-0705-X (Vol. 551, 1997 paper)
International Standard Book Number ISBN 0-7619-0704-1 (Vol. 551, 1997 cloth)
Manufactured in the United States of America. First printing, May 1997.

The articles appearing in THE ANNALS are indexed in *Academic Index, Book Review Index, Combined Retrospective Index Sets, Current Contents, General Periodicals Index, Public Affairs Information Service Bulletin, Pro-Views,* and *Social Sciences Index.* They are also abstracted and indexed in *ABC Pol Sci, America: History and Life, Automatic Subject Citation Alert, Book Review Digest, Family Resources Database, Higher Education Abstracts, Historical Abstracts, Human Resources Abstracts, International Political Science Abstracts, Managing Abstracts, Periodica Islamica, Sage Urban Studies Abstracts, Social Planning/Policy & Development Abstracts, Social Sciences Citation Index, Social Work Research & Abstracts, Sociological Abstracts, United States Political Science Documents,* and/or *Work Related Abstracts, Westlaw,* and are available on microfilm from University Microfilms, Ann Arbor, Michigan.

Information about membership rates, institutional subscriptions, and back issue prices may be found on the facing page.

Advertising. Current rates and specifications may be obtained by writing to THE ANNALS Advertising and Promotion Manager at the Thousand Oaks office (address above).

Claims. Claims for undelivered copies must be made no later than twelve months following month of publication. The publisher will supply missing copies when losses have been sustained in transit and when the reserve stock will permit.

Change of Address. Six weeks' advance notice must be given when notifying of change of address to ensure proper identification. Please specify name of journal. Send address changes to: THE ANNALS, c/o Sage Publications, Inc., 2455 Teller Road, Thousand Oaks, CA 91320.

THE ANNALS

of The American Academy *of* Political *and* Social Science

ALAN W. HESTON, *Editor*
NEIL A. WEINER, *Assistant Editor*

―――――――― **FORTHCOMING** ――――――――

STRENGTHENING TRANSITIONAL
DEMOCRACIES THROUGH CONFLICT RESOLUTION
Special Editors: Raymond Shonholtz and Ilana Shapiro
Volume 552   July 1997

TRANSPORT AT THE MILLENNIUM
Special Editor: Stanley G. Long
Volume 553   September 1997

UNDERSTANDING THE NGO PHENOMENON
Special Editors: Jude Fernando, Alan W. Heston,
and Abigail McGowan
Volume 554   November 1997

―――――――――――――――――――――――――――――――――――――

See page 2 for information on Academy membership and
purchase of single volumes of **The Annals.**

CONTENTS

BOOK DEPARTMENT CONTENTS

PREFACE

Under the onslaught of globalization, North American cities are changing dramatically. This process—anything but new—today exhibits a new character and intensity that places cities within dramatically transforming economic and social networks. Hyperactive flows of investment, seamlessly penetrating the city, transform aging downtowns into glittering consumption landscapes. Business decisions thousands of miles away close plants and factories, thereby sending cities into tailspins. Cities compete desperately and ferociously to attract jobs and investment in a fight for survival. And the dizzying arrival of new commodities and fashions reverberates through the urban everyday to resculpt cultural fabrics. In this city, a heightened commodification and search for global purpose alter urban culture, politics, and civic life in fundamental ways.

But this poignant change is merely one in a historical set of transformations that has altered North American cities. What is different about this one? Most fundamentally, it creates an unparalleled scale of operation—the global—that links places like never before. The North American city hooks up with faraway control points that render places pieces in a global whole. Furthermore, city life, inexorably colliding with a global culture of consumption, becomes startlingly commodified. With a frenetic international financial system and media flowing exuberantly through daily life's circuitry, commodification now penetrates the everyday's furthest corners. To this set of changes, Jerry Mander declares that globalization involves the most fundamental redesign of political and economic arrangement since the Industrial Revolution.[1]

Globalization stems from the ruptured and rebuilt international economy of the 1970s. Out of ominous economic stagnation, enterprise decisions to "globalize" supported by governments and technology recrafted economic stabilization and orderly profit taking. Banks, financial companies, service providers, and manufacturers spawned global webs of operation, with spaces of operation rendered far-flung and increasingly replaceable. Like interchangeable pieces in a puzzle, spaces could be assembled and disassembled to ensure orderly entrepreneurialism. Like other landscapes, cities frequently became discardable staging grounds for business usage. If a city was "uncooperative" or outgrew its usefulness, another staging ground could be found. In this way, globalization has dramatically de-linked business enterprises from their place-based employees.

Cities become victims, beneficiaries, or survivors in this new reality. Renouncing community roots, enterprises stake out desires and expect them

1. Jerry Mander, "The Dark Side of Globalization: What the Media Are Missing," *Nation*, 15-22 July 1996, pp. 8-16

to be met. Not to meet them is to risk ruthless punishment by the withholding or withdrawal of the lifeblood of cities: jobs and investment. Of course, economic enterprises, recognizing their crucial municipal role, have always made demands on the North American city. Increasingly, however, these demands are uncompromising and threatening. Threats to go elsewhere (the suburbs, out of state, abroad), a common reality, now typically leverage massive tax abatements, land write-downs, and provision of physical infrastructure. In this context, city-company bargaining assumes a new ominousness; its outcome can replenish or devastate cities.

Yet cities do devise strategies to attract and retain investment and jobs, sometimes very successfully. Recent entrepreneurialism in Cleveland and Indianapolis is testimonial. Cleveland, "the Comeback City" and "the Big Plum," rose from the ashes of industrial decimation to strengthen and diversify its economy. Indianapolis, long dubbed "Indiana-no-place" for its lackluster ambiance and economy, today revels in a "Jewel of the Rustbelt" moniker. Marketing itself as an amateur sports capital and recreational haven, the city has seen resounding economic and job growth. It is small wonder, then, that stepped-up efforts by cities to sell investment climates and livability have coincided with the global economy's emergence. But for too many places, a disadvantaged setting in the global economy makes turn-around difficult; entrepreneurial embellishment can take them only so far.

The impact of the new hypermobile business enterprise on the North American city is also complicated by its uneven intra-urban effect. The North American city is, typically, a diverse entity with disparate populations, neighborhoods, and economic sectors. New York and Toronto, for example, contain over forty economic sectors; some boom and others stagnate amid globalism. Microelectronics firms, to illustrate, recently underwent spectacular growth, unlike heavy manufacturing and aerospace firms. Moreover, within each sector, people in different occupational slots unevenly benefit. Typically, corporate executives benefit more than middle-level managers and workers. At the bottom of the rung, low-level workers benefit least. They are the people often left out of the global bounty, much as deteriorating neighborhoods hungry for investment see the creation of nearby glossy consumption districts.

IMPACTS OF GLOBALIZATION

The impacts of globalization on the North American city are numerous. Most visibly, it is creating the new fractured and fragmented city. Business and industry, increasingly tied to global chains, wall themselves off and create vast detached spaces in the city. In this process, these land users, once rooted to place, increasingly link to distant control cities rather than to local downtowns or neighborhoods. For example, high-technology parks fenced off from decline and abandonment busily churn out specialized products often for a global market. Banks tied to global networks, moreover, draw their brain power from a global labor pool and invest their assets in Third World countries. Such nodes, localized in appearance only, are at the heart of the fragmenting North American city, with its vibrant points engulfed by neglected interstitial spaces. Most perniciously, vast swaths of land abandoned by the vagaries of the global economy continue to expand.

At the same time, residential segregation in the city is intensifying (but see the article in this volume by Bashi and Hughes). On top of an already immense and calcified pattern of segregation, the major beneficiaries of globalization—corporate managers and executives—continue to live in, and reinforce the exclusivity of, posh suburban areas and gentrified enclaves. For these people, the metropolitan area is ripe for residential plucking. Lesser beneficiaries of globalization—service workers and laborers—continue to live in lesser urban neighborhoods. At the lowest end of the continuum, low-wage and chronically unemployed workers (sometimes called the urban underclass) often live within eyeshot of gleaming office towers or spectacular homes but are miles from these worlds materially. Among the many barriers that confine them to dilapidated neighborhoods—steering by real estate agents; municipal zoning; provision of squalid public housing—low wages in the global economy are a dominant underpinning.

Globalization is also changing the city's political and social fabric. Politically, the city is increasingly managed in a larger influencing setting. It toils to find its place in a harsh global reality, with politics increasingly about city selling: government efficiency, civic entrepreneurialism, public-private partnerships, and business growth. Public provision of welfare and services is subsumed by a more outward-looking stance emphasizing economic development and city growth. Once distinctive private sector responsibilities now fall to government: salesmanship, profit seeking, risk taking, and the selling of locality. The city now anchors the "urban entrepreneurial machine," the nexus of institutions that scramble to secure resources for city survival. While a politics of resource distribution and a politics of growth can coexist, currently the latter dominates the former.

Now city leaders work feverishly to attract resources. City leaders commonly present residential quality of life as bound up with the attracting (rather than the distribution) of city resources. With businesses flaunting their mobility, city leaders labor to convert the urban populace to their cause. Their mission, they proclaim, is the residents' mission: to improve quality of life for all via building new upscale housing, recreational facilities, cultural complexes, and urban malls. With often little explanation, these are trumpeted as the keys to a benefiting of everyone regardless of race, ethnicity, and economic standing. This ideology of urban aestheticization, as I have called it elsewhere, presents everyone as having the same needs and tastes.[2] In the end, the principle of what we can get, rather than how resources are distributed or who benefits, becomes the dogma of the day.

2. David Wilson, "Metaphors, Growth Coalition Discourses, and Black Poverty Neighborhoods in a U.S. City," *Antipode*, pp. 72-96 (Jan. 1996).

This transformed politics, sometimes called "the new urban politics," is underlain by the crucial symbolic remaking of what the city is and strives for.[3] The city and its "dreams," offered to the public through the crafting of social "objects," become the grid of representations through which urban entrepreneurialism is unswervingly pursued. Such symbolic objects—what the city is, what growth is, what the urban gentry is, what urban planners are—form a matrix of meanings whose consumption by the public legitimates this political agenda. The city, then, becomes iconographically remade to suit its current interests, a point aptly described by Jonathan Rabin: "The city goes soft; it awaits the imprint of an identity . . . it invites you to remake it, consolidate it into a shape you can live in . . . decide who you are and the city will again assume a fixed form around you."[4]

The city is also changing socially. Most fundamentally, social worlds in cities are converging in a commodified homogenization that is, ironically enough, deeply rooted and difficult to explain. On the one hand, the local culture's deepened commodification breeds a uniform set of meanings and values. People now eat the same food, consume the same media images, wear the same clothing, and think the same thoughts about people and processes in their city. In its most garish manifestations, as Helena Norberg-Hodge notes, Barbi and Madonna are accepted icons and the Marlboro Man and Rambo define the male ideal.[5] Such icons are piped nonstop into homes that make everyone gazers and absorbers of commodified culture. More penetratingly, however, the very character of cities, their problems, and possibilities are seen similarly and in a distinctive way. People come to apprehend their city through the lens of the growth machine's needs that purportedly give the city vibrancy.

This sameness suits the requirements of business and government enterprises, which profit from the homogeneity of visions and the predictability of standardized consumption. Urban people across vast spaces are increasingly interchangeable, thinking the same thoughts about their lives, their neighbors, their cities, and their worlds. Spatial barriers become artifacts of the past, simple administrative units that enclose globally tinged inhabitants. Culture now becomes central to the city-building and profit-making apparatuses, a relationship that undermines cultural diversity and uniqueness.

On the other hand, global capitalism's multitextured complexities make this convergent social world less easy to read. Electronic images traveling in hyper time bombard the senses with sophisticated codings about people, places, and processes. In the hands of corporate advertising and media, such representations are multilayered and deeply textured. Techniques like simile,

3. Kevin Cox, "Globalization, Competition and Politics of Local Economic Development," *Urban Studies*, 32:213-24 (1995).

4. Quoted in Linda McDowell, "The Transformation of Cultural Geography," in *Human Geography: Society, Space, and Social Science*, ed. D. Gregory, R. Martin, and G. Smith (Minneapolis: University of Minnesota Press, 1994), pp. 146-73.

5. Helena Norberg-Hodge, "Break Up the Monoculture," *Nation*, 15-22 July 1996, pp. 20-23.

metaphor, metonymy, and sanitary coding offer new and complex tropes that complicate signification. Through these representations (rather than a "real" reality), people make sense of their world, which structures their understanding of themselves, others, city problems, and city possibilities.

The perniciousness of this process is obvious. The age-old problems of the city persist—poverty, substandard housing, crumbling infrastructure, crime—but their sources are difficult to pinpoint. As Nigel Thrift notes, the Four Horsemen of the Apocalypse—poverty, famine, war, disease—still stalk the social scene but all we can see are the hoofprints.[6] People stumble through life acutely aware of its complexities but dimly aware of the causes behind them. People experience what Thrift identifies as a kind of vertigo, a sense of an unseen abyss in the collective social fabric whose origins are a mystery.[7] In this new world, the archetypal person is thrown into a maelstrom of sophisticated significations. People work through a city life whose speed and complexity seem to indicate a world spiraling out of control. It is not only that the world is more complex; the representations that organize our world are also more complex.

ARTICLES IN THIS ISSUE

This issue of *The Annals* illuminates globalization and the North American city from a range of viewpoints and in their diverse dimensions. Our focus is on broad characteristics, concrete effects, associated problems and possibilities, and policy implications. In the investigations that follow, two themes cut through all. First, globalization is a powerful urban influence rooted in economic restructuring. It has complex dimensions—social, political, spatial—steeped in new economic reaches, ways of producing, and things that are produced. Second, cities are never passive in the face of globalization but always mediate it and negotiate it in complex ways. In this sense, cities are unpredictable landscapes that shape globalization's character as they also reflect it.

In the first article, Paul Knox provides an overview of globalization, urban economic change, and city evolution. International economic change is seen to lie at the heart of an emergent global space and a restructured North American city. Its producing of global commodity chains eclipses the traditional role of the city as local producer and distributor. Roots that were once local are increasingly severed and supplanted by global economic imperatives, altering the character of labor forces, political currents, and built environments. While some cities have become global directorships, managing and maintaining commodity chains, other places are constituent participants. Their economic fortunes are based on finding and securing a niche in commodity chains, a task that such cities compete for and struggle through.

6. Nigel Thrift, "A Hyperactive World," in *Geographies of Global Change: Remapping the World in the Late Twentieth Century*, ed. R. J. Johnston, P. J. Taylor, and M. J. Watts (Cambridge, MA: Basil Blackwell, 1995), p. 256.

7. Ibid., p. 20.

Susan Clarke and Gary Gaile examine a basic dimension of the changing North American city, "the new urban politics." They argue that this politics—oriented to attracting external investment and jobs—is best understood in terms of the ideas and understandings concerning globalization produced. Local politics is more than a matter of new interests or desires prompted by globalization; it is the causal stories about globalization through which people come to understand life. These stories, spun differently across urban places, implant globalization's influence in the everyday. From this, the public forges notions of city problems, possibilities, villains, and saviors amid urban change. Economics, then, is always social, a set of processes known through representation and situated within common understandings.

Peter Muller examines another basic dimension of the changing North American metropolis, the new urban mosaic and the emerging outer suburb. Miller scrutinizes five dominant perspectives in current urban theory and contends that they all provide an undeniable interpretation: globalization is accelerating outer suburban growth. Here, Muller believes, a new urban future is being built that is powering metropolitan and "world city growth." Suburban business complexes control and coordinate global networks—particularly in the largest metropolitan areas—that constitute the nub of metropolitan economic growth. The outer suburbs continue to prosper; the city continues to struggle. This development, the continuation of long-term trends, promises to be further exacerbated. Its social and economic implications, according to Muller, will be enormous.

Jeffrey Morenoff and Marta Tienda begin a foray into the problems associated with globalization. They examine the links between a changing urban ecology and the rise of globalization in Chicago. Five new ecological trends—the underclass's increasing social isolation, its growing spatial isolation, the eclipse of working-class areas, the rise of identifiable Hispanic neighborhoods, the presence of race-specific kinds of neighborhood upgrading—are identified and situated within the global trend of falling wages. Cities like Chicago are more than ever globally influenced. Intensified poverty and socioracial polarization follow from a growing global inequality that disadvantages vast places and populations. To Morenoff and Tienda, this situation is likely to worsen as globalization accelerates.

In a similar vein, Kingsley Haynes and Roger Stough probe the dilemma of insufficient federal policy to combat the forces of globalization. To Haynes and Stough, there is not yet a coherent and well-articulated response to regional transformation under globalization. Instead, federal sectoral policies have been relied on: transportation, housing, environment, and national defense. Using the national capital region as a particular case, Haynes and Stough unearth general outcomes of this response. They find the results mixed and inconclusive, and suggest the need for more generally cast and encompassing policy to cope with globalization's restructuring tendencies.

Changing the focus to globalization's impacts, Glenda Laws, Vilna Bashi, and Mark Alan Hughes address the closely linked issues of racial segregation and socioeconomic marginalization but with different visions. Whereas Laws places globalization at the center of socioeconomic marginalizing, Bashi and Hughes dismiss its influence on racial segregation. To Laws, the global economy's tentacles strangle the social footing of many. Its increasingly coordinated uneven development and production of poverty leaves many people poor, forced to migrate, and subsequently mired in deprivation. Bashi and Hughes, in contrast, place segregation squarely in the realm of local housing dynamics and racial attitudes. They contend that globalization does not affect everything and has little impact on racial segregation. Four leading conceptions of globalization are probed and found to be wanting as causal constructs.

David Bartelt, Greg Dimitriadis, and George Kamberelis continue the exploration of globalization's impacts by examining the issues of urban housing and urban education. Bartelt implicates globalization in the accelerated disinvestment and decline of vast portions of Philadelphia. Housing quality, a crucial life determinant, is purportedly structured more by transnational systems and organizations than by local entrepreneurs. Philadelphia's housing quandaries—spiraling abandonment, lessened affordability, growing homelessness—are logical by-products of transnational corporate power and their imperatives to accumulate that are manifested in new global capital flows, migration streams, and transnational business relocation patterns. Bartelt believes Philadelphia is unique in important respects, but its housing conditions are fundamentally shaped by place in a global hierarchy.

Dimitriadis and Kamberelis review discourses in urban educational curricula, linking their content to the process of mass globalization. They examine key themes—the educational needs of marginalized children, preparing students for the information age, reshaping schools to fit changing demographics, countering the influence of mass media images—as responses to the reality of local immobility and capital hypermobility. In a world of restless capital flows, the spontaneous spread of information, and poignant commodification, human concerns become inscribed in school curricula. Curricula here are human constructions generated in a power-laden and inequality-plagued world. Although they frequently embody a rhetoric of social democracy, school curricula often mirror and thus reproduce prevailing social conditions, powers, and concerns. To be more effective agents of social change, Dimitriadis and Kamberelis argue, curricula must be more responsive to the material conditions of students and schools and more wary of their rhetorical dimensions.

Michael Dear, Steven Flusty, and Jan Nijman begin a probing of globalization in international cities, examining Los Angeles and Miami. Dear and Flusty see Los Angeles as the quintessential U.S. postmodern city, a balkanized collage of spaces devoid of conventional centers. Los Angeles, to Dear and Flusty, is the prototype of the acutely fragmented but globally specialized urban form. It is splintered, amorphous, and assiduously specialized in economic purpose, making it simultaneously disordered and ordered, shapeless but acutely patterned. Three thousand miles from Los Angeles, Miami is unveiled in a strikingly similar way. Nijman situates Miami at the intersection of globalization's materialist imperatives and its unplanned social consequences. Its social fabric, complex and fragmented, is thinly held together by the ideology of multiculturalism, which is warily received by many. Miami, to Nijman, is a controlled chaos, a place of turbulence whose economic niche fits uncomfortably onto a straining population.

Continuing the focus, Richard Greene and Ray Bromley examine the dynamics of Chicago and New York City. Greene investigates the interconnections of globalization's producing flexible manufacturing and producer services with newly arriving immigrant lives. He discovers that new immigrants to Chicago encounter a new employment landscape of reduced wages and nominal job security. At the same time, traditional inner-city assimilationist neighborhoods are increasingly closed to them, being occupied by entrenched poor populations. Bromley unveils the Bronx's rich tapestry of neighborhoods and their ties to globalization with focus on one section, Community Board 6. Here is the other side of New York's globalization, the spaces commonly depicted as simple sources of labor and consumption. A steady influx of immigrants, changing economic composition, and fluid social worlds make this area a dynamically lived home intimately tied to national and increasingly global forces. Globalization, to Bromley, cuts through all and leaves no part of lived urban experience untouched.

A final set of articles narrows the focus to the regional city. In the first two, Barney Warf, Brian Holly, and Carolyn Adams examine the changing character of Cleveland and Philadelphia. Warf and Holly trace Cleveland's fight to rebound from a traumatic deindustrialization of the 1970s. The city's unexpected renaissance is tied to fortuitous circumstances: a changing competitive position within a national and increasingly global division of labor. Cleveland's much-hyped astute city-selling is seen as secondary to the serendipitous evolution of place in the global economy that made conditions ripe for economic resurgence. Adams, similarly, traces global influences on Philadelphia, finding the growing manifestations of globalization but also an increasingly locally oriented economy. The manifestations of globalization—increased foreign investment, aligning business partnerships, growing international labor, an expanding informal economy—are tempered by the rise of local consumer services as they replace shrinking manufacturing.

The final article, by Kenneth Reardon, examines the changing character of the quintessential abandoned city in America, East St. Louis. Reardon reconstructs the city's past as a prelude to understanding its current circumstance, a city slowly upgrading through prudent government intervention. Its decline, climaxing in a 1991 economic collapse that rendered it incapable of providing basic services, left it reeling and bankrupt. Reardon places this urban problematic in a global context and believes enlightened response to globalization's ills arrested its decline. Human action, in the end, has an important role to play in the fight against urban abandonment. Without it, Reardon contends, cities like East St. Louis are destined to suffer immensely under globalization's devastating effects.

DAVID WILSON

ANNALS, *AAPSS*, **551**, May 1997

Globalization and Urban Economic Change

By PAUL L. KNOX

ABSTRACT: The reorganization of global space that has been set in motion over the past quarter century by processes of international economic change has had some important consequences for North American cities. Traditionally, cities' economic functions have been to organize and facilitate production and distribution within local, regional, and national spaces. Increasingly, these functions are being eclipsed by cities' roles as nodal points in global commodity chains. In this context, a few cities have acquired world city status because of their involvement in linking and shaping whole complexes of commodity chains. In most other cities, the globalizing world economy can be seen in the changes of economic fortune attached to the ebbs and flows of foreign direct investment, imports, and exports, and in the local economic restructuring and spatial reorganization driven by a new international division of labor.

Paul Knox is currently University Distinguished Professor and professor of urban affairs and planning at Virginia Tech. His publications include The Restless Urban Landscape *(1993) and, coedited with Peter Taylor,* World Cities in a World-System *(1995).*

A T the beginning of the 1990s, before he became U.S. labor secretary, Robert Reich wrote:

We are living through a transformation that will rearrange the politics and economics of the coming century. There will be no national products or technologies, no national corporations, no national industries. There will no longer be national economies, at least as we have come to understand that concept. . . . As almost every factor of production—money, technology, factories, and equipment—moves effortlessly across borders, the very idea of an American economy is becoming meaningless, as are the notions of an American corporation, American capital, American products, and American technology.[1]

Reich was not alone in voicing the breadth and depth of change associated with economic globalization. It had already become a major theme throughout the social sciences, raising some vexed questions for traditional disciplinary approaches, especially in politics and economics. Without national borders and national institutions as natural frameworks for the circulation and reproduction of capital, a lot of conventional academic wisdom, along with its apparatus of analysis, becomes less convincing. The realities of globalization have forced us to rethink many of our theories of economic change and to reconsider our ideas about people, place, and culture. Among other things, they have forced us to reconsider the effects of globalization on cities. In a globalizing world, systems of cities are com-

1. Robert Reich, *The Work of Nations: Preparing Ourselves for Twenty-First Century Capitalism* (New York: Vintage Books, 1991), pp. 3, 8.

ing into their own as the natural frameworks for the circulation and reproduction of capital.

GLOBALIZATION

Globalization is not entirely new, of course. The basic framework for globalization has been in place since the nineteenth century, when the competitive system of national states fostered the emergence of international agencies and institutions, global networks of communication, a standardized system of global time, international competitions and prizes, international law, and internationally shared notions of citizenship and human rights. Within this global framework, the roles of cities have been continuously revised and reorganized in response to the opportunities and constraints presented by successive technology systems and geopolitical regimes. In the process, cities themselves experienced successive rounds of physical and economic restructuring.

What is distinctive about the globalization of the past 25 years or so is that there has been a decisive shift in the proportion of the world's economic activity that is transnational in scope. Transnational corporations first began to appear in the nineteenth century, but until the mid-twentieth century there were only a few, most of them U.S.- or European-based transnationals that were concerned with obtaining raw materials such as oil or minerals for their domestic manufacturing operations. After World War II, an increasing number of large corporations began to invest in overseas production and manufacturing operations as a means of establishing a foothold in foreign consumer markets. Between 1957 and 1967, 20 percent of all new U.S. machinery plants, 25 percent of all new chemical plants, and over 30 percent of all new transport equipment plants were located abroad. By 1970, almost 75 percent of U.S. imports were transactions between the domestic and foreign subsidiaries of transnational conglomerates. By the end of the 1970s, overseas profits accounted for a third or more of the overall profits of the 100 largest transnational corporations. By the early 1980s, 40 percent of all world trade was in the form of intra-firm trade (that is, between different branches and companies of the same transnational conglomerate).

Between 1990 and 1995, U.S. overseas investment in manufacturing grew at twice the rate of exports of U.S.-manufactured goods. By the mid-1990s, there were nearly 40,000 transnational corporations in the world, 90 percent of which were headquartered in the United States, Japan, or the European Union. Between them, these corporations control about 180,000 foreign subsidiaries and account for over $6 trillion in worldwide sales. They have been central to the major new phase of global geographical restructuring that has been under way for the last 25 years or so, during which time an unprecedented amount of economic, political, social, and cultural activity has spilled beyond the geographic and institutional boundaries of national states.

The reason for this growth in the number and scale of transnational

conglomerate corporations was that international economic conditions had changed. Postwar restrictions on the international currency market were lifted in the 1960s, opening new possibilities for trade and investment. A recession in the 1970s, triggered by a massive increase in the price of crude oil, meant that companies everywhere had to reexamine their strategies. At the same time, technological developments in transport and communications provided larger companies with the flexibility and global reach to exploit the steep differentials in labor costs that exist between core countries and peripheral countries. (By 1995, U.S.-based companies employed about 5.5 million workers overseas, 80 percent of whom were in manufacturing jobs.) These same developments in transport and communications meanwhile made for a homogenization of consumer tastes and made it possible for companies to cater to global markets.

It was the consequent burst of transnational corporate activity that formed the basis of the recent globalization of the world economy. In effect, the playing field for large-scale businesses of all kinds had been marked out anew. Companies have had to rationalize their operations in a variety of ways, restructuring their activities and reorganizing and redeploying their resources between different countries, regions, and places. Local patterns of economic development have been recast and then recast again as these processes of restructuring, reorganization, and redeployment have been played out.

One particularly important dimension of this economic restructuring from the point of view of urban change has been the globalization of finance. Banking, finance, and business services are now no longer locally oriented ancillary activities but important global industries in their own right. The new importance of banking, finance, and business services was initially a result of globalization of manufacturing, an increase in the volume of world trade, and the emergence of transnational corporate empires. It was helped along by advances in telecommunications and data processing. Satellite communications systems and fiber-optic networks made it possible for firms to operate key financial and business services 24 hours a day, around the globe, handling an enormous volume of transactions.

But as banking, finance, and business services grew into important global activities, they were themselves transformed into something quite different from the old, locally oriented ancillary services. The global banking and financial network now handles trillions of dollars every day (estimates in 1995 ranged from $3 trillion to $7 trillion), no more than 10 percent of which has anything to do with the traditional world economy of trade in goods and services. International movements of money, bonds, securities, and other financial instruments have now become an end in themselves because they are a potential source of high profits from speculation and manipulation. There has, meanwhile, been a truly global shift in the location of major international banks. In 1973, three of the four largest banks in the world were headquar-

tered in the United States. By 1993, BankAmerica, which was the largest of all in 1973, had slipped to 43d place. Nine of the top 10 banks were Japanese, as were 15 of the top 20. The highest-ranked U.S. bank was Citibank, with total assets of about one-third the size of those of Tokyo's Fuji Bank, the largest bank in the world. Banks and financial corporations with the size and international reach of Citibank or Nomura or Salomon Brothers are able to influence local patterns and processes of economic development throughout the world, just like the major transnational conglomerates involved in globalized assembly lines.

All this adds up to an intensification of global connectedness and the beginnings of the world as one place. Or, to be more precise, it adds up this way for the 800 million or so of the world's population who are directly tied to global systems of production and consumption, and who have access to global networks of communication and knowledge. At first glance, it might seem that this global connectedness might render geography obsolete, reducing the differences between cities and leading to an ultimate convergence of function and appearance. High-technology communications and the global marketing of standardized products seem as if they might soon wash away the distinctiveness of people and places, permanently diminishing the importance of differences between cities.

Far from it. The new mobility of money, labor, products, and ideas actually increases the significance of place in some very real and important ways. The greater the reach of transnational corporations, the more easily they are able to respond to place-to-place variations in labor markets and consumer markets, and the more often and more radically that economic geography has to be reorganized. The more universal the diffusion of material culture and life-styles, the more valuable local identities become. The faster the information highway takes people into cyberspace, the more they feel the need for a subjective setting—a specific place or community—that they can call their own. All in all, the reality is that globalization is variously embraced, resisted, subverted, and exploited as it makes contact with specific settings. In the process, cities are modified and reconstructed, rather than being effaced or homogenized.

AMERICAN CITIES IN
THE WORLD ECONOMY

Today's world economy is constituted through a myriad of commodity chains that criss-cross global space. Commodity chains are networks of labor and production processes whose origin is in the extraction or production of raw materials and whose end result is the delivery and consumption of a finished commodity. They are, effectively, global assembly lines that are geared to produce global products for global markets. These assembly lines often span countries and continents, linking the production and supply of raw materials, the processing of raw materials, the production of components, the assembly of finished products, and the distribution of finished products into vast webs of interdependence.

It is within the context of these constantly changing chains of economic interdependence that urban restructuring must be understood. Some North American cities have come to occupy key strategic roles, effectively linking and shaping whole complexes of commodity chains. Others have humbler and more transient roles, reflecting this or that dimension of the global economy in microcosm.

There are in fact very few cities that can be said to occupy key strategic roles within the globalizing economy. These are the cities that have acquired the kind of infrastructure that is essential for the delivery of services to clients with an international scope of activity: specialized office space, financial exchanges, teleports, and communications networks. They have also established a comparative advantage in the mix of specialized firms and expert professionals that are on hand and in the high-order cultural amenities that are available (both to highly paid workers and their out-of-town business visitors). Above all, they have established themselves as centers of authority, with a critical mass of people-in-the-know about market conditions, trends, and innovations—people who can gain one another's trust through frequent face-to-face contact, not just in business settings but also in the informal settings of clubs and office bars. These places have become world cities—places that, in the globalized world economy, are able not only to generate powerful spirals of local economic development but also to act as pivotal points in the reorganization of global space: control centers for the flows of information, cultural products, and finance that, collectively, sustain the economic and cultural globalization of the world.

Ever since the evolution of a world economy in the sixteenth century, certain cities have played key roles in organizing space beyond their own national boundaries. In the first stages of the growth of the world economy, these key roles involved the organization of trade and the execution of colonial, imperial, and geopolitical strategies. The world cities of the seventeenth century were London, Amsterdam, Antwerp, Genoa, Lisbon, and Venice. In the eighteenth century, Paris, Rome, and Vienna also became world cities, while Antwerp and Genoa became less influential. In the nineteenth century, Berlin, Chicago, Manchester, New York, and St. Petersburg became world cities, while Venice became less influential.

Today, with the globalization of the economy, the key roles of world cities are concerned less with the deployment of imperial power and the orchestration of trade and more with transnational corporate organization, international banking and finance, supranational government, and the work of international agencies. These world cities represent the mega-cephalic corporate and financial dimension of globalization: centers of transnational corporate headquarters, of their business services, of international finance, of transnational institutions, and of telecommunications and information processing.

In New York, the United States has one of the three preeminent world cities, the other two being London and Tokyo. Their distinctive social and political attributes notwithstanding, the chief significance of world cities is their role as centers of authority and as settings conducive to the transaction of transnational business. Such functions are nearly impossible to quantify, though a reputational survey of 500 corporate executives in 32 countries placed 5 U.S. cities among the world's top 10 settings for transnational business.[2] In addition to New York, Atlanta, Chicago, San Francisco, and Miami made the top 10.

World cities also provide an interface between the global and the local. They contain the economic, cultural, and institutional apparatus that channels national and provincial resources into the global economy and that transmits the impulses of globalization back to national and provincial centers. As such, there are several functional characteristics of world cities:

1. They are the sites of most of the leading global markets for commodities, commodity futures, investment capital, foreign exchange, equities, and bonds.

2. They are the sites of clusters of specialized, high-order business services, especially those that are international in scope and that are attached to finance, accounting, advertising, property development, and law.

3. They are the sites of concentrations of corporate headquarters—not just of transnational corporations but

2. William Saporito, "The World's Best Cities for Business," *Fortune*, 14 Nov. 1994, pp. 112-18.

also of major national firms and large foreign firms.

4. They are the sites of concentrations of national and international headquarters of trade and professional associations.

5. They are the sites of most of the leading nongovernmental organizations and intergovernmental organizations that are international in scope (for example, the World Health Organization, UNESCO, the International Labor Organization, and the International Federation of Agricultural Producers).

6. They are the sites of the most powerful and internationally influential media organizations (including newspapers, magazines, book publishing, and satellite television), news and information services (including newswires and on-line information services), and cultural industries (including art and design, fashion, film, and television).

If the very peak of the global urban system is dominated by the three world cities whose influence is truly global (London, New York, and Tokyo), the second tier of the system consists of world cities with influence over large regions of the world economy. These include, for example, Brussels, Frankfurt, Los Angeles, Paris, Singapore, and Zurich. North American cities in this category include Chicago, Los Angeles, and Washington, D.C. A third tier consists of important international cities with more limited or more specialized international functions, including Amsterdam, Madrid, Mexico City, Seoul, and Sydney and, in North America, Houston, Miami, San Fran-

cisco, Toronto, and Vancouver. There is a fourth tier, which comprises cities of national importance and with some transnational functions, including Barcelona, Manchester, Munich, and Melbourne and, in North America, Boston, Dallas, Montreal, and Philadelphia.

Some commentators, recognizing the increasing interdependence of the global and the local, would add a fifth tier, which includes the likes of Atlanta, Georgia; Rochester, New York; Columbus, Ohio; and Charlotte, North Carolina, places where an imaginative and aggressive local leadership has sought to carve out distinctive niches in the global marketplace. Columbus, for example, with a substantial informational infrastructure that includes CompuServe, Sterling Software/Ordernet, Chemical Abstracts, the Online Computer Library Center, and the Ohio Supercomputer Center, managed to get itself designated as an infoport by the U.N. Conference on Trade and Development, which is seeking to foster international trade through the use of computer networks and electronic data interchange.

THE WORLD ECONOMY IN AMERICAN CITIES

Most North American cities have humbler and more transient roles within the webs of commodity chains that constitute the globalizing economy. Nevertheless, the world economy has been inscribed into local economies almost everywhere in one way or another, and in some cases local economies have reshaped the world economy. A few towns do re-

TABLE 1

**METROPOLITAN EMPLOYMENT IN MANUFACTURING AND SERVICES,
SELECTED CITIES, 1970 AND 1995 (Percentage)**

	Manufacturing		Services	
	1970	1995	1970	1995
Atlanta	20.7	11.5	14.6	29.3
Baltimore	24.8	8.8	17.0	35.5
Boston	22.1	12.4	24.7	38.3
Chicago	31.8	16.9	16.9	30.0
Dallas	24.6	14.5	15.2	28.5
Denver	17.5	9.5	18.1	30.5
Detroit	38.1	21.6	14.3	30.1
Houston	18.6	10.6	18.2	29.1
Kansas City	25.1	12.5	15.7	28.0
Los Angeles–Long Beach	28.9	16.8	18.7	32.2
Miami	15.8	8.8	15.8	32.0
Minneapolis–St. Paul	27.4	18.0	17.7	28.8
New York City	21.1	8.6	20.1	35.1
Newark	31.5	15.2	17.1	30.2
Pittsburgh	32.3	12.9	18.3	33.9
Portland	22.7	16.4	17.9	27.0
St. Louis	30.9	16.2	17.2	30.8
San Diego	17.9	11.6	14.8	31.8
San Francisco	15.9	8.1	17.6	34.8
Seattle	24.8	15.7	15.8	27.9

SOURCE: U.S. Department of Labor, *Employment and Earnings* (monthly reports for 1970 and 1995).

main primarily export platforms for low-value-added, labor-intensive products made by unskilled cheap labor. Many more, though, have had a traditional industrial core hollowed out and are in the process of restructuring their economies, making higher-value-added items that employ sophisticated technologies and require a more extensively developed, tightly integrated local industrial base. In general terms, the composition of American metropolitan labor forces has changed quite dramatically since 1970, with service employment expanding and manufacturing employment diminishing in relative importance (Table 1).

Meanwhile, the complex of flows associated with the commodity chains that pass through larger urban economies have become powerful decentering forces that have established new and diverse infozones, technoregions, and glocalities: intensive points of interaction between the global and local scales of operation, places where firms involved in global commodity chains can find a market in which to develop and finance new products, find access to high-quality communication networks to manage extended production functions, and find access to risk finance to sustain the elongated chains through which the company's products are produced and marketed around the globe.

All this has already had a substantive impact on the structure and performance of urban economies.[3] For example, Charlotte, North Carolina, has become the third most important commercial banking center in the United States, surpassed only by New York and San Francisco. Orlando ranks just behind Los Angeles and New York in television and film production and has become a world-class center for electro-optics and laser research. Provo, Utah, now boasts the second-largest concentration of computer software jobs in the United States after California's Silicon Valley.

For many cities, of course, economic globalization has meant, above all else, an escalation in the stakes involved in economic development. Faced with increasing international competition and the hollowing-out of traditional economic structures, many towns and cities have sought to reposition themselves through municipal foreign policy: promoting international trade and investment, sending trade missions to foreign countries, and creating favorable zoning ordinances and local tax breaks for foreign investors. Spartanburg, South Carolina, provides a good example. Anticipating the decline of the local textile industry through competition from low-cost foreign suppliers, Spartanburg actively sought foreign direct investment. The city now hosts 60 firms from 12 different countries, whose local investments add up to more than $1 billion and a roster of more than 7000 employees.[4]

Within metropolitan settings, the positive effects of economic restructuring can be seen most clearly in edge cities: nodes of commercial development located on metropolitan fringes. These places, with lower rents and a slightly more laid-back ambience than big-city downtowns, have become particularly conducive to entrepreneurial innovation within restructuring economies. A survey conducted in 1994 for *American Demographics* magazine showed that the 20 population centers with the highest proportion of companies with 50 or fewer employees were all edge cities, with Walnut Creek, California, a San Francisco edge city, leading the list.

The expansion of edge cities is connected to another, more general aspect of urban economic restructuring. While the globalization of finance has consolidated certain world city functions in a few cities, the transformation of finance, banking, and business services, combined with the availability of new telecommunications technologies, has led to a massive decentralization of back-office functions from most U.S. central cities. Some of this decentralization has been metropolitan in scale, with edge cities being the main beneficiaries; some has been regional in scale, with less-expensive metropolitan settings like Charlotte, North Carolina, being the main beneficiaries; and some has been international in scale, with coun-

3. See, for example, David H. Kaplan and Alex Schwartz, "Minneapolis-St. Paul in the Global Economy," *Urban Geography*, 17:44-59 (1996); Richard Walker, "Another Round of Globalization in San Francisco," ibid., pp. 60-94; Thomas Harvey, "Portland, Oregon: Regional City in a Global Economy," ibid., pp. 95-114.

4. Heidi Hobbs, *City Hall Goes Abroad* (Thousand Oaks, CA: Sage, 1994), p. 3.

tries like Ireland being the main beneficiaries of economic development.

Back-office functions are record-keeping and analytical functions that do not require frequent personal contact with clients or business associates. The accountants and financial technicians of main street banks, for example, are back-office workers. Developments in computing technologies, database access, electronic data interchanges, and telephone call routing technologies are enabling a larger share of back-office work to be relocated to a specialized office space in cheaper settings, freeing up space in the high-rent locations occupied by the bank's front office. For example, the U.S. Postal Service is using optical character readers (OCRs) to read addresses on mail, which is then barcoded and automatically sorted to its appropriate substation. Addresses that the OCRs cannot read are digitally photographed and transmitted to a computer screen where a person manually types the address into a terminal. In Washington, D.C., OCR sorting takes place at the central mail facility, but the manual address entry is done in Greensboro, North Carolina, where wage rates are lower. Workers in Greensboro view images of letters as they are sorted in Washington and enter correct addresses, which are in turn electronically transmitted back to be barcoded on the piece of mail.

Among the more prominent examples of back-office decentralization from U.S. metropolitan areas have been the relocation of back-office jobs at American Express from New York to Salt Lake City, Fort Lauderdale, and Phoenix; the relocation of Metropolitan Life's back offices to Greenville, South Carolina; Scranton, Pennsylvania; and Wichita, Kansas; the relocation of Hertz's data entry division to Oklahoma City, Dean Witter's to Dallas, and Avis's to Tulsa; the relocation of Citibank's Master-Card and Visa divisions to Tampa and Sioux Falls; and of Eastern Airlines' back-office jobs to Miami and North Carolina. Some places have actually become specialized back-office locations as a result of such decentralization. Omaha and San Antonio, for example, are centers for a large number of telemarketing firms, while Roanoke, Virginia, has become something of a mail-order center.

By decentralizing back-office functions to offshore locations, companies can save even more in labor costs. Several New York–based life insurance companies, for example, have established back-office facilities in Ireland, situated conveniently near Ireland's main international airport, Shannon Airport. The companies ship insurance claim documents from New York via Federal Express, process them, and beam the results back to New York via satellite or transatlantic fiber-optic line.

CONCLUSION

Globalization has affected most North American cities in one way or another: directly, through the ebbs and flows of foreign direct investment, imports, and exports; and indirectly, through the consequent flows of ideas and people. All of the larger North American metropolitan areas are both cause and effect of the restructuring associated with economic globalization. In their labor markets, their demographics, and their built environment, they register the strategic shifts of transnational capital— some of which they host, and an increasing amount of which they control. Meanwhile, the globalizing economy is increasingly inscribed into the economies of most smaller urban places in North America through their roles in extended commodity chains. All this is part, as Robert Reich and others have pointed out, of a transformation that will rearrange both the economics and the politics of the coming century. It certainly portends a continual transformation not only of the economic structure of North American cities but also of their politics, demographics, social formations, and culture.

Local Politics in a Global Era:
Thinking Locally, Acting Globally

By SUSAN E. CLARKE and GARY L. GAILE

ABSTRACT: Given the contested meanings of the local global context, it is important to see local political processes as more than a matter of new interests or claims prompted by globalization or even new institutions such as public-private partnerships. We argue that local politics in a global era are best understood in terms of the ideas, institutions, and interests shaping local policy processes. They are shaped by the causal stories that different groups and organizations use to politicize issues linking the local and the global, to seek new institutional venues, and to promote some solutions over others. We draw on our national surveys in 1989 and 1996 of large and medium-sized American cities to examine these causal stories about globalization and localism and the policy choices they privilege. Five local strategies are especially salient: classic locational approaches, the world-class community orientation, the entrepreneurial mercantilism strategy, asset-based human capital strategies, and the sustainable development orientation.

Susan E. Clarke is professor of political science at the University of Colorado at Boulder. Her current research is on local human capital and economic development policies. Gary L. Gaile is associate professor of geography at the University of Colorado at Boulder. His research is on urban and regional planning and international development issues. They are coauthors of The Work of Cities.

RECONSIDERING local politics in terms of globalization processes is yielding fresh thinking that promises to reinvigorate the study of globalization as well as analyses of localities. In the continuing debate over the nature and extent of global economic integration and spatial reorganization of the economy, issues of scale are paramount. Bringing localities into analyses of globalization forces us to recognize "the concrete economic complexes situated in specific places" through which globalization exists.[1] Taking localities seriously turns attention from the broad sweep of, among other things, economic shifts and technological changes constituting globalization processes to, as Sassen puts it, the array of local practices constituting and enabling globalization. This necessarily pushes the analytic focus beyond global cities to encompass the many types of places in which "the work of globalization gets done."[2]

Similarly, taking globalization seriously challenges the modernist urban political economy framework. While still significant, these approaches hinder local political analyses to the extent that they emphasize economic interpretations of local global impacts. This limits our understanding of globalization and community: we overlook other systems of stratification and domination generating social complexity and tend to view "the global context of urban life" as "some objective structure existing 'out there'" rather than a socially constructed process.[3] Given the contested meanings of the local global context, it is important to see local political processes as more than a matter of new interests or claims prompted by globalization or even new institutions such as public-private partnerships. The politics of ideas are fundamental: local politics center on creating, changing, and struggling over the ideas and interpretations that mediate our understanding of the local global context. This does not mean that globalization is not real; rather, it means our ideas about globalization, about how and why globalization is defined as a problem for local communities, are at the heart of local politics.

In this article, we argue that local politics in a global era are best understood in terms of the ideas, institutions, and interests shaping local policy processes rather than assuming that they simply reflect aggregations of interests—global or otherwise.[4] We see the local political world as constituted by these elements and contend that local political change in a globalization context stems from the intersection of ideas, interests, and institutions. Thus we reject privileging any one of these elements in explaining local politics, particularly reading off interests and institutional change

1. Saskia Sassen, "Cities and Communities in the Global Economy: Rethinking Our Concepts," *American Behavioral Scientist*, 39:630 (Mar.-Apr. 1996).

2. Ibid. See also Paul Knox, "Globalization and Urban Change," *Urban Geography*, 17:115-17 (1996).

3. Michael Peter Smith, "Postmodernism, Urban Ethnography, and the New Social Space of Ethnic Identity," *Theory and Society*, 21:503 (1992).

4. Hugh Heclo, "Ideas, Interests, and Institutions," in *The Dynamics of American Politics: Approaches and Interpretations*, ed. Lawrence C. Dodd and Calvin Jillson (Boulder, CO: Westview Press, 1994), pp. 366-92.

from macroeconomic globalization processes. Rather, we sketch the contested ideas about localism and globalism that advantage some interests and organizations and the changing institutional venues in which they interact to describe the different ways in which localities are responding to the global context.

INTERPRETING GLOBALIZATION: THE EPISTEMIC COMMUNITY

Political change is as much about attention shifts and timing as it is about preferences and interests.[5] In responding to their changing environment, local decision makers select certain dimensions of the situation, or context, for attention and direct problem-solving efforts to particular definitions of the problem of globalization. If we acknowledge that local officials seek to solve problems as well as satisfy preferences—their own and those of powerful interests—the interesting political questions center on which aspects of globalization practices are interpreted as causal stories about political problems rather than inadvertent conditions beyond intervention.[6]

The politics of ideas involve the differing causal stories about globalization and its local impacts and the contested solutions to those problems. These causal stories emerge from a loose epistemic community of academics and policymakers with expertise and shared interests in understanding globalization processes; some are advocates of particular solutions almost independent of the problem (trade liberalization, job training), while others reflect more evolutionary policy thinking.[7] The causal stories emerging from this epistemic community frame issues for local decision makers: for example, the stories attribute blame to certain aspects of the situation, they resonate with other values and beliefs important to citizens and decision makers, and they privilege some solutions over others.

Competing stories: The two faces of globalization

There are a multitude of stories to choose from, some more optimistic than others. Most present globalization as recasting distance and locational constraints on communities through economic and technological changes attendant to globalization. These changes alter economic space and raise the prospect of the "death of distance" as a significant factor in investment calculations. For many communities, this new space economy opens up economic opportunities. Furthermore, the most important value-added processes in the global economy depend on human capital and are inherently localized. As a consequence, there is a distinctive new geography of human capital

5. Bryan Jones, *Reconceiving Decision-Making in Democratic Politics: Attention, Choice, and Public Policy* (Chicago: University of Chicago Press, 1994).

6. Deborah Stone, "Causal Stories and the Formation of Policy Agendas," *Political Science Quarterly*, 104:281-300 (1989).

7. The notion of epistemic communities is developed in Peter Haas, "Do Regimes Matter? Epistemic Communities and Mediterranean Pollution Control," *International Organization* (Summer 1989).

in the United States and a new localism rejuvenating local politics.[8] Understanding this new localism, however, depends on interpreting the causal stories behind the two faces of globalization.

The new localism story

As Margit Mayer sees it, the economic and spatial trends underlying globalization bring into question the ability of central governments to orchestrate the necessary local conditions of production required by global capital.[9] To some, this is a "hollowing out" process akin to corporate restructuring: significant decision responsibilities move up to supranational and regional bodies and down to subnational and local entities.[10] Trade liberalization also reduces the prospects for national intervention in the flow of both capital and commerce and thus creates new economic spaces for cities.[11] This new localism

does not imply the withering away of the national state but it underscores the increased salience of other scales where globalization materializes.[12]

These new localism causal stories resonate with cultural values of growth, wealth, power, opportunity, individualism, localism, and, increasingly, consumer sovereignty. From this perspective, the lesson for communities is to find a niche in the global urban hierarchy. City officials take on strategic broker roles, aiming to create settings for "the work of globalization."[13] This new role centers on steering local governments toward improving the city's economic and social situation through negotiations with a wider set of actors. With its greater salience, local government acts as a catalyst of processes of innovation and cooperation. Underlying these causal stories is an assumption that global integration will bring a convergence in growth prospects and that cities can upgrade their position in a global urban hierarchy by their strategic interventions.

*The dark side of the
new localism story*

A darker side of globalization makes the new localism more problematic. The hypermobility of capital, the international division of labor, and the "death of distance" due to

---

8. In 1996, the National League of Cities created the Committee on New Localism to "rethink the role of cities." See Christine Becker, "NLC Panel Sketches Its Vision for Cities' Future Role," *Nation's Cities Weekly*, 20 May 1996, p. 1. See also Edward Goetz and Susan E. Clarke, *The New Localism* (Newbury Park, CA: Sage, 1993).

9. Margit Mayer, "Post-Fordist City Politics," in *Post-Fordism: A Reader*, ed. Ash Amin (Cambridge, MA: Basil Blackwell, 1994), pp. 316-37.

10. Bob Jessop, "Towards a Schumpeterian Workfare State? Preliminary Remarks on Post-Fordist Political Economy," *Studies in Political Economy*, 40:7-39 (1993). This argument is developed further in Susan E. Clarke and Gary L. Gaile, *The Work of Cities* (Minneapolis: University of Minnesota Press, forthcoming).

11. See Peter Karl Kresl, "The Determinants of Urban Competitiveness: A Survey," in *North American Cities and the Global Econ-*

omy: Challenges and Opportunities, ed. Peter Karl Kresl and Gary Gappert (Thousand Oaks, CA: Sage, 1995), pp. 45-68. See also Rosabeth Moss Kanter, *World Class: Thriving Locally in the Global Economy* (New York: Simon & Schuster, 1995).

12. Sassen, "Cities and Communities in the Global Economy," p. 631.

13. Ibid., p. 630.

information technologies appear to undermine local autonomy. In addition, international trade liberalization agreements such as the North American Free Trade Agreement reduce national authority, expose regions and cities to more global competition, and constrain local autonomy.[14] Recent trade agreements allow preemptions of state and local government powers in economic development, environmental regulation, and other areas if they appear to privilege local firms or producers and thus would act as barriers to the "equal treatment" necessary for mobile trade and investment.[15]

The concomitant rise in consumerism generates new local stratification patterns based on links to the global economy. An emergent world class of Cosmopolitans has weak community ties since their interests and resources transcend communities.[16] In contrast, most citizens remain Locals, defined by particular places and limited opportunities; although many are weakly linked to a global web through their involvement in global practices, their well-being is dependent on decisions of world-class citizens. For Kanter, the smart question for individuals and cities is, What does it take to become world class? But to others, the rise of a world class signals an erosion in links between people, place, and identity; it contributes to an increased civic fragmentation because there are fewer incentives to invest in a community's civic society.[17]

This is obvious for Cosmopolitans, but Locals who see little gain from globalization may also find fewer incentives to contribute to civic society. The new economic changes appear to bring few benefits to central-city residents and newcomers: most new jobs go to suburban residents, and a two-tiered wage structure and segmented labor market offer little promise. Globalization practices at the local level often bring about social polarization, job displacement, wage compression, intensified property speculation, informal economies, immigration pressures, and the continued economic and social isolation of the poor in the central city. Despite gaining majority status in many large cities and achieving some political incorporation, the economic and social gains of African Americans and Hispanics relative to those of whites and even some recent immigrant groups remain low. The map of the local political terrain increasingly features greater social and economic polarization, intensified multiethnic competition for jobs, housing, and political resources, and eroding citizenship.[18]

14. John Kincaid, "Cities and Citizens in Flux: Global Consumer Integration and Local Civic Fragmentation," in *North American Cities and the Global Economy*, ed. Kresl and Gappert, pp. 69-85.

15. Charles S. Colgan, "International Regulation of State and Local Subsidies," *Economic Development Quarterly*, 9:107-18 (1995).

16. This argument is developed in Kanter, *World Class*.

17. Kincaid, "Cities and Citizens in Flux."

18. For an account of the power of ideas and images in this volatile political context, see Sheila Croucher, *Imagining Miami: Ethnic Politics in a Postmodern World* (Charlottesville: University Press of Virginia, forthcoming). See also Michael A. Pagano and Ann O'M. Bowman, *Cityscapes and Capital: The Politics of Urban Development* (Baltimore, MD: Johns Hopkins University Press, 1995).

Yet shifting electoral demographics encourage the abandonment of cities by national policymakers. Through the 1980s and into the 1990s, national policies embraced a neoliberal policy of facilitating capital mobility and cutting community programs that might distort private investment decisions. The Clinton administration's Empowerment Zone program includes more social funding than previous proposals, but stirs only modest local expectations. The remaining community programs are to be funded through "performance partnerships" tying local funds to achieving benchmarks rather than local needs.[19] Place-based funding is increasingly replaced by transfer payments to individuals, particularly the nonurban middle class and elderly. In 1996 Clinton proposed that 61 percent of federal aid to states and local governments go directly to individuals, compared to 35 percent in 1960; 16 percent in capital grants to state and local governments, compared to 47 percent in 1960; and 22 percent in other state and local grants, compared to 17 percent in 1960.[20]

These more pessimistic causal stories bring in cultural values of equity, obligation, rectitude, sustainability, and fairness. For some, local communities seem to have little choice but to cater to the demands of the global marketplace. To others, striving to become a world-class community is irrelevant; localities must address social citizenship issues. This darker side of globalization hints that growth prospects may become more uneven over time; cities initially positioned to benefit from globalization trends enhance their position at the expense of others, so the likelihood of upgrading a city's position in the global urban hierarchy is more remote.

Shifting institutional venues

Despite the conflicting assessments of the two faces of globalization, there is broader agreement within the epistemic community on the institutional changes promoted by globalization practices. These social and cultural aspects of economic change include more numerous and more diverse local actors seeking cooperation in the face of greater complexity, the emergence of a third sector of nonprofit organizations, and the reconstruction of the local institutional infrastructure to accommodate different bargaining and negotiating processes.

The expansion of the local sphere and the increase in the different types of actors exacerbates the dilemma of generating "enough cooperation" to get things done.[21] Bringing the necessary actors to the table and then moderating differences and negotiating cooperation is a new local government responsibility. This has prompted a variety of new bargaining systems and institutions. In each instance, the objective is to find new

19. Alice M. Rivlin, "Performance Partnerships: Summary and Guiding Principles" (Memorandum, Executive Office of the President of the United States, Office of Management and Budget, 28 Mar. 1995).

20. "Long Term Shifts Will Burden Cities," *Nation's Cities Weekly*, 25 Mar. 1996, p. 8.

21. Clarence Stone, *Regime Politics* (Lawrence: University Press of Kansas, 1989).

institutional and organizational arrangements with sufficient scope, responsiveness, and flexibility to accommodate these competing ideas and interests. Often, however, they operate outside formal government structures; the public sector may no longer be the center of negotiations and decision making about public resources.

Embedded in this expanded local sphere is the emergence of a third sector between state and market. To Drucker, this is the social transformation of our times.[22] Less romantically, there is a clear increase in the use of nonprofit organizations as service delivery mechanisms. As Mayer points out, local government becomes the enabler in negotiations with nonstate actors rather than the provider of services or local field office of national programs.[23] In addition to their service delivery and catalytic role, nonprofits, ironically, permit the enlargement of the sphere of local politics in the face of declining local public sector functions: local officials must play a more activist role in interactions with nonstate sectors by moderating and managing areas of interest and providing resources on a conditional basis.[24]

Some claim that the character of the local institutional infrastructure distinguishes between localities in terms of their effectiveness in coping with changing economic realities.[25]

Institutions are the legacy of past conjunctures of interests and ideas as well as the framework for current politics: they articulate working agreements on what can and cannot be done, how reforms will be implemented, and how costs and benefits are to be distributed.[26] The thicker the institutional fabric, the more likely the local milieu will support features seen as necessary in a global era: institutional stability, commonly held knowledge, institutional flexibility, high innovative capacity, trust and reciprocity, and, potentially, a sense of inclusiveness. But it is not clear that institutional thickness is necessary or sufficient for local economic change. Indeed, it could support sclerosis and resistance to change as well as innovation.

It is evident that communities are searching for a new "institutional fix," for institutional arrangements compatible with a changing economic base and social structure.[27] It appears easy to encourage more inter-institutional interactions but more difficult to generate collective representation or shared understandings. Not all institutions are of equal weight; noneconomic groups may be

22. Peter F. Drucker, "The Age of Social Transformation," *Atlantic Monthly*, pp. 53-80 (Nov. 1994).

23. Mayer, "Post-Fordist City Politics."

24. Ibid.

25. Ray Hudson, "Institutional Change, Cultural Transformation, and Economic Re-generation: Myths and Realities from Europe's Old Industrial Areas," in *Globalization, Institutions, and Regional Development in Europe*, ed. Ash Amin and Nigel Thrift (New York: Oxford University Press, 1995), pp. 196-216.

26. David C. Paris, *Ideology and Educational Reform: Themes and Theories in Public Education* (Boulder, CO: Westview, 1995), p. 17.

27. Jamie Peck and Adam Tickell, "Searching for a New Institutional Fix: The After-Fordist Crisis and the Global-Local Disorder," in *Post-Fordism: A Reader*, ed. Ash Amin (Cambridge, MA: Basil Blackwell, 1995), pp. 280-315. See also Mayer's argument on compatibility in "Post-Fordist City Politics."

plentiful and interactive but fragmented, underfunded, and unlikely to share a collective understanding of an agenda that does not support their constituencies.

IDEAS, INTERESTS, AND INSTITUTIONS: MORE COMPLEX LOCAL POLITICS

All these stories are true. For local officials, the dilemma is to sort out these causal stories and map the strategic consequences of these trends. In the process, attention shifts to new problem definitions and new solutions, prompting the local policy strategies that we will note in the following. Ideas do not bring about agendas and outcomes independently, of course, but they are constitutive of outcomes. Nor are ideas mere rationalizations of self-interested groups with fixed preferences; perceptions of interest can emerge from debates, and conflicts over ideas shape interests. As a consequence, local politics are shaped by the causal stories that different groups and organizations use to politicize issues linking the local and the global, to seek new institutional venues, and to promote some solutions over others. Our research indicates that the following local strategies are especially salient: classic locational approaches, the world-class community orientation, the entrepreneurial mercantilism strategy, asset-based human capital strategies, and the sustainable development orientation.[28]

The city limits story

Analyses of local American politics are invariably marked by the long shadow of Paul Peterson's *City Limits*.[29] Peterson's elegant deductive argument emphasizes the city limits— the constraints on local action—built into the American decentralized federal system: cities are relatively free from central oversight but fiscally dependent on the health of the local economy for their tax revenues. In Peterson's model, economic forces drive local policies: they act as structural constraints and create a systemic bias toward business interests. In the context of these political and fiscal structures, businesses and residents seek places with the most favorable ratio of taxes paid to services received. Local developmental policies enhance that ratio; in Peterson's view, cities have a unitary interest in stimulating economic activity that employs residents, generates tax revenues, and contributes to attractive locational sites for capital and households.

Correspondingly, local redistributional policies distort that ratio by directing services and benefits to those paying fewer taxes. The logic of interjurisdictional competition and necessary sensitivity to cost-benefit ratios implies that redistribution of local funds is not in a city's interest, given the burden such transfers place on the productive members of the

---

28. We draw on our national surveys in 1989 and 1996 of local economic development strategies in American cities with populations

above 100,000 in 1975. For further study details, see Clarke and Gaile, *Work of Cities*. Mara Sidney, Brad Hall, and Art Hingerty assisted in the 1996 follow-up survey, with the support of the Department of Political Science, University of Colorado.

29. Chicago: University of Chicago Press, 1981.

community. Such groups can threaten to exit if they perceive that the benefit-tax ratio is no longer favorable. Furthermore, in the absence of viable mechanisms such as coherent party structures or stable social change coalitions, local demands for redistribution are not easily translated into redistributive policies.[30]

To many, this notion of city limits is only exacerbated by globalization. The economic logic of federalism and globalization suggests that the menu of local choices will shrink in the face of greater global competition, with local communities putting increasing emphasis on entrepreneurial economic development and the subordination of social policies.[31] It appears irrational for local communities to do otherwise. But this new local terrain is constituted by ideas, interests, and institutions unanticipated by the city limits model.[32] These deductive models, for example, assume that policy choices stem from the self-interest of officials predominantly concerned with reelection chances and tax-based budgets. But we have seen that globalization has expanded the

sphere of local political action, broadened local economic horizons, and escalated the competing understandings of localism and global competition. Increasingly, local politics are characterized by nonelected public, private, and nonprofit actors as well as decision organizations and partnership arrangements that cannot be labeled as strictly public or private. Hewing to the city limits story ignores these contextual cues and inhibits the search for new solutions.

*Locational
  strategies*

Nevertheless, many cities balk at discarding the city limits story of a unitary interest in economic development. As Peterson's model predicts, local officials continue to diagnose local development problems in terms of an economic growth model emphasizing the importance of factor costs—basically, the costs of land, labor, and capital—in production processes. Cities adopt policies to reduce those costs relative to other cities, such as providing subsidies for firms, tax abatements, and below-market land costs. Although disparaged as "smoke-stack chasing" and "corporate-centered" strategies, these public policies are justified by the claim that the benefits spread to the community as a whole through jobs and tax revenues. Critics argue otherwise, pointing to the questionable cost-effectiveness of these deals and the skewed distributional benefits.

Given the prevalence of locational strategies, many cities clearly continue to cope with changes in their

30. Paul E. Peterson and Mark C. Rom, *Welfare Magnets: A New Case for a National Standard* (Washington, DC: Brookings Institution, 1990).

31. For example, see Mayer, "Post-Fordist City Politics"; Jessop, "Towards a Schumpeterian Workfare State?"

32. For recent analyses of more diverse local agendas, see Rowan Miranda and Donald Rosdil, "From Boosterism to Qualitative Growth," *Urban Affairs Review*, 30:868-79 (1995); Edward Goetz, "Expanding Possibilities in Local Development Policy: An Examination of U.S. Cities," *Political Research Quarterly*, 47:85-109 (1994); Robert D. Atkinson, "The Next Wave in Economic Development," *Commentary* (Spring 1993).

environment by applying decision rules and programmatic solutions that worked in the past. In that sense, city development responses may be path dependent:[33] they lock in the protected interests of certain sectors of the business community as well as solution sets linked to factor costs. This limits the city's ability over time to adjust to changing constituencies and to address emergent problems unrelated to factor-cost issues. Local institutions continue to reflect this legacy of interests and economic growth models, particularly those articulated by past federal programs. They hamper new agreements on what can and cannot be done and new allocations of costs and benefits.

World-class
community orientations

Although these classic locational strategies are pervasive, our research indicates that the worldview of many local officials is changing— away from the focus on attracting firms encouraged by the city limits viewpoint, to a concern with facilitating economic growth processes. Cities still pursue development as predicted by the deductive models but in line with the new localism story: local economic well-being is attributed to gaining a niche in the global economy and becoming a world-class community. The diagnosis of local economic

problems focuses on innovation capacities and transaction costs rather than solely on factor costs. Indeed, the locational factors cited by international businesses show little correlation with the production-cost features typically ranked highly by domestic firms: 24 percent of new foreign-owned companies in Colorado ranked the opportunity for acquisitions or joint ventures as the main reason for selecting a particular country, followed by "cost or suitability of space," "strategic location," and "personal preference" tied at 22 percent, with local transportation advantages cited by 17 percent. The local issues of greater concern included labor quality (cited by 52 percent), labor availability (48 percent), the education of employees (39 percent), and the state and local tax system (33 percent).[34]

The world-class-community orientation singles out qualitatively different intervention styles featuring public entrepreneurship, public-private partnerships, the encouragement of research and development activities, new business starts, foreign investment, and small-business formation. This third wave demands entrepreneurial public roles and a broader range of nongovernmental and market actors.[35] From this perspective, local governments enter-

---

33. For illustrative uses of the path dependency concept, see Jones, *Reconceiving Decision-Making*; D. Wilsford, "Path Dependency, or Why History Makes It Difficult But Not Impossible to Reform Health Care Systems in a Big Way," *Journal of Public Policy*, 14:251-83 (1994).

34. KPMG Peat Marwick, *Colorado: 1996 Foreign Investment Study* (Denver: KPMG Peat Marwick, 1996), pp. 14, 17.

35. See Atkinson, "Next Wave in Economic Development." See also David Harvey, "From Managerialism to Entrepreneurialism: The Transformation of Urban Governance in Late Capitalism," *Geografisker Annaler,* 71:3-17 (ser. B, 1989). For empirical analyses, see Susan E. Clarke and Gary L. Gaile, "The Next

tain more risk and seek new growth opportunities by marketing themselves in the global economy.

One element of this world-class local entrepreneur story involves developing information infrastructure relevant to the new global roles of cities. In our 1996 survey, over two-thirds of the communities recognized this as a new element on their economic development agenda. Nearly every community reported having or creating a home page on the World Wide Web; over 75 percent reported that some or all city hall offices were linked by E-mail; and most provided job and education information through publicly accessible computer terminals in libraries and at kiosks. This new path to global competitiveness is prompting the reconfiguration of local growth coalitions around "electronic public spaces" rather than traditional land-use issues.[36] Partnerships such as the Greater Austin Area Telecommunications Network often include city, county, and state officials as well as public school districts, institutions of higher education, and local utilities. City partnerships or contracts with private corporations such as Time Warner Cable and SpectraNet raise issues of universal access, which must be provided by public utilities. Yet local initiatives to build and operate municipal fiber-optic systems are

challenged by private firms on the grounds of unfair competition. Furthermore, many cities are limited in planning for the virtual city by state laws and prohibitive costs. To avoid these political and fiscal hazards, cities are adopting new organizational structures: Milpitas, California, set up the country's first municipal telecommunications commission in 1995; San Diego is seeking private sector proposals for a public-private partnership to build a regional telecommunications network called San Net; while 21 northeastern Ohio communities are considering formation of a nonprofit corporation to operate a telecommunications network.[37]

Entrepreneurial mercantile orientations

Another twist on the new localism story entails solutions based on entrepreneurial mercantilism. Entrepreneurial mercantilism aims for more diversified growth built on local initiative and indigenous assets; selected intervention in the market encourages new and existing small businesses that would provide greater local benefits from economic development.[38] In St. Paul, Mayor Latimer's Homegrown Economy Initiative in 1976 launched the city's mercantilist approach with substantial intergovernmental support and foundation funds. This early proto-

---

Wave: Local Economic Development Strategies in the Post-Federal Era," *Economic Development Quarterly*, 6:189-98 (1992).

36. See Stephen Graham and Simon Marvin, *Telecommunications and the City* (London: Routledge, 1996), for an extensive analysis of local telecommunication issues, including the notion of "electronic public space" (p. 359).

37. These examples are drawn from Stephanie Neumann, "Telecommunication: The Experience of Other Cities" (Manuscript, City of Littleton, CO, n.d.)

38. David L. Imbroscio, "Overcoming the Economic Dependence of Urban America," *Journal of Urban Affairs*, 15:173-90 (1993).

type sought to promote local owner- ship, job quality, economic diversifi- cation, and small businesses; in con- trast to the world-class community path, the emphasis is on enhancing local self-reliance through emphasiz- ing local benefits from investments, community and employer ownership, the net tax benefits of public subsi- dies, and attracting capital and funds from outside through export indus- tries.[39] In Minneapolis, officials re- port they are determined "to grow what we have, to expand what we have rather than pursue companies from outside the city and state."[40] Similarly, Davenport, Iowa, recently refocused its incentives to what city officials describe as "primary busi- ness, those bringing wealth into our community."

Chicago's entrepreneurial mer- cantilism was neighborhood ori- ented. Responding to his electoral coalition of African Americans, white liberals, and Latinos, Mayor Harold Washington advocated increased job opportunities for local residents, pro- moted the balanced growth of the downtown and neighborhoods, as- sisted neighborhoods in participating in partnerships and coordinated in- vestment, and encouraged more citi- zen participation. His "new populist" approach redirected funds toward smaller-scale neighborhood projects; it decentralized power to community- based and nonprofit organizations to increase local autonomy and develop

local assets.[41] This agenda encapsu- lated the entrepreneurial mercantil- ist tenet that a local government can stimulate an alternative develop- ment strategy by providing seed money for community-based develop- ment and bringing neighborhoods and small businesses to the table on economic development deals.

Nonprofits have taken the lead in other cities. In the struggle over the redevelopment of the Tenderloin area in San Francisco, successful chal- lenges to the city's redevelopment in- itiatives came from a network of non- profit organizations that constituted a "social and political infrastructure" in the impoverished Tenderloin neighborhood.[42] This infrastructure had its roots in the growth of non- profit housing development corpora- tions (HDCs) in the late 1970s to build affordable housing. Ironically, San Francisco HDCs were supported by grants from the city, other redevel- opment mitigation funds, founda- tions, and sweat equity. While these HDCs were essential for federal housing programs requiring non- profit partners (80 percent of the low- income housing in the United States now involves HDCs), they also became a source of neighborhood activism. Based on these groups, an anti-regime emerged, demanding downzoning to low-rise residential use in the Ten- derloin, mitigation of the effects of further commercial development, and redefinition of environmental sustainability to include socioeco- nomic elements. Robinson asks if

39. Dennis Judd and Randy L. Ready, "En- trepreneurial Cities and the New Politics of Economic Development," in *Reagan and the Cities*, ed. George Peterson and Carole Lewis (Washington, DC: Urban Institute, 1986).

40. From interviews in surveys done for Clarke and Gaile, *Work of Cities*.

41. Judd and Ready, "Entrepreneurial Cities."

42. This example is drawn from Tony Robinson, "Gentrification and Grassroots Re- sistance in San Francisco's Tenderloin," *Urban Affairs Review*, 30:483-513 (1995).

such coalitions of tenants' unions and nonprofit housing organizations could provide an entrepreneurial coalition capable of responding to the darker side of globalization. In San Francisco, grassroots action pressured local government to shift attention to the social consequences of displacing the poor, the homeless, and immigrant families. As Robinson puts it, even transnational capital is grounded in communities and must contend with local activism.

*Asset-based human
    capital strategies*

In response to the dark side of globalization, there has been a resurgence of human capital initiatives and poverty-reduction efforts at the local level. These efforts are counter to the predictions of the city limits story. Indeed, these human capital strategies differ from past initiatives.[43] While the federal Private Industry Council job training model remains important, many communities in our 1996 survey report local policy designs to target specific concerns. Minneapolis, for example, set up a task force to work on linking human capital and economic development; pushed by state legislation requiring reports on jobs created with public funds, the city is tying some economic development assistance to the creation of living-wage jobs. Other cities also report making development assistance contingent on specific job

creation and training efforts. Portland, Oregon's efforts to link new and expanding businesses with local labor pools in the late 1980s evolved into a separate Workforce Development Department by the mid-1990s. With the incentive of state funding support, Oregon counties can form alliances to support workforce development and training programs. The sheer cost of human capital efforts limits what cities can do; cities are drawing on general funds, Community Development Block Grants, debt financing, state support, payroll taxes, and even lottery funds to support these programs.

Many local efforts are premised on explicitly reframing local poverty issues in terms of underutilized assets rather than social needs and pathologies. Michael Porter faults past models for treating the central city as an island isolated from the rest of the city and focusing on public subsidies rather than on the creation of wealth via private investment.[44] Porter advocates building on the competitive advantage of the central city by identifying the clusters of activities that would gain from a central-city location. He targets the development of critical masses of economic activities that would respond to local demand (such as specialty foods, financial services), link with other regional clusters, and export goods and services to broader markets. Porter argues that private sector models and leadership can build on the competitive advantages and underutilized assets of these distressed areas. While it

43. For an overview, see Michael Rich, "Empower the People: An Assessment of Community-Based, Collaborative, Persistent Poverty Initiatives" (Paper delivered at the annual meeting of the Midwest Political Science Association, Chicago, 1995).

44. Michael E. Porter, "The Competitive Advantage of the Inner City," *Harvard Business Review*, pp. 55-71 (May-June 1995).

could be argued that disinvestment by these private institutions created much of the difficulty facing these areas, Porter relegates government to a supportive role to business leadership.

In contrast, John L. McKnight and John P. Kretzmann's influential model of asset-based community organizing relies on strong public and civic leadership.[45] They, too, reject past policy designs, characterizing them as "needs-driven" deficiency models creating client neighborhoods and ensuring only survival. In their alternative view, poor people are the underutilized assets. Kretzmann and McKnight argue explicitly for shifting attention away from deficiency cues and toward an internal focus on rediscovering local assets as the means to development solutions. This involves mapping and developing strategies to knit together the individual skills, associations, and institutions in the neighborhood. The literally hundreds of examples they provide include arrangements for street markets in Cleveland to accept food stamps to encourage local buying, church investments of pension funds in revolving loan funds for community-based housing projects in Massachusetts, and community development credit union loans to low-income residents for financing the purchase and repair of used cars in Chicago.

In Baltimore, electoral mobilization overcame some of the city limits constraints. New constituencies arose from discontents over the corporate-centered strategies bringing about Baltimore's revitalization but having little impact on citizens' lives.[46] BUILD, an Alinsky-type community-based organization, emerged in the 1970s based on churches but also including labor unions, the teachers' union, and the school employees' union. It focused on educational needs ignored by the revitalization plans; their Baltimore Commonwealth plan promoted education as an economic necessity. While building up their independent power base and electoral clout through voter registration and mobilization, BUILD also sought allies in the business community and the mayor's office. Neither venture was successful until new leadership in the business and public sector emerged in the late 1980s and concurred with BUILD's linking of economic development and human capital. As Orr notes, neither the mayor nor the business community initiated these strategies, but both were necessary to consolidating the agenda status of human capital.

Sustainable development

Although often seeming more rhetoric than reality, issues of local sustainable development are increasingly visible. They are one of the areas where transnational organizations are influential in American local politics. Local sustainable de-

45. John P. Kretzmann and John L. McKnight, *Building Communities from the Inside Out: A Path Toward Finding and Mobilizing a Community's Assets* (Chicago: ACTA, 1993).

46. This account is provided in Marion Orr, "Urban Regimes and Human Capital Policies: A Study of Baltimore," *Journal of Urban Affairs*, 14:173-87 (1992).

velopment agendas stem from a definition of sustainability as current use
of resources that does not threaten
future generations; local decision
making and governance are focused
on sustainability values, including
intergenerational and intragenera-
tional equity concerns, rather than
the city limits emphasis on short-
term growth goals.[47] In 1986, the
World Health Organization inaugu-
rated the Healthy Cities initiative,
which now includes over 1000 communities. These activities are
tracked by organizations such as
the Global Tomorrow Coalition in
Washington, D.C., and the Community Sustainability Resource Institute in Maryland.[48]

In cities as disparate as St. Paul,
Jacksonville, San Diego, Chattanooga, Seattle, and Vancouver, sustainability is a key agenda issue. In
Chattanooga, the sustainable development path was promoted as an in-
sider strategy by local leaders seeking an urban revitalization strategy.
In the 1970s, Chattanooga was one of
the most polluted cities in the United
States. With the help of local founda-

tion support from a public-private
task force, the city adopted an ecosys-
tem approach to urban management
that put sustainability as the primary agenda item. Reintegration of
urban functions through clustering
was seen as the key; in 1984 an initiative for urban ecology encouraged
neighborhood networks and citizen
participation to renovate the riverfront, attack air pollution, and
close the production loop through
recycling.[49]

In cities where traditional business and government interests remain locked in, local groups have mo-
bilized and pushed their objectives
from the outside. In San Diego, citizens used "ballot box planning" to
overcome the growth machine alliance; they continually threatened to
put their growth management concerns on the ballot through the initiative process if elected officials refused
to respond.[50] Many such sustainable
development initiatives are now supported through programs such as the
Healthy Communities Initiative and
the President's Council on Sustainable Development.

Sustainable development concerns also take regional forms, such
as the Cascadia alliance in the Pacific
Northwest. The commonality and interdependence of environmental interests in the Georgia Basin–Puget
Sound bioregion ("one forest, one wa-
terway, one airshed") led to the creation of new institutional structures to
protect the quality of life in the area

47. The sustainable development concept
was introduced at the 1972 U.N. Conference
on Human Environment but gained currency
through World Commission on Environment
and Development, *Our Common Future* (New
York: United Nations, 1987), also known as the
Bruntland Report. This report linked poverty,
inequality, and environmental degradation
and emphasized the need to balance economic
and environmental concerns.

48. Much of this activity is described in
John K. Davies and Michael P. Kelly, *Healthy
Cities: Research and Practice* (London: Rout-
ledge, 1993); World Health Organization,
*World Health Organization Healthy Cities Proj-
ect: A Project Becomes a Movement* (Geneva:
World Health Organization, 1990).

49. See Robert Frenay, "Chattanooga Turn-
around," *Audubon*, 98:82 ff. (1996).

50. Nico Calavita, "Growth Machines and
Ballot Box Planning: The San Diego Case,"
Journal of Urban Affairs, 14:1-24 (1992).

referred to as Cascadia in response to global growth pressures.[51] With the advent of the North American Free Trade Agreement, the North-South trade links through Cascadia increased. This spurred the growth of binational alliances and multiparty groups and forums concerned with the impacts on the local environment. The Cascadia alliance, a regional alliance coordinating growth management and strategic planning efforts in Alaska, British Columbia, the Yukon, Alberta, Oregon, Washington, Montana, and Idaho, exemplifies a new institutional fix emerging in response to globalization and interdependence. The British Columbia/ Washington Environmental Cooperation Council was set up in 1993 to bring together regional government groups for cooperation on environmental and growth management strategies. To planners and citizen groups, these new institutions were essential: traditional structures of government appeared less effective in dealing with issues of interdepen-

51. Alan F. J. Artibise, "Achieving Sustainability in Cascadia: An Emerging Model of Urban Growth Management in the Vancouver-Seattle-Portland Corridor," in *North American Cities and the Global Economy*, ed. Kresl and Gappert, pp. 221-50.

dence and in responding to the demands of these new groups. The Cascadia alliance reflects the influence of transnational groups; these institutions also shape new transnational environmental and trade interests over time.

CONCLUSION

Redirecting our attention to the political dynamics of ideas, interests, and institutions highlights the ways in which communities are thinking locally and acting globally. Local officials make strategic choices between the causal stories generated by an epistemic community with expertise in globalization studies. They adapt these interpretations to fit the political and economic context in which they work. In doing so, they are reconstructing local policy agendas to take account of human capital needs, information technologies, and environmental issues. Many of these local responses to the spatial and political implications of economic change are unanticipated; local efforts to accommodate the work of globalization are contributing to political practices and institutional venues that challenge our current theoretical approaches.

ANNALS, *AAPSS*, 551, May 1997

The Suburban Transformation
of the Globalizing American City

By PETER O. MULLER

ABSTRACT: As the American metropolis has turned inside out since 1970, the emerging outer suburban city has captured critical masses of leading urban activities from the central city that spawned it. Globalization increasingly shapes U.S. urban development in the 1990s, yet research to date has focused on the central city and mainly ignores the outer ring, where a growing majority of metropolitan residents live and work. Following a brief review of the unprecedented recent suburbanization of major economic activities, this article explores the rapidly expanding international role of suburban business complexes in large metropolitan areas, particularly Greater New York. Among the perspectives discussed are the world city hypothesis, relationships between telecommunications and urban form, high-technology industrial location processes, the influence of corporate headquarters on global information-flow networks, and the foreign presence in suburban America. It is concluded that globalization forces intensify and accelerate the suburban transformation of the American city. A new urban future is being shaped as fully developed suburbs become the engine driving metropolitan and world city growth.

Peter O. Muller is professor and department chair of geography at the University of Miami in Coral Gables, Florida. He was previously affiliated with Temple and Villanova universities, has served as a fellow of the Urban Land Institute, and is book review editor of Urban Geography. *He is the author of* Contemporary Suburban America, *coauthor of* Suburban Business Centers: Employment Implications, *and has written numerous articles, book chapters, and commentaries on the consequences of post-1970 suburbanization and the accompanying transformation of metropolitan America.*

CONSIDER the following list: Silicon Valley, Hollywood, Boeing's jetliner manufacturing complex, Walt Disney World and Disneyland, and the corporate headquarters of IBM, AT&T, and Microsoft. Each ranks among America's most powerfully connected global institutions; collectively, they daily generate and/or attract massive flows of technology, capital, information, people, and prestigious, world-class products. What they also have in common is that all are located in the suburban ring of a major metropolitan area.

To many readers this will not come as a surprise because the United States, in terms of where its people live and work, has been a decidedly suburban nation for the past three decades. In essence, the American city has turned inside out since about 1970, thereby constituting the most profound social and economic transformation in its history. Undoubtedly, the triggering processes of intra-urban deconcentration and restructuring are related to even larger forces that accompany the ongoing transition to a postindustrial, globally organized world dominated by ever increasing information flows within state-of-the-art telecommunications networks. A large literature on the latter has accumulated in recent years, and much of it is discussed in this issue of *The Annals*. Curiously, however, that body of research, while recognizing the growing role of suburbs, has almost exclusively focused on the globalization of the central city. The purpose of this article is to (1) briefly review the latest episode of U.S. suburbanization, (2) pull together what

we have learned about the rapidly expanding international connections of suburban America, and (3) discuss the consequences of the globalization of suburban business complexes for the development of the twenty-first-century metropolis.

THE SUBURBAN TRANSFORMATION OF METROPOLITAN AMERICA

The November 1975 issue of this journal was one of the first scholarly publications to recognize the then-new urbanization of the suburbs, and its 13 articles constitute a benchmark overview of suburbanization as the metropolis began to turn inside out.[1] The profound significance of this structural transformation was reviewed by the renowned planner David Birch,[2] who noted several key trends: (1) suburbs were becoming places of self-generating urban growth; (2) the intrametropolitan hierarchy of activity centers, dominated by the central city's downtown central business district (CBD), was disintegrating; (3) many suburbs were inheriting functions previously reserved for the CBD; and (4) certain suburbs were developing complete economic bases of their own, thereby eliminating their dependency on the nearby central city for a growing array of goods and services. Moreover, Birch foresaw that the future success

1. Louis H. Masotti, ed., *The Suburban Seventies*, vol. 422, *The Annals* of the American Academy of Political and Social Science (Nov. 1975).

2. David L. Birch, "From Suburb to Urban Place," *The Annals* of the American Academy of Political and Social Science, 422:25-35 (Nov. 1975).

of mushrooming suburban economic centers would depend on their linkages—via new networks of highways, air routes, cables, satellites, and computers—to a large number of urban places throughout the nation and, importantly, the world.

Although Birch identified most of the forces affecting the restructuring of the metropolis, he did not examine the spatial pattern of all this suburbanization. Even during the 1970s, however, it was apparent that retailing, office employment, commercial-services provision, and light manufacturing were concentrating around strategic locations on the metropolitan freeway network, especially where radial and circumferential expressways intersected. Here, often anchored by prestigious new regional shopping malls, multifunctional activity centers swiftly materialized, and by the mid-1980s many fully merited such labels as "suburban downtown" and "edge city."[3] Over the

past ten years, their development has continued to surge at the direct expense of the CBD—which has now lost its regionwide centrality advantage as superior accessibility to the rest of the metropolis has become a ubiquitous geographic commodity in every suburban freeway corridor.

As burgeoning suburban downtowns become coequals of the CBD, today's intrametropolitan spatial organization deviates sharply from those traditional models of urban structure that described a single-centered, dominant core city surrounded by a belt of subordinate bedroom suburbs. Not only does the metropolis now exhibit the expected polycentric form (Figure 1); it is also splitting asunder into a set of increasingly self-contained urban realms, each (including the central city) a tributary area served more or less exclusively by its own downtown.[4] There is also evidence that, like the central cities of an earlier era, suburban downtowns are evolving into more complex and sophisticated activity centers. The 1980s saw the landscapes of these centers increasingly marked by high-rise office

3. These centers have now become commonplace in the outer rings of large metropolitan areas, and many have achieved national recognition, such as Tyson's Corner (outside Washington, D.C.), King of Prussia (Philadelphia), Schaumburg (Chicago), Costa Mesa (Los Angeles), and Bellevue (Seattle). Their evolution is discussed in Peter O. Muller, *Contemporary Suburban America* (Englewood Cliffs, NJ: Prentice Hall, 1981), pp. 120-28, 162-75; Christopher B. Leinberger and Charles Lockwood, "How Business Is Reshaping America," *Atlantic Monthly*, pp. 43-52 (Oct. 1986); Joel Garreau, *Edge City: Life on the New Frontier* (Garden City, NY: Doubleday, 1991); Truman A. Hartshorn and Peter O. Muller, "The Suburban Downtown and Urban Economic Development Today," in *Sources of Metropolitan Growth*, ed. Edwin S. Mills and John F. McDonald (New Brunswick, NJ: Rutgers University, Center for Urban Policy Research, 1992), pp. 147-58.

4. The urban realms model was devised more than three decades ago by James E. Vance, Jr., in his monograph, *Geography and Urban Evolution in the San Francisco Bay Area* (Berkeley: University of California, Institute of Governmental Studies, 1964). It has been further refined in idem, *This Scene of Man: The Role and Structure of the City in the Geography of Western Civilization* (New York: Harper's College Press, 1977), pp. 409-16; Muller, *Contemporary Suburban America*, pp. 8-11, 173-81; Truman A. Hartshorn and Peter O. Muller, "Suburban Downtowns and the Transformation of Metropolitan Atlanta's Business Landscape," *Urban Geography*, 10:375-95 (July-Aug. 1989).

buildings and high-technology research-and-development facilities; in
the 1990s, many suburban downtowns are maturing into full-fledged
urban centers as their land-use complexes diversify and perform ever
more important economic, social,
civic, and recreational functions.[5]

As Figure 1 shows, the reconfiguration of the metropolis is confining
the local influence of the CBD to the
innermost, central-city realm; concurrently, the metropolitan ring is becoming a true outer city, whose increasingly independent realms are
decidedly no longer "sub" to the "urb"
at the core that spawned them. This
changed geographic reality enhances
the locational freedom of employers
within the metropolis, and so many
have opted to leave or avoid the central city that most job sectors today
have attained critical-mass proportions (greater than 50 percent of the
metropolitan total) in the suburbs.[6]
Moreover, the elimination of cost differentials between central cities and

suburbs has enabled noneconomic
factors to come to the forefront in
locational decision making, and they
strongly reinforce the deconcentration of economic activity as employers respond to the pull of suburban
amenities, perceived improvements
in the quality of workplace life, and
commuting conveniences as well as
the push of higher pressures, congestion, and costs of doing business in
the CBD.

The rapid economic development
of the outer city, particularly as a
corporate haven, gave early impetus
to the notion that the new suburban
business centers were capable of
making their own international connections (as David Birch noted in
these pages 22 years ago). Writing in
the *Harvard Business Review* in
1977, David Heenan discussed the
rise of three "global cities," one of
which was Miami's prestigious suburb of Coral Gables (the other two were
Paris and Honolulu). Coral Gables had
recently become the Latin American
division headquarters for more than
fifty of the nation's largest corporations, capitalizing on its proximity to
Miami's gateway International Airport, superior residential amenities,
strong business community, and diversity of its well-educated labor
force. Presciently, as we are about to
discover in the following pages,
Heenan also noted that the ability of
certain suburbs to provide a congenial,
stress-free home for multinational corporations gives them special advantages over the central city.[7]

5. Hartshorn and Muller, "Suburban
Downtown," pp. 151-52.

6. Obtaining comprehensive data between
decennial censuses on the intra-urban location
of employment facilities is not possible, but the
Census Bureau's annual *County Business Patterns* may be used for eight large metropolitan
areas whose suburban rings coincide with
county boundaries. Philadelphia is one of
them, and it is a good indicator of trends because this metropolis is often used as an economic microcosm of the nation. Total employment achieved critical mass in suburban
Philadelphia as far back as 1972 and is estimated to be 71.5 percent in 1997. Disaggregated by sector, the 1997 suburban percentage
of metropolitan employment in manufacturing
is estimated to be 83.5; wholesale trade, 81.8;
retail trade, 79.0; finance, insurance, and real
estate, 61.3; services, 66.4; business services,
85.6; and health services, 64.2.

7. David A. Heenan, "Global Cities of Tomorrow," *Harvard Business Review*, pp. 79-92
(May-June 1977).

FIGURE 1
URBAN REALMS AND DOWNTOWNS IN THE POLYCENTRIC METROPOLIS

Urban Realms Model

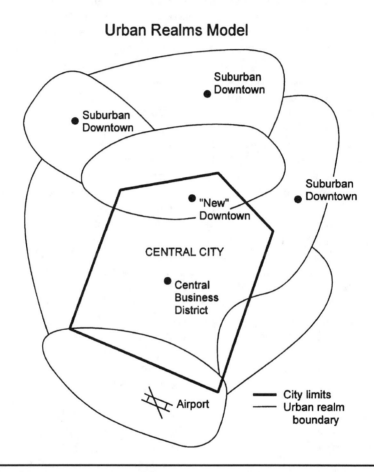

SOURCE: Truman A. Hartshorn and Peter O. Muller, "Suburban Downtowns and the Transformation of Metropolitan Atlanta's Business Landscape." Reprinted with permission from *Urban Geography,* Vol. 10, 1989, p. 378. Copyright V.H. Winston & Son, Inc., 360 South Ocean Blvd., Palm Beach, FL 33480. All rights reserved.

THE EXPANDING
INTERNATIONAL
CONNECTIONS OF
SUBURBAN AMERICA

The transformation of the metropolis described in the foregoing has been accompanied by restructur-ing at broader geographic levels. At the national level, the United States is completing its transition to a postindustrial civilization in which new social, economic, and technological forces are reshaping the nature and purpose of the city, which is becoming a node in the flow of information rather than commodities.[8] More important for our concerns in this article, at the intercontinental level a profound, transnational reorganization of the world economy is well under way—a still-intensifying globalization trend that we shall examine for its impact on the functioning of the outer suburban city.

It is not yet possible to directly isolate the international linkages of suburban business complexes (or those of the CBD, for that matter), but a number of indirect approaches are useful because a sizable literature on the globalization of the American city has accumulated since 1985. Some refinement, however, is needed in applying that body of research here since most of it focuses on the CBD and is often unclear in its usage of "city" when that term really refers to the entire metropolis. In fact, through the early 1990s, much of this work pointedly de-emphasized the role of suburbs by stressing their residential character and by (incorrectly) perpetuating fuzzy notions of a continuing subsidiary position vis-à-vis the central city. Only during the past five years has the outer city come to be recognized as the powerhouse that in 1995 prompted the Office of Technology Assessment of the U.S. Congress to conclude that for at least the next two decades many outer suburbs "will continue to be the

healthiest part of the metropolitan economy and the strongest parts of the national economy."[9]

As the metropolitan spatial economy turns inside out, it is reasonable to expect that its international functions and connections are included in the tide of activity suburbanization. It is the aim of this section to bring into sharper focus these suburban dimensions of the globalization of the American city. Our discussion is organized within the framework of five perspectives: (1) the world city hypothesis, (2) relationships between telecommunications and urban form, (3) high-technology industrial location processes, (4) corporate headquarters as control points in transnational information-flow networks, and (5) the foreign presence in suburban America.

The world city hypothesis

One of the hallmarks of the contemporary globalization phenomenon is the emergence of a world economic system whose operations are commanded by a handful of powerful cities atop an international hierarchy of control centers.[10] Researchers have labeled these "world cities," and their work to date suggests that such status is achieved only when a major metropolis simultaneously becomes a

8. A particularly concise statement of the urban significance of this revolutionary change is offered in Edward Blakely, "The New Technology City: Infrastructure for the Future Community," in *Cities of the Twenty First Century: New Technologies and Spatial Systems,* ed. John Brotchie et al. (New York: Halsted Press/Wiley, 1991), pp. 229-36.

9. U.S., Congress, Office of Technology Assessment, *The Technological Reshaping of Metropolitan America,* OTA-ETI-643 (Washington, DC: Government Printing Office, 1995), p. 123.

10. For background on the development of this concept, see Paul L. Knox, "Globalization and Urban Economic Change," this issue of *The Annals* of the American Academy of Political and Social Science.

center of international finance, transnational corporate headquarters, related high-level business (producer) services, information processing, and advanced telecommunications. Although a number of U.S. and foreign cities presumably meet these criteria, most of the attention in the literature has thus far been directed toward the three highest-ranking occupants of this global urban hierarchy: London, New York, and Tokyo.[11] Accordingly, examples from the Greater New York region will be used in the remainder of this article whenever possible.

The word "region" is important here because, as John Friedmann (who coined the term "world city") reminds us in his 1995 retrospect, "world cities are large, urbanized regions that are defined by dense patterns of interaction rather than by political-administrative boundaries."[12] That property of world cities was not widely considered in the initial research of the 1980s and early 1990s, which tended to focus almost exclusively on the central city. But in the mid-1990s, metropolitan characteristics are coming to the forefront, particularly in the newest work of

leading theoretician Saskia Sassen.[13] Here she examines the shift to a polycentric urban structure, asserting that the CBD and the new nodes of the outer ring together constitute the spatial base for cities atop the global hierarchy. This conceptualization has much to do with ongoing telecommunications changes, whose impact on urban form we shall elaborate in a moment.

But first let us recognize that this new research thrust opens the door to the incorporation of suburban downtowns into the world city model. From their inception in the 1970s, these outlying activity complexes have been attracting high-order functions previously reserved for the CBD, and a growing number—ranging from corporate producer services to cutting-edge telecommunications— are today achieving critical-mass proportions. In fact, as will be seen later, all of the criteria that define a world city can now either be met or substantially exceeded at certain locations in the vast outer city surrounding New York's Manhattan.

*Relationships between
telecommunications
and urban form*

The most powerful economic centers atop the new international urban hierarchy secured their positions by making themselves the world's

11. Urban geographers are no longer comfortable with this limitation, and their most recent investigations have begun to shed light on the globalization process in other, smaller, less well-known metropolitan areas. See the case-study articles in this issue of *The Annals* as well as Barney Warf and Rodney Erickson, eds., *Globalization and the U.S. City System*, special issue, *Urban Geography*, 1 Jan.-14 Feb. 1996.

12. John Friedmann, "Where We Stand: A Decade of World City Research," in *World Cities in a World-System*, ed. Paul L. Knox and Peter J. Taylor (New York: Cambridge University Press, 1995), p. 23.

13. Saskia Sassen, "On Concentration and Centrality in the Global City," in *World Cities in a World-System*, ed. Knox and Taylor, pp. 63-75. Sassen's most important earlier work was *The Global City: New York, London, Tokyo* (Princeton, NJ: Princeton University Press, 1991).

foremost producers and processors of the massive flows of information that circulate instantaneously within global, state-of-the-art telecommunications networks. For the central city, however, this telecommunications breakthrough is proving to be a mixed blessing: whereas at the intercontinental and national levels it drives the ever further urban concentration of high-level services and information-related activities, at the metropolitan level the new technology simultaneously propels the decentralization of these functions. In other words, to maintain their supremacy, these metropolises must constantly upgrade their electronic infrastructures—which, of course, improves internal as well as external linkages and keeps suburban access to the global networks on a par with that of the world city's CBD.

This is underscored in a study by Mitchell Moss, entitled "New York Isn't Just New York Anymore," in which he discovered that New York City's suburbs accounted for a surprisingly high one-third of the metropolitan region's ongoing international telecommunications traffic as far back as 1982.[14] That proportion is almost certainly closer to one-half in the late 1990s, and the implications of such a trend have been anticipated by Sassen:

Arguably, a new phase of innovation in telecommunications technology might make the current infrastructure obsolete and lead to the equivalent of the earlier suburbanization of large-scale manufac-

turing that resulted from the obsolescence of the physical structures that housed manufacturing in large [central] cities. At that point we could, conceivably, enter a whole new phase in the development of the urban economic system.[15]

Sassen's most recent work on the impact of telecommunications technology on urban form has begun to consider just such a restructuring of the metropolitan economic system.[16] This inquiry is based on the following assumptions: (1) the CBD is no longer the only first-order metropolitan center; (2) a grid of nodes of intense business activity, all fully interconnected by state-of-the-art electronic means, now predominates; and (3) these centers are directly linked to the global network in which the metropolis is a primary control point. Collectively, these developments permit the suburban ring to achieve its full growth potential as a "new space of centrality" that emerges from "the decentralized reconcentration of economic activity on the urban periphery."[17]

High-technology
industrial
location processes

The notion that suburbia will increasingly be the predominant spatial form of the American city is also one of the conclusions drawn by Manuel Castells in his landmark study on the transforming urban space-economy, *The Informational*

14. Mitchell L. Moss, "New York Isn't Just New York Anymore," *InterMedia*, 12:10-14 (1984).

15. Sassen, *Global City*, p. 330.

16. The points in this paragraph are drawn from Sassen, "On Concentration and Centrality," pp. 70-73.

17. Ibid., pp. 72-73.

City.[18] In fact, this leading scholar of high-technology industrial location theory begins his most recent book by conjuring up a signature image (on a par with the smoke-belching factory for the nineteenth-century industrial economy) for the new postindustrial economy: "It consists of a series of low, discreet buildings, usually displaying a certain air of quiet good taste, and set amidst impeccable landscaping in that standard real-estate cliché, a campus-like atmosphere."[19]

Not surprisingly, the distribution of high-tech industrial activity in the United States is overwhelmingly suburban. Indeed, its very hearth is Silicon Valley, lying between San Francisco and San Jose, and home of the largest pool of venture capital on Earth. Its other major centers bring to mind such places as the Route 128 corridor girdling Boston and Research Triangle Park next to Raleigh, North Carolina, not to mention all those would-be Silicon Valleys in suburban Dallas (Silicon Prairie), Denver (Silicon Mountain), Portland and Seattle (Silicon Forest), Phoenix (Silicon Desert), and several other metropolitan areas.

Castells and Hall have adapted the French term *technopole* to describe such science-park complexes, which involve the planning and promotion, in a single concentrated area, of technologically innovative, industry-related production. Collectively, these engines of the new global round of economic development form the organizing nodes of the postmodern world's "new industrial space," and their function is nothing less than the generation of the basic materials of the informational economy.[20] In their exhaustive survey, these authors document the rise of technopoles in every corner of the developed world; most exhibit a preference for the urban periphery, and they may well be harbingers of the intensifying globalization of the suburbs in many countries besides the United States.

*Corporate control points
  on transnational
  networks*

As we have noted, world cities are the premier locations for the command and control functions of the global economic system. Among these functions, the headquarters of the largest transnational corporations stand out because decisions made there have an enormous impact on worldwide flows of capital, commodities, and information. These facilities have a particular locational affinity for urban business complexes because they are highly dependent on a plethora of specialized legal, financial, and other business activities, which we may call producer, or corporate, services.

The annual compilations by *Fortune* magazine of the 500 largest firms allow us to monitor the locational behavior of the leading U.S. corporations. Nationally, in 1994, 233 (47 percent) of the *Fortune* 500 were

18. Manuel Castells, *The Informational City: Information Technology, Economic Restructuring, and the Urban-Regional Process* (Cambridge, MA: Basil Blackwell, 1989).

19. Manuel Castells and Peter Hall, *Technopoles of the World: The Making of Twenty-First-Century Industrial Complexes* (New York: Routledge, 1994), p. 1.

20. Ibid., pp. 1-9.

headquartered in the suburbs compared to 56 (11 percent) in 1969 and 170 (34 percent) in 1978. Greater New York has for decades been the dominant headquarters metropolis, but the suburban shift there has lately surged far ahead of the national pattern. Manhattan, which as recently as 1983 led suburbia in *Fortune* 500 head offices, has seen its total plunge from 138 in 1968 to 73 in 1980 to 29 in 1994; alternatively, the suburbs were home to 52 headquarters (64 percent of the metropolitan total) in 1994, most of them clustered at a few locales in southwesternmost Connecticut, northern New Jersey, and the New York State suburbs north of the central city. There may be more than one way to interpret this quintessential intra-urban deconcentration trend, but one certainly cannot ignore how closely it seems to fit Sassen's postulation of a new space of centrality emerging around a grid of nodes.

As the location cost differential between the metropolitan core and ring equalized around 1970, a corporate suburbanization movement was launched that has still not run its course. With noneconomic factors taking over, headquarters shifts have been guided by perceived improvements in the quality of workplace life, the geographic prestige of new suburban business milieus, and overall convenience for a workforce whose majority already resided in the suburbs.[21] Although many commentators warned that corporations would be geographically disadvantaged by

locating outside the CBD, ever greater numbers of them thrive in the outer city. This also appears to be the case for companies with increasingly internationalized operations. Joel Garreau has pointed out that AT&T's headquarters complex around Basking Ridge, New Jersey (approximately 30 miles west of Manhattan), quite effectively controls its world communications network from there; he even speculates that this global information hub "may someday erupt like a historic boomtown" on the order of Detroit when automobiles were new.[22] Most recently, Tenneco, ranked 34th on the 1994 *Fortune* list, might have sparked the newest trend: in late 1995 it announced a relocation of its corporate headquarters from Houston to suburban Greenwich, in the southwestern corner of Connecticut, primarily so it could be closer to its European markets (not to mention Manhattan and Kennedy Airport, less than an hour's drive to the southwest)![23]

The continuing ascendancy of New York's suburban corporate community is reinforced by the steady deconcentration of supporting corporate services. These activities, which through the recent past were always tightly agglomerated in the CBD, include highest-order legal, financial, banking, data-processing, accounting, management, and other specialized business services. Today Manhattan remains the chief metropolitan supplier of corporate services, but its position is steadily eroding as corporations leave New York City and

21. Peter O. Muller, "The Suburbanization of Corporate Headquarters: What Are the Trends and Consequences?" *Vital Issues* (Center for Information on America), Apr. 1978.

22. Garreau, *Edge City*, p. 27.

23. Allen R. Myerson, "Tenneco Pulling Out of Houston for a New Base in Greenwich," *New York Times*, 16 Sept. 1995.

as their supporting activities discover they no longer require a CBD location to be successful.[24]

This exodus was undoubtedly heightened in the aftermath of the stock market crash of 1987 and the national economic recession of the early 1990s, both of which severely affected all of Manhattan's office industries. At the same time, the city's undereducated resident labor force is increasingly mismatched to the jobs that are available in the CBD, which require the importing of ever greater numbers of suburban workers who do possess the necessary skills. Tellingly, the *New York Times* recently reported that New York City no longer attracts bright young professionals from elsewhere in the country, for the first time in memory becoming a net exporter of talent.[25] This suggests that a new generation of highly skilled workers does not want the big-city lifestyle, preferring to live where work can be balanced with other pursuits. This particularly affects the Wall Street–based securities industry, which since 1987 has experienced the outflow of thousands of jobs, billions of dollars, and the economic power that goes with them.

Manhattan's declining role in the metropolitan corporate-service complex is reflected in the latest employment data. Table 1 shows that the business services sector attained critical mass in the suburbs during the 1980s and still continues to steadily decentralize. In Table 2, those data are disaggregated to highlight a number of key components. Note that only the Madison Avenue–centered advertising business is assured of a critical mass in Manhattan through the foreseeable future; the other producer services, most significantly computer and data processing services, exhibit a relentless suburbanization trend that could soon pass a point of no return and signal the unraveling of New York City's remaining corporate community. That possibility is also suggested in Table 3, which shows parallel employment trends in the closely related finance, insurance, and real estate sector. This is the crucial sector that contains the Wall Street financial community, accounts for the lion's share of Manhattan's massive post-1987 job losses, and appears poised to achieve critical mass in the suburban ring by the turn of the century. When the latter does occur, it will lend more credence than ever to the warning recently voiced by Markusen and Gwiasda: "New York [City] increasingly lacks the layering of urban functions—political, industrial, financial, educational—that is the essence of [world] cities and their ability to continue as seedbeds of innovation and generators of new types of employment."[26]

24. An analysis of the situation at the end of the 1980s is provided in Alex Schwartz, "The Geography of Corporate Services: A Case Study of the New York Urban Region," *Urban Geography*, 1 Jan.-14 Feb. 1992, pp. 1-24. Schwartz's optimism for the CBD, however, is now harder to justify against data trends through the mid-1990s on Manhattan's corporate and employment losses.

25. Sam Roberts, "New York Exports Its Talent as a Migration Tide Turns," *New York Times*, 6 Mar. 1994.

26. Ann Markusen and Vicky Gwiasda, "Multipolarity and the Layering of Functions in World Cities: New York City's Struggle to Stay on Top," *International Journal of Urban and Regional Research*, 18:168 (1994).

The foreign presence in suburban America

Our final perspective is the most difficult to capture, but there is a lot of (admittedly fragmentary) anecdotal evidence that suggests a steadily growing foreign presence in the outer metropolitan ring. Urban geographers, especially, cannot help noticing the internationalization of certain suburban landscapes in many parts of the nation. Thomas Harvey's current reconnaissance of suburban Portland catalogues what may be an increasingly typical roster of foreign-owned businesses and real estate enterprises, dominated here by the Japanese but also including those operated by investors from such exotic places as Kuwait and the South Pacific's Nauru.[27] In the Dallas–Fort Worth metroplex, in fact, about half of the foreign-owned firms are found outside the central cities. The growing predilection of foreigners for American suburbs is underscored in a vignette offered by Garreau, who was astonished to discover one of the nation's largest Japanese malls and cultural centers on the New Jersey bank of the Hudson across the river from Manhattan; he quickly learned the facility serves the 60,000-plus Japanese working for their global companies in the New York area, most of whom live in the city's northern and western suburbs.[28]

The course of development of such foreign communities is perhaps best illustrated by two examples from

TABLE 1
CENTRAL CITY AND SUBURBAN PERCENTAGES OF METROPOLITAN EMPLOYMENT IN THE BUSINESS SERVICES SECTOR, GREATER NEW YORK REGION, 1974-96

Year	New York City	Suburban Ring
1974	57.3	42.7
1984	48.4	51.6
1988	45.4	54.6
1992	40.9	59.1
1996 (est.)	36.7	63.3

SOURCE: U.S., Department of Commerce, Bureau of the Census, *County Business Patterns* (annually). Percentages based on the 1993 definition of the New York Consolidated Metropolitan Statistical Area by the Office of Management and Budget.

suburban Los Angeles, which may be harbingers for other metropolitan areas. Business communities tend to cluster in the same suburban sector, though often dispersing locally along freeway corridors. Such is the case with the nine Japanese automakers, which have located near Interstates 5 and 405 south and east of central Los Angeles. These office campuses concentrate not on manufacturing but on research-and-development operations. Interviews with managers (who tend to be Americans—as are most other employees) reveal that the purpose of locating here in the giant marketplace of pacesetting Southern California is to study American styles of living so as to better design new automotive products.[29] Foreign residential communities tend to be more tightly agglom-

27. Thomas Harvey, "Portland, Oregon: Regional City in a Global Economy," *Urban Geography*, 1 Jan.-14 Feb. 1996, pp. 98-102.

28. Garreau, *Edge City*, pp. 22-23.

29. Doron P. Levin, "Motor City for Japanese in California, Their Strategy: 'When in Rome . . . ,'" *New York Times*, 7 May 1990.

TABLE 2

CENTRAL CITY AND SUBURBAN PERCENTAGES OF METROPOLITAN EMPLOYMENT IN SELECTED PRODUCER SERVICES, GREATER NEW YORK REGION, 1984-96

	Year	New York City	Suburban Ring
Advertising	1984	84.8	15.2
	1992	76.8	23.2
	1996 (est.)	72.5	27.5
Legal services	1984	60.2	39.8
	1992	56.3	43.7
	1996 (est.)	53.7	46.3
Computer and data processing services	1984	31.6	68.4
	1992	24.6	75.4
	1996 (est.)	19.8	80.2
Engineering and management services	1984	49.9	50.1
	1992	41.2	58.8
	1996 (est.)	37.9	62.1

SOURCE: Bureau of the Census, *County Business Patterns* (annually). Percentages based on the 1993 definition of the New York Consolidated Metropolitan Statistical Area by the Office of Management and Budget.

TABLE 3

CENTRAL CITY AND SUBURBAN PERCENTAGES OF METROPOLITAN EMPLOYMENT IN THE FINANCE, INSURANCE, AND REAL ESTATE SECTOR, GREATER NEW YORK REGION, 1974-96

Year	New York City	Suburban Ring
1974	68.0	32.0
1984	62.8	37.2
1988	58.3	41.7
1992	56.1	43.9
1996 (est.)	51.8	48.2

SOURCE: Bureau of the Census, *County Business Patterns* (annually). Percentages based on the 1993 definition of the New York Consolidated Metropolitan Statistical Area by the Office of Management and Budget.

erated. The quintessential example is the city of Monterey Park, just east of Los Angeles. It is the nation's "first suburban Chinatown," whose majority Asian population includes immigrants from Taiwan, Hong Kong, Southeast Asia, and, most recently, China.[30] This affluent community has even been called an extension of Pacific-Rim Asia, because its transplanted residents seek to re-create their homeland lives here. As a result, Monterey Park and nearby towns in the San Gabriel Valley are transforming as Asian investments pour in and are channeled into high-rise apartment buildings, retail centers, and a variety of business ventures.

30. Timothy P. Fong, *The First Suburban Chinatown* (Philadelphia: Temple University Press, 1994); Seth Mydans, "Asian Investors Create a Pocket of Prosperity: California Valley Avoids Region's Slide," *New York Times*, 17 Oct. 1994.

GLOBALIZED SUBURBS IN THE TWENTY-FIRST-CENTURY METROPOLIS

The five perspectives considered in this article all point toward the same interpretation: globalization intensifies and accelerates the suburban transformation of the American city. The world city model, whose city is actually a polycentric metropolis of realms, articulates the role of the CBD and its surrounding constellation of suburban downtowns as primary control points in global economic networks. The relationship between telecommunications and urban form reinforces this new grid of nodes by assuring them equal access to international information flows via metropolitan-wide, state-of-the-art electronic infrastructures. High-technology industrial complexes, particularly the pacesetting technopoles, are heavily shaped by global forces and their marked preference for campuslike, outer-city locations. Transnational corporate headquarters continue to relocate outside New York and other large central cities, and in the 1990s there is much evidence that corporate-services complexes are suburbanizing as well. In addition, as businesses and people become ever more internationally mobile, foreign-settler communities are on the rise in metropolitan rings from Los Angeles to New York to Miami.

The consequences of these developments will surely have a decisive impact on the layout and functioning of the twenty-first-century metropolis. As more and more high-order activities achieve critical mass in the suburbs, it is not hard to envision that in a few years the economies of many central cities will have fully turned inside out. Although private-sector and public policies have for decades encouraged the deconcentration of intrametropolitan activity, the most recent decline in the power and prestige of the CBD is also the result of its having been shaped by economic-geographic factors in an urban-industrial era that has now ended. With no long-term forces on the horizon to resurrect its once dominant centrality—or even to bind its remaining functions—the CBD for the first time will confront a situation in which none of its activities must be located there. Thus growth strategies to carve out a new role for the central city in a new age must be sensitive to this new footlooseness within a metropolitan economy increasingly led from the outer ring. They may even require that major investments be diverted from the CBD to outer areas adjacent to suburbia. Airport zones might be candidates as well as such suburban-like central-city fringes as Philadelphia's Far Northeast, New York City's Staten Island, and Los Angeles's San Fernando Valley (perhaps not coincidentally, the latter two faced serious secession movements when this issue went to press).

As fully urbanized suburbs take over as the engine that drives metropolitan and world city growth, the implications for American economic and social life will be enormous. Many scholars have speculated on urban futures that presume the continued dominance of the central city, but very few have projected scenarios from the line of reasoning followed in this article. Among the latter is planning theorist Edward Blakely, of the University of California, Berkeley, and his vision merits wider attention in the urban studies arena. Tomorrow's cities will have cleanly broken with a past dominated by "agri-industrial" urban centers enmeshed in webs of interconnections geared to the distribution of goods and supporting services. Replacing the latter is the "new technology city," which will function externally as a leading transmission point and control center in global information networks. Its internal configuration will be based on economic and social factors discussed earlier, marked by a mosaic of new communities (that merge living, working, shopping, education, and recreation) and enveloped by a technology infrastructure that will facilitate a thorough reorganization of urban space.[31]

The new city will emerge on the periphery of the current metropolitan areas. It will begin with a rich technology system that communicates with the world. It will gradually take over other functions and emerge as the central node away from the old CBD. It will, in fact, become a city or community based on the notion of shaping its development rather than reacting to externalities. The new city has the promise of providing the kind of living and working environments that planners desire. It has the problem of creating a greater differentiation among communities and economic classes.[32]

Some may find this to be a startling forecast, but its gathering elements have been detectable to researchers for years. This article has sought to assess how far we have advanced toward that kind of urban future and how local expressions of globalization forces are likely to hasten the emergence of a totally new American city.

31. Blakely, "New Technology City."

32. Ibid., p. 236.

ANNALS, *AAPSS*, **551**, May 1997

Underclass Neighborhoods in Temporal and Ecological Perspective

By JEFFREY D. MORENOFF and MARTA TIENDA

ABSTRACT: This article places the growth of an urban underclass in the broader context of trends in inequality and the stratification of place in global cities. Using Chicago as a case study, we construct a multidimensional typology of urban neighborhoods to illuminate trends in the spatial distribution of opportunity, the impact of immigration on the city's ecological structure, and modal patterns of neighborhood change. Our empirical analysis documents (1) the increasing spatial polarization of Chicago's neighborhoods, fueled by a concentration of both affluence and socioeconomic disadvantage; (2) the erosion of working-class areas as an ecological category; (3) the emergence of Hispanic neighborhoods as a distinct ecological type; and (4) the existence of race-specific patterns of neighborhood upgrading. These trends have broader implications for the study of spatial inequality in advanced industrial cities.

Jeffrey D. Morenoff is a Ph.D. candidate in the Department of Sociology at the University of Chicago. His research interests focus on race and ethnic stratification, human ecology, and criminology. He is completing a dissertation on birth outcomes of minority populations.

Marta Tienda is Ralph Lewis Professor of Sociology, University of Chicago. She is former editor of the American Journal of Sociology *and coauthor, with Frank D. Bean, of* The Hispanic Population of the United States *(1987).*

NOTE: This research was supported by funds to the Center for the Study of Urban Inequality and the Ogburn-Stouffer Center of the University of Chicago. We are grateful for institutional support from the Population Research Center of the National Opinion Research Center and the University of Chicago.

S EVERAL global trends have altered the spatial distribution
of opportunities in major cities
throughout the world. One global
trend is rising inequality, which has
been mainly driven by falling real
wages. Another is deindustrialization, namely, the relative decline of
well-paying industrial jobs and concomitant rise of unskilled service
jobs. In the United States, for example, manufacturing employment fell
by 26 percent between 1980 and 1990
in large central counties of Frostbelt
areas.[1] Many central city jobs migrated to nearby suburban communities, but others were transferred to
low-wage labor markets within the
United States or overseas. Chicago, a
prototypical Rustbelt city, lost 60 percent of its manufacturing jobs between 1967 and 1987.[2] In some countries, three additional trends have
altered the spatial distribution of opportunities: (1) population decline in
urban centers most affected by deindustrialization, (2) increased international migration to a few large
metropolitan areas, and (3) uneven
rates of job growth between rural and
urban areas and between major regions.

In response to these macrolevel
trends, a vast social science literature has sought to understand the
social consequences of changes in the
spatial distribution of economic opportunity.[3] William J. Wilson was the
first to observe that concentrated
poverty is associated with extreme
forms of social disorganization, manifested in high rates of violent crime,
nonmarital fertility, infant mortality,
chronic joblessness and welfare dependence, and dismal scholastic outcomes. According to Wilson, these social dislocations, which he dubbed
"concentration effects," are produced
by the constraints on opportunities
faced by residents of extreme poverty
neighborhoods.

Unfortunately, by focusing almost
exclusively on how macro demographic and economic forces affected
the most disadvantaged segments of
the population, most of the research
about urban inequality ignored
broader changes in the ecology of advanced industrial cities. In fact, since
the publication of Wilson's *Truly Disadvantaged*, the notion of "social
transformation" has become virtually synonymous with the concentration of urban poverty. Thus the explosion of research on urban poverty
during the 1980s and early 1990s had
the unintended consequence of ne-
glecting the wider context of urban
inequality characterizing large cities
worldwide. More specifically, by limiting the scope of investigation to a
subset of underclass areas of a few
global cities, researchers have ignored other important forces of urban
change, such as the spatial concentration of affluence and the impact of
recent waves of immigration in transforming global urban centers.[4]

1. John Kasarda, "Industrial Restructur-
ing and the Changing Location of Jobs," in
State of the Union: America in the 1990s, ed.
Reynolds Farley (New York: Russell Sage
Foundation, 1995), 1:215-68.

2. William J. Wilson, *When Work Disappears* (New York: Alfred A. Knopf, 1996).

3. William Julius Wilson, *The Truly Disadvantaged: The Inner City, the Underclass,*
and Public Policy (Chicago: University of Chicago Press, 1987).

4. For a noteworthy exception, see Kath-
erine McFate, Roger Lawson, and William
Julius Wilson, eds., *Poverty Inequality and the*

Accordingly, in this article, we briefly review the literature on urban transformations and the spatial distribution of opportunity, and then, using Chicago as a case study, we conduct an empirical analysis that addresses three significant yet neglected questions about trends in urban inequality. The first concerns temporal transformation in the ecological structure of urban neighborhoods. Specifically, has there been a trend toward the concentration of affluence paralleling the concentration of poverty, and if so, what changes in Chicago's ecological structure have driven the spatial polarization of inequality? Second, how does neighborhood change transform the ecological structure of cities? More specifically, what types of neighborhoods are most likely to (1) downgrade and join the ranks of ghetto underclass areas, (2) upgrade through gentrification, or (3) remain ecologically stable over time? Third, what implications does urban ecological transformation portend for specific demographic groups? For example, are black middle- and working-class neighborhoods always less likely to remain economically stable than similar white neighborhoods? Where do emerging immigrant neighborhoods fit into the ecological structure of the city, and what types of neighborhoods are they likely to succeed?

Chicago is an important case study because it replicates many features of the national population. As the third-largest city, it is a major destination of recent immigrants and the

only U.S. city that combines both Mexicans and Puerto Ricans among its Hispanic residents. The findings reported in this article, while particular to Chicago, illuminate trends in inequality and the stratification of place that may have generalizable consequences for other advanced industrial cities. These include the spatial polarization of inequality and the concomitant erosion of working-class neighborhoods.

Wilson's notion of "social transformation" characterizes a wave of social change that hit older industrial cities in the 1970s and left residents of inner-city neighborhoods more disadvantaged than poor residents of other city and suburban neighborhoods and than poor residents of the same neighborhoods in previous decades. Wilson identified two principal causes of social transformation: the decline in job opportunities associated with deindustrialization; and the exodus of middle- and upper-income black families from the inner city, which removed a "social buffer" that might have deflected the full impact of economic dislocations.[5] Wilson called attention to how increases in poverty trigger out-migration of nonpoor residents from mixed-income neighborhoods. In fact, he argued that selective out-migration was the key mechanism underlying the increase of concentrated poverty in Chicago during the 1970s, although his evidence was highly inferential.

Besides the spatial concentration of poverty and social disadvantage, another research theme in the modern urban poverty literature concerns the demographic mechanisms

---

Future of Social Policy: Western States in the New World Order (New York: Russell Sage Foundation, 1995).

5. Wilson, *Truly Disadvantaged*, p. 56.

undergirding the geographic expansion of concentrated poverty. Wilson recognized that a variety of mechanisms may operate simultaneously, including the possibilities that residents of previously nonpoor neighborhoods increasingly fall into poverty and that these neighborhoods attract poor migrants from other areas of the city.[6] Still, he maintained support for the hypothesis that "the significant increase in the poverty concentration in these overwhelmingly black communities is related to the large out-migration of nonpoor blacks."[7]

Douglas Massey and his colleagues attempted to dismantle Wilson's out-migration hypothesis by showing that residential segregation prevents middle- and upper-income blacks from leaving the inner city.[8] Massey argued that racial segregation leads to the geographic concentration of poverty by ensuring that exogenous economic shocks, which increase the poverty rate, are confined to poor minority neighborhoods. Thus, while Wilson's out-migration thesis envisions the depopulation of emerging poverty areas, Massey's explanation predicts an increase in the number of segregated black families that fall into poverty (but is ambivalent with respect to population change).

Jargowsky and Bane expanded on this debate by delineating four mechanisms that can account for the rise in concentrated poverty: (1) poor residents moving from other areas of the city into the ghetto; (2) nonpoor persons moving out of mixed-income neighborhoods; (3) no net migration, but an overall increase in the poverty rate among those who live in mixed-income neighborhoods, causing some areas to be reclassified; and (4) some combination of the foregoing, including the effect of differential rates of fertility, mortality, and changes in family structure.[9] These authors showed that the rise in ghetto poverty between 1970 and 1980 could be attributed only to the economic deterioration of neighborhoods that had been mixed income in 1970 but were reclassified as high in poverty in 1980.[10] In addition, the mixed-income areas in all four cities studied experienced substantial population decline. Thus Jargowsky and Bane concluded that out-migration was the most prominent demographic mechanism operating in the 1970s. Although this debate has yet to be settled conclusively, more recent research substantiates the idea that the demographic mechanisms underlying the concentration of poverty are multidimensional and more complex than previously recognized.[11]

In sum, although there is indisputable evidence that urban inequality

6. Ibid., p. 49.
7. Ibid., p. 50.
8. Douglas S. Massey and Nancy Denton, *American Apartheid: Segregation and the Making of the Underclass* (Cambridge, MA: Harvard University Press, 1993).

9. Paul A. Jargowsky and Mary Jo Bane, "Ghetto Poverty in the United States, 1970-1980," in *The Urban Underclass*, ed. Christopher Jencks and Paul E. Peterson (Washington, DC: Brookings Institution, 1991), p. 261.
10. Ibid., pp. 266-67.
11. Katharine Nelson, "Racial Segregation, Mobility and Poverty Concentration" (Paper delivered at the annual meeting of the Population Association of America, Washington, DC, 1991); Douglas S. Massey, Andrew A. Gross, and Kumika Shibuya, "Migration, Segregation and the Concentration of Poverty," *American Sociological Review*, 59:425-45 (1994).

increased during the 1970s and 1980s, as proven by sharp increases in the concentration of various measures of economic deprivation and social disadvantage, there have been surprisingly few attempts to place this trend toward concentrated poverty within the broader context of urban social change and the spatial polarization of inequality. The remainder of this article redresses this shortcoming of prior studies by devising a method for reclassifying neighborhoods using a multidimensional clustering technique.

TYPOLOGIZING URBAN TRANSFORMATION

The goals of our empirical analysis, as stated previously, are to examine changes in Chicago's ecological structure, to analyze the patterns of neighborhood change that undergird transformations in that structure, and to understand the implications of this ecological change for different racial and ethnic groups. We use the word "ecological" to signify that our analytic units are spatially defined aggregates, neighborhoods, in our application, that are proxied by census tracts. Hence the term "ecological structure" refers to the stratification of neighborhoods. Likewise, "ecological characteristics" refers to neighborhood-level measurements rather than their microlevel analogues. For example, many sociodemographic characteristics, such as poverty, unemployment, and race, reflect categorical distinctions at the individual level but, when translated into ecological constructs, are typically expressed as percentages or rates.

Relying on tract-level census data for the city of Chicago from 1970 to 1990, our empirical strategy entailed constructing a typology of Chicago neighborhoods that groups census tracts into ecological categories at each of three time periods. The conventional approach is to sort neighborhoods based on arbitrary cutoff points in the distribution of a single variable, usually poverty. Typically, neighborhoods with poverty rates of 40 percent and over are classified as "ghetto poor," while those with rates of between 20 and 40 percent may be labeled simply as "poor," and those with poverty rates of under 20 percent are usually classified as "nonpoor." Changes in the concentration of poverty are then assessed by the number of neighborhoods that enter these categories over time.

This approach is lacking in three respects. First, it focuses on neighborhoods at one tail of the distribution, namely, those with the highest poverty rates, revealing little about potentially important distinctions between near-poor and nonpoor neighborhoods. Second, the cutoff points are usually imposed arbitrarily. Finally, a single-indicator approach to inequality neglects other important sociodemographic dimensions of a city's ecological structure, such as age composition and residential stability, that are decisive in shaping trajectories of neighborhood change.

Therefore, we devised a strategy that allows us to construct ecological categories across a multidimensional array of empirically observed neighborhood characteristics, including measures of socioeconomic status, residential stability, family structure, and age composition. More specifically, we conducted a cluster analysis on 825 Chicago census tracts (collected for the census years 1970, 1980, and 1990) with a set of 10 variables. These include rates of poverty, public assistance, unemployment, college graduates, white-collar workers, female-headed families, owner occupancy, residence in same house for at least five years, and two indicators of age structure (residents aged 17 and younger, and those aged 75 and older). Cluster analysis is a method that groups cases (in our case, census tracts) into hierarchical categories on the basis of their "proximity" to one another, which can be calculated by a variety of different algorithms.[12]

CHICAGO AS A CASE
STUDY OF NEIGHBORHOOD
TRANSFORMATION:
EMPIRICAL RESULTS

Our cluster analysis yields a fourfold typology of Chicago neighborhoods from 1970 to 1990 consisting of the following ecological categories: (1) stable middle-class neighborhoods; (2) gentrifying yuppie neighborhoods; (3) transitional working-class neighborhoods; and (4) ghetto underclass neighborhoods.[13] The

clustering procedure provides no insights into the meaning of the categories it creates; it simply groups neighborhoods based on their similarities. Our labels for the four clusters reflect our interpretation of neighborhood types based on the salience of various characteristics. To arrive at our interpretations, we examined descriptive statistics for each of the clusters, as presented in Table 1.[14] Although measures of racial and ethnic composition were not used in the cluster analysis, their mean values are also displayed in order to show how the resulting ecological types vary with respect to race. As a baseline reference for comparing the clusters, the first column of Table 1 displays means and standard deviations for the entire city.[15]

Table 1 shows that the first cluster consists mainly of residentially stable middle-class neighborhoods with aging populations. Neighborhoods in this category tend to be of high socioeconomic status, as indicated by the low rates of poverty, public assistance, unemployment, and female-headed families relative to the citywide means. The only factors that detract from the high socioeconomic status of these neighborhoods are the moderate levels of both college graduates and, to a lesser extent, white-collar workers. These neighborhoods con-

12. We relied on Ward's minimum variance algorithm to compute the similarity measures. See SAS, *SAS/STAT User's Guide, Version 6* (Cary, NC: SAS Institute, 1990).

13. Individual neighborhoods can move through different ecological categories over time because the unit of analysis is not the tract per se but, rather, the tract-year. As a result, the categories themselves can grow or decline in size over time, in terms of the number of neighborhoods that compose them.

14. We also examined how the characteristics of each cluster changed over time, but in the interest of parsimony these tables are not reported.

15. Citywide tabulations do not represent the true mean values for the entire city because they are calculated to reflect average characteristics of census tracts from different time periods and with varying population sizes, and thus they contain aggregation bias.

TABLE 1
DESCRIPTIVE STATISTICS BY NEIGHBORHOOD TYPE

Variable	Citywide		Stable Middle-Class		Gentrifying Yuppie		Transitional Working-Class		Underclass	
	Mean	(Standard deviation)	Mean	(Standard deviation)	Mean	(Standard deviation)	Mean	(Standard deviation)	Mean	(Standard deviation)
Used in clustering										
% poor	18.1	(16.9)	7.2	(6.3)	8.8	(7.9)	20.7	(10.4)	43.3	(16.6)
% public assistance	14.7	(15.9)	6.1	(6.5)	5.6	(5.8)	13.4	(8.5)	41.4	(14.3)
Unemployment rate	10.5	(9.2)	6.7	(4.7)	5.2	(3.7)	9.1	(4.9)	24.6	(10.5)
% college graduate	15.9	(15.9)	13.7	(8.6)	48.8	(17.7)	10.0	(7.5)	6.4	(4.9)
% white-collar	55.3	(18.9)	56.8	(13.4)	79.3	(12.6)	42.7	(12.6)	53.4	(21.9)
% female head	23.7	(17.8)	14.0	(9.2)	17.7	(12.4)	22.1	(10.1)	50.5	(16.9)
% aged 17 and under	29.1	(11.1)	25.2	(6.4)	14.8	(7.4)	35.6	(7.8)	38.0	(10.1)
% aged 75 and older	11.1	(6.4)	14.4	(6.3)	12.2	(6.6)	7.9	(3.9)	8.4	(5.6)
% same house 5 years	55.1	(15.0)	63.9	(10.2)	38.2	(11.0)	48.0	(13.3)	61.1	(11.2)
% owner occupancy	36.1	(24.4)	56.7	(22.0)	21.0	(14.5)	25.1	(14.9)	22.5	(16.6)
Not used in clustering										
% black	37.5	(43.9)	17.8	(35.9)	17.6	(24.5)	39.3	(42.9)	90.1	(22.9)
% Hispanic	14.8	(22.2)	9.9	(15.7)	10.2	(10.8)	29.1	(29.0)	6.5	(17.5)
% foreign-born	10.3	(13.1)	9.7	(11.2)	13.4	(11.6)	14.5	(16.5)	2.7	(7.0)

SOURCE: U.S. Census, 1970-90, City of Chicago.

tain high percentages of elderly and small to moderate-sized youth populations. Average rates of owner occupancy and residential stability are both very high in this category. Neighborhoods of this type contained relatively few blacks and Hispanics.

Gentrifying yuppie neighborhoods are also characterized by relatively high socioeconomic status. However, these neighborhoods differ from stable middle-class neighborhoods in their distinctive age structures and unstable residential character. Youths are relatively underrepresented in these areas, and although the percentage of elderly is slightly higher than the citywide average, unreported tabulations revealed that the elderly population declined over time. Another distinguishing feature of this cluster is its low level of residential stability. Less than 40 percent of persons residing in gentrifying yuppie neighborhoods lived in the same house for at least five years, and the mean owner occupancy rate is only 21 percent. Rates of poverty, public assistance, unemployment, and female headship are low in these neighborhoods, while the share of college-educated residents and white-collar workers is higher than in stable, middle-class areas of the city. Whites predominate in these neighborhoods.

The third cluster, denoted transitional working-class neighborhoods, plays a pivotal role in the process of neighborhood change. Compared to the previous two neighborhood types, these neighborhoods exhibit lower socioeconomic status but are close to citywide averages along many dimensions. For example, the poverty rate in these neighborhoods is just above the citywide mean, while rates of public assistance, unemployment, and female headship fall just below the citywide averages. However, the most distinctive socioeconomic characteristics of these neighborhoods are their low shares of college-educated residents and white-collar workers. Demographically, these neighborhoods are characterized by high percentages of youths and low percentages of elderly. Levels of residential stability and owner occupancy also fall below the citywide averages, which underscores the transitional nature of these neighborhoods. Perhaps the most distinguishing characteristic of this neighborhood type is its race and ethnic composition, which became increasingly dominated by Hispanics and immigrants over time. The Hispanic presence in this cluster increased from 14 to 58 percent of the population between 1970 and 1990.

The final neighborhood type comprises socially and economically disadvantaged neighborhoods, what have come to be known as "underclass" neighborhoods, or areas of ghetto poverty that suffer from severe socioeconomic deprivation. Rates of poverty, unemployment, public assistance, and female-headed families are very high in this cluster, while the proportion of college graduates is very low. Of the socioeconomic characteristics considered, only the proportion of white-collar workers ranks near the city average. The structural context of disadvantage in this cluster is further compounded by high rates of residential entrenchment (the percentage of people living in the same house for at least five years) and low rates of owner occupancy. The age structures of these neighborhoods are characterized by a high proportion of youths and low proportion of the elderly. These areas are racially homogeneous, averaging 90 percent black.

ECOLOGICAL TRANSFORMATION AND THE PATHS OF NEIGHBORHOOD CHANGE

To examine the growth and decline of the ecological categories, we cross-classified the four types of neighborhoods over successive time periods. Like mobility tables, the cross-tabulations displayed in Table 2 depict inflows and outflows among ecological categories over time. The top panel depicts patterns of change in the 1970s, the middle panel shows mobility in the 1980s, and the bottom panel displays neighborhood trajectories from 1970 to 1990. These panels reveal that both the stable middle-class and transitional working-class categories diminished in size over time. The transitional working-class category was the most dominant neighborhood type in 1970, when it comprised 45 percent of all tracts (374 out of 825), but it diminished considerably over each decade and accounted for only 14 percent of all neighborhoods (tracts) in 1990. The stable middle-class category also experienced a decline, though not as drastic, shrinking from 41 percent (342 out of 825) of all tracts in 1970 to 34 percent (278 out of 825) in 1990.

An equally prominent insight is that categories at the two poles of the socioeconomic distribution—the gen-

trifying yuppie and ghetto underclass neighborhood types—gained increasing shares of the city's neighborhoods over time. Most of the growth in the ghetto underclass category occurred during the 1970s, when it expanded from just 22 tracts (3 percent of the city total) in 1970 to 187 tracts (23 percent of the city total) in 1980. The gentrifying yuppie category also expanded over time, particularly during the 1980s, when it grew from 90 to 175 tracts (increasing its share from 11 to 21 percent of the city's tracts). Thus, in terms of socioeconomic status, the ecological structure of Chicago's neighborhoods became more polarized over time, with the erosion of the middle ground occupied by transitional working-class areas, and the concomitant emergence of more impoverished areas in the 1970s and gentrifying neighborhoods in the 1980s.

Table 2 also shows a tendency for neighborhoods to remain in the same ecological category over time. This pattern is particularly pronounced among the gentrifying yuppie and ghetto underclass neighborhoods and, to a lesser extent, for stable middle-class areas. Transitional working-class neighborhoods were the most fluid of all clusters. Panel C shows that only 17 percent of the neighborhoods in this category in 1970 remained there in 1990. Thus these neighborhoods served as turning points in neighborhood trajectories. From this type, many neighborhoods either downgraded and joined the ghetto underclass category, or upgraded and joined either the stable middle-class or the gentrifying yuppie category. Most of the downgrad-

TABLE 2

NEIGHBORHOOD MOBILITY THROUGH ECOLOGICAL CATEGORIES

A. Neighborhood Mobility 1970-80

1970 Category	1980 Category				
	Middle-class	Yuppie	Working-class	Underclass	Total
Middle-class	270	8	50	14	342
Yuppie	9	63	13	2	87
Working-class	52	19	152	151	374
Underclass	0	0	2	20	22
Total	331	90	217	187	825

B. Neighborhood Mobility 1980-90

1980 Category	1990 Category				
	Middle-class	Yuppie	Working-class	Underclass	Total
Middle-class	248	41	31	11	331
Yuppie	0	90	0	0	90
Working-class	26	40	82	69	217
Underclass	4	4	3	176	187
Total	278	175	116	256	825

C. Neighborhood Mobility 1970-90

1970 Category	1990 Category				
	Middle-class	Yuppie	Working-class	Underclass	Total
Middle-class	211	44	**50**	37	342
Yuppie	2	77	4	4	87
Working-class	**65**	**54**	62	**193**	374
Underclass	0	0	0	22	22
Total	278	175	116	256	825

ing of these transitional neighborhoods occurred during the 1970s, when 40 percent of these neighborhoods moved into the ghetto underclass category, while most of the upgrading took place over the following decade, when 30 percent of the transitional neighborhoods moved to either the stable middle-class or gentrifying yuppie category. These substantial outflows were somewhat counterbalanced by a smaller inflow of neighborhoods into this category, particularly from the stable middle-class neighborhood type. In fact, 43 percent of the neighborhoods that were in this category in 1990 began the 1970s in the stable middle-class category.

To understand the implications of neighborhood change for different demographic groups, we inspected in closer detail the cells with bold numbers in Panel C of Table 2. Descriptive statistics for these numbers are shown in Table 3. We report racial and ethnic composition, as well as an index of socioeconomic status and an index of residential stability, which provide summary indicators of most variables listed in Table 1 that were used in the cluster analysis.[16] Positive values of these indices reflect higher levels of socioeconomic status and residential stability, respectively, and the scale is measured in positive or negative standard deviation units from the mean.

The vast majority of neighborhoods that were in the transitional working-class category in 1990 followed one of two modal paths: either they moved there from the stable middle-class category (cell 13) or they began the period (1970) in the transitional working-class category and remained there in 1990 (cell 33). Both trajectories are important for understanding the emergence of Hispanic neighborhoods in Chicago. The top panel of Table 3 reveals that transitions from stable middle-class to transitional working-class neighborhoods were associated with a rapid growth of the Hispanic population, increasing on average from 6 percent Hispanic in 1970 to 45 percent in 1990. At the same time, the non-Hispanic white composition of these neighborhoods declined dramatically, from 94 percent in 1970 to 27 percent in 1990. This means that many Hispanic neighborhoods

16. The socioeconomic status index was calculated by first standardizing and then averaging the following set of variables: the poverty rate (–), the percentage of families on public assistance (–), the unemployment rate (–), the percentage of college graduates (+), and the percentage of white-collar workers (+). The resulting index was then standardized to a mean of zero and a standard deviation of 1. The residential stability index was computed in the same way as the previous index, using the indicators of owner occupancy (+) and the percentage residing in the same house five years ago (+).

evolved out of formerly white, stable, middle-class areas of Chicago. This transition was accompanied by moderate declines in both socioeconomic status and residential stability. The second modal path associated with Hispanic neighborhood change is represented by those neighborhoods that remained in the transitional working-class category throughout the period under consideration. These neighborhoods, which increased from 34 percent Hispanic in 1970 to 70 percent in 1990, were early ecological footholds for Chicago's Hispanic population. Neighborhoods that followed this trajectory were of lower socioeconomic status and were less residentially stable than those emerging from the stable middle-class category (compare the first and second panels of Table 3).

Although most neighborhoods that left the transitional working-class type became underclass areas by 1990, a substantial number also upgraded by moving to either the stable middle-class or gentrifying yuppie category. Given the tendency to equate the ghetto underclass with black neighborhoods, it is pertinent to ask whether all black neighborhoods that were on the cusp of ghetto poverty in 1970 did eventually tip and become underclass, or whether there was also a substantial counter-trend toward neighborhood upgrading that was ignored in the urban poverty literature. Our results show that upgrading did occur among both black and white neighborhoods, but in race-specific patterns: black neighborhoods that upgraded were more likely to join the stable middle-class category, while white neighborhoods

TABLE 3

DESCRIPTIVE STATISTICS BY PATTERN OF NEIGHBORHOOD CHANGE

Pattern of Neighborhood Change	1970		1980		1990	
	Mean	(Standard deviation)	Mean	(Standard deviation)	Mean	(Standard deviation)
Cell 13 (Middle class to working class)						
% black	0.3	(1.0)	7.0	(16.3)	21.7	(29.9)
% non-Hispanic white	93.7	(6.1)	56.9	(21.4)	27.4	(18.7)
% Hispanic	6.2	(7.2)	31.4	(18.6)	45.2	(24.2)
SES index	0.37	(0.16)	0.02	(0.22)	−0.03	(0.33)
Residential stability index	0.18	(0.40)	−0.08	(0.54)	−0.16	(0.39)
Cell 33 (Working class to working class)						
% black	5.5	(16.8)	5.1	(14.1)	6.6	(14.0)
% non-Hispanic white	60.5	(22.0)	30.8	(18.4)	20.5	(15.1)
% Hispanic	34.5	(19.3)	62.0	(21.0)	70.5	(20.5)
SES index	0.02	(0.20)	−0.40	(0.28)	−0.23	(0.30)
Residential stability index	−0.50	(0.35)	−0.55	(0.42)	−0.35	(0.36)
Cell 31 (Working class to middle class)						
% black	48.8	(39.8)	59.9	(44.4)	61.8	(45.0)
% non-Hispanic white	40.0	(33.0)	20.9	(28.5)	16.2	(25.0)
% Hispanic	11.9	(18.5)	18.5	(28.0)	19.6	(31.0)
SES index	−0.27	(0.39)	−0.21	(0.42)	0.03	(0.39)
Residential stability index	−0.27	(0.54)	0.54	(0.84)	0.66	(0.69)
Cell 32 (Working class to yuppie)						
% black	18.3	(30.1)	20.1	(28.2)	18.9	(25.9)
% non-Hispanic white	58.4	(25.9)	47.4	(21.9)	54.5	(24.8)
% Hispanic	20.5	(13.4)	24.7	(17.0)	17.5	(15.0)
SES index	0.14	(0.27)	0.15	(0.47)	0.67	(0.54)
Residential stability index	−0.80	(0.49)	−0.73	(0.49)	−0.79	(0.46)
Cell 34 (Working class to underclass)						
% black	78.3	(35.6)	84.9	(29.3)	86.8	(27.2)
% non-Hispanic white	13.8	(24.3)	5.2	(11.4)	2.9	(7.3)
% Hispanic	7.2	(15.4)	9.4	(20.8)	9.7	(22.5)
SES index	−0.25	(0.32)	−0.99	(0.40)	−1.04	(0.42)
Residential stability index	−0.54	(0.51)	−0.13	(0.53)	−0.09	(0.58)

SOURCE: U.S. Census, 1970-90, City of Chicago.

NOTE: Cell numbers refer to Panel C of Table 2.

were more likely to enter the gentrifying yuppie category.

The third and fourth panels of Table 3 shed more light on these paths of neighborhood change. Neighborhoods that moved out of the transitional working-class category and into the stable middle-class category were nearly 50 percent black in 1970, and this rose to over 60 percent by

1990. Likewise, neighborhoods in this cell witnessed overall declines in white population, from 40 percent in 1970 to 16 percent in 1990. In terms of socioeconomic status, these neighborhoods lost some ground over time, but they remained slightly above the citywide average in 1990. Neighborhoods that made this transition also became more residentially stable over time. The second mode of upgrading—neighborhoods that moved from transitional working-class to gentrifying yuppie—was dominated by white neighborhoods. The socioeconomic status of these neighborhoods increased substantially during the 1980s, and residential stability remained at very low levels throughout the entire period.

As widely documented in the urban poverty literature, Table 3 confirms that the process of ghetto formation was almost exclusively confined to blacks. Neighborhoods that moved from the transitional working-class category to the underclass category became increasingly homogeneous in racial composition over time. These neighborhoods witnessed dramatic declines in socioeconomic status, particularly during the 1970s.

CONCLUSION

Having established both a temporal and ecological perspective on neighborhood change, we now return to our initial questions. First, by utilizing a multidimensional typology of urban neighborhoods, we documented a dramatic spread of ghetto underclass neighborhoods during the 1970s, confirming the general findings of the urban poverty literature. Moreover, we contextualized the growth of ghetto underclass neighborhoods by revealing how the expansion of poverty proceeded in conjunction with several other important ecological trends. One of these is the spatial concentration of affluence, exemplified by the spread of gentrifying yuppie neighborhoods during the 1980s. The net effect of these two transformations was to heighten the spatial polarization of inequality in Chicago neighborhoods. Another trend was the erosion of the transitional working-class areas that occupied the middle ground in Chicago's ecological structure. However, the city's burgeoning Hispanic population appears to have transformed these areas into a new ecological niche that shows signs of persisting. Finally, a more subtle temporal shift was the gradual decline of stable middle-class areas, along with their ecological transformation into black middle-class enclaves.

The second question inquired about the modal patterns of neighborhood change undergirding these ecological transformations. We noted that the transitional working-class neighborhood marked an important turning point in the trajectories of many neighborhoods. Although many of these neighborhoods tipped and thus fueled the growth of the underclass category, our mobility tables also revealed a substantial countertrend toward neighborhood upgrading. At the poles of the ecological distribution—in the ghetto underclass and gentrifying yuppie categories—these transitions were typically rare, implying that once neighborhoods entered these categories, they were unlikely to leave. This pattern of ecological persistence accentuated the spatial polarization of Chicago neighborhoods.

Our last set of questions asked how these changes differentially affected specific demographic groups. As an important corrective to the urban poverty literature, we noted that among black neighborhoods, the process of neighborhood change is not unidirectional. However, when neighborhoods do upgrade, they appear to follow race-specific patterns. Whereas upgrading white neighborhoods tend to follow the path of gentrifying yuppie neighborhoods, emerging black middle-class neighborhoods take on an ecological character more consistent with stable middle-class areas of the city. Our final observation concerns the understudied process of Hispanic neighborhood change. Here we observed that Hispanic neighborhoods followed two modal trajectories. On the one hand, Hispanic populations followed the classic ecological pattern of establishing an early foothold in transitional working-class areas of the city. On the other hand, many Hispanic neighborhoods succeeded white populations in formerly stable middle-class areas of Chicago.

Although our findings shed light on ignored dimensions of urban transformation, they also raise several new questions with more global implications. Is the phenomenon of spatial polarization yet another manifestation of the trend toward global inequality? More research attention should be focused on the spatial concentration of affluence. This research should proceed from the recognition that substantial heterogeneity exists among neighborhoods that for too long have been thought of simply as nonpoor. Another challenge for future research is to specify a set of causal mechanisms that may determine the direction that neighborhood trajectories will take when they reach their turning points. Understanding more about the processes of neighborhood upgrading and downgrading is a crucial first step toward addressing policy issues that might stem the tide toward the spatial concentration of the urban underclass. Finally, researchers should be careful not to equate the ecological experience of Hispanics and other recent immigrant groups with that of blacks in U.S. cities. Recognition of the unique aspects of Hispanic neighborhood change and its role in transforming a growing number of American cities is long overdue.

ANNALS, *AAPSS*, **551**, May 1997

The Federal Urban Policy Agenda: Recent Past and New Realities

By KINGSLEY E. HAYNES and ROGER R. STOUGH

ABSTRACT: After reviewing changes in housing policy and the impact of U.S. metropolitan decentralization on jobs and the demand for transportation, the authors examine the role of the new high-technology economy in urbanization. Specifically, they suggest that the patterns of public and private metropolitan infrastructure investments continue to support decentralized expansion. Using the Washington, D.C., region as an example, they explore the increased separation of suburbs and core cities in metropolitan regions. They explore the different policy perspectives of economic dependency versus specialized economic functions in an interdependent metropolitan region. They argue that present federal urban policy reflects the former but that new urban regional dynamics are driven by the realities of the latter.

Kingsley E. Haynes is University Professor of Public Policy and director of the Institute of Public Policy at George Mason University, Fairfax, Virginia. He has written widely on transportation and urban policy and has been an overseas adviser on these topics in Southeast Asia, the Middle East, and Latin America.

Roger R. Stough is the Northern Virginia Endowed Professor in Local Government and director of the Center for Regional Analysis at George Mason University, Fairfax, Virginia.

FOR years, the federal agenda for urban policy has been sideline cheering or outright benign neglect. This began to change under the Bush administration's Housing and Urban Development (HUD) secretary, Jack Kemp, but has been completely retargeted under Clinton's HUD appointment, Henry Cisneros. The older approach was to ignore cities where possible and to focus issues on the national economy with the view that a good national economic tide would raise all ships or, in this case, metropolitan areas. The 1993 National Urban Policy Report, released at the end of the Bush administration, *Rediscovering Urban America*, focused on metropolitan America, with only one chapter on the hard-to-ignore inner city.[1]

PEOPLE AND HOUSING

America is urban and metropolitan. Eighty percent of Americans are housed in metropolitan areas, and over half live in the largest forty urban centers (each center having a million or more in population). Twenty percent of Americans reside in the five largest metropolitan regions: New York, Los Angeles, Chicago, San Francisco, and Philadelphia.[2] Policy toward housing this population is to some degree urban policy almost by definition. Changes

in the pattern of housing and the federal role in supporting expansion of the housing supply as well as the matching of housing needs to income, location, and jobs are central to any urban policy strategy.

The consequences of the non-region-specific and nonurban strategy of the 1980s was that public housing and its immediate counterpart, center-city neighborhoods, were the victims of neglect. In a period of national dwelling-unit expansion and rise in housing quality, suburbs benefited and lower-income central-city areas were left behind. Moreover, the gap widened. HUD's scandal-ridden housing programs of the 1980s were implemented during a period of extraordinary expansion of apartment and single-family housing. The expansion of the former—multifamily housing—was driven by tax-exempt housing bonds and favorable tax provisions of the Economic Recovery Act of 1981 (phased out in 1987), and the latter—single-family housing—was aided by housing interest rates that at first stalled housing starts with double-digit levels and then released pent-up demand with the lowest levels in 25 years.[3] These policies were driven by a sectoral economic strategy that supported the construction industry.

The Tax Reform Act of 1986 halted the tax-fueled expansion of the multifamily housing sector with lengthened depreciation periods, abandonment of accelerated depreciation, and removal of real estate loss write-offs against other income. Further, with the revision of the tax-exempt hous-

1. Jack Sommer and Donald A. Hicks, eds., *Rediscovering Urban America: Perspectives on the 1980s* (Washington, DC: Department of Housing and Urban Development, Office of Policy Development and Research, 1993).

2. Henry R. Richmond, "Rationale and Program Design" (Manuscript, National Land Use Policy Institute, 1994).

3. Gretchen Armijo et al., "Demographics and Economic Trends," *Journal of Housing Research*, 1(1):21-42 (1990).

ing revenue bonds and with increasingly restrictive rules by the Internal Revenue Service to support lower qualifying incomes, the rent stream became too small to support construction costs through tax-exempt mortgages alone.[4] With the loss of these benefits, the multifamily housing boom fizzled.

The financial crisis of the late 1980s also affected multifamily housing production, forcing commercial banks and savings and loans to consolidate their real estate lending in general and their investment in multifamily construction in particular. During this period of contraction, HUD shifted from support of project construction subsidies to tenant subsidies.[5] This shift slowed the growth in supply while expanding demand.

The only supply-side encouragement of multifamily housing in the first half of the 1990s was the low-income housing tax credit (LIHTC) and the block grant HOME program of the National Affordable Housing Program of 1990.[6] Both could be used to complement the section 8 housing voucher program, and HOME grants could be used for tenant rental assistance or new low-income multifamily

housing construction under very restrictive circumstances. Due to high transaction costs, together with HUD fees and profit caps, and the need to integrate these tax credit programs with other tax subsidies, total costs rose, the risk to developers rose, and government management costs increased.[7] The result was that tax credit utilization for support of housing supply expansion became quite limited, and the distribution of housing resource support also remained limited.[8] Despite the modest expansion of apartment completions since 1990 (1991-94), LIHTC low-income units have accounted for close to a quarter of this construction.[9]

The LIHTC HUD program for affordable housing has made $3 billion in annual support available to state housing authorities since the late 1980s. LIHTC project sizes have increased from an average of 28 units to 42 units since 1993, with a split of 60 percent for new construction to 40 percent for rehabilitation. The latter, of course, is much higher in central cities. Financially, only 6 percent of recent units used bond financing. However, there has been a rise in nonprofit project sponsors from 9 to 23 percent in the mid-1990s as the

4. Richard Peiser, "The Decline of Housing Revenue Bond—Financial Development," *Real Estate Finance Journal*, 3(4):77-116 (1988).

5. Richard Peiser, William C. Baer, and Lee Fairman, "Housing Markets and Patterns," in *Rediscovering Urban America*, ed. Sommer and Hicks.

6. Karl E. Case, "Investors, Developers and Supply-Side Subsidies: How Much Is Enough," *Housing Policy Debate*, 2(2):341-56 (1991). The term "HOME" refers to the Housing Ownership Partnership Investment portion of Title II of the National Affordable Housing Act of 1990.

7. ICF, Inc., "Evaluation of Low-Income Housing Tax Credit, Final Report" (Department of Housing and Urban Development, 1991).

8. Kathryn Nelson and Jill Khadduri, "To Whom Should Limited Housing Resources Be Directed," *Housing Policy Debate*, 3(1):1-55 (1992).

9. Department of Housing and Urban Development, "New Data on the Low-Income Housing Tax Credit," *US Housing Market Conditions* (Department of Housing and Urban Development, Office of Policy Development and Research), pp. 3-8 (1996).

complexity of LIHTC financing becomes better understood. In terms of location, these projects are primarily nonsuburban (54 percent central city and 19 percent nonmetropolitan), although this tracks closely to the national rental market averages of 47 percent in central cities and 14 percent in nonmetropolitan areas.[10] Specifically, 37 percent of all properties are in "difficult to develop areas" or qualified census tract designation areas (low income, high construction cost). Overall, 65 percent of all LIHTC units are in low-income neighborhoods, and one-third are in areas of concentrated poverty, although LIHTC units are in poor neighborhoods with a high proportion (56 percent) of owner occupancy.[11] The impression is that LIHTC has begun to be an effective system of support for low-income housing after a long and shaky start.

PEOPLE AND JOBS

Garreau's popular edge-cities perspective is an accurate articulation of the metropolitan pattern of economic growth in the United States of the 1980s.[12] For many of the reasons he

10. Department of Housing and Urban Development, Office of Policy Development and Research, *American Housing Survey* (Washington, DC: Government Printing Office, 1989).
11. These data are a comparison of the ICF report and the Abt report. ICF, Inc., "Evaluation of Low-Income Housing Tax Credit"; Abt Associates, "Development and Analysis of the National Low-Income Housing Tax Credit Database" (Report prepared for Department of Housing and Urban Development, Office of Policy Development and Research, 1996).
12. Joel Garreau, *Edge City: Life on the New Frontier* (New York: Doubleday, 1991).

outlines, infrastructure investments flowed to the metropolitan periphery, leaving central cities behind. Over 100 edge cities were created, each with a dependent population of 100,000 or more across metropolitan America. This expansion ground to a halt due to overbuilding and the real estate crash of the late 1980s. Although many of the excesses of this system of expansion are in trouble, its basic pattern will survive for some time. This expansion was fueled by the Reagan Tax Act (1981) and economic restructuring leading to the information economy of the late twentieth century.

These new centers of information-oriented, retail, and commercial employment grew on the edge of metropolitan areas during the 1980s. They were supported by a highly subsidized, peripherally oriented beltway transportation system and the demand for low-threshold-cost suburban sprawl as the post–World War II baby-boomers entered the housing market during the period of 1985-95. The decentralized metropolitan areas began to focus around new nodes external to the historic urban centers in terms of jobs, commercial space, retailing quality, variety, ambiance, and cultural offerings. These edge centers were more automobile friendly, had higher-quality schools, were homogeneous in terms of income-based class, and offered family-oriented functional support (at high prices) integrated into a parklike environment. They were supported by rising incomes, two-income families, low-energy costs, safety considerations, and new technology that reduced the friction of distance and the cost of spatial separation. This pattern was also driven by negative factors such as congestion, crime, racism, urban scale, and heterogeneity typical of older urban centers.

This bright new urban periphery is bought at the expense of a dark urban core. The lack of functional and spatial accessibility of the poor to the legitimate economy means that unemployment rises and illegitimate, often antisocial activity related to crime, violence, and drugs fills the financial gap. This antisocial illegitimate economy has to own health risks expressed in high-mortality rates driven by drugs, alcoholism, and AIDS reflected in a high prevalence of tuberculosis, pneumonia, and various other infectious diseases.[13] Rising educational requirements for employment compound the effects of the already excessively high educational dropout rates exacerbating the functional accessibility gap.[14]

METROPOLITAN PERSPECTIVE

Present federal urban policy focuses on the metropolitan region as the new center of economic activity, and discussion of regionally centered national economies abounds.[15] Metropolitanization has become synonymous with regionalization of the

national economy.[16] This has evolved into a view of the national economy as a federalism of regional economies or a regional common market—a market where regions compete and cooperate as an interdependent system. To quote HUD policy secretary and urban research scholar Michael Stegman, "Detroit's real competition is not its suburbs but the metropolitan regions of Baden-Wurtemburg in Germany and Kyushu in Japan."[17] This is the new metropolitan perspective of Clinton's Cisneros-led HUD. Regions are economically competitive, interdependent, and organized around a central city. The central city must be taken care of to make a successful region that can compete in a world economy built of regions.[18]

The new urban policy agenda in intellectual terms comes to grips with the earlier metropolitan perspective but adds the view of the regional economic base and the idea of the system of regions and places them into a global perspective of international trade and competition. Most important, it refocuses this regional metropolitan perspective back to the sum of its parts by indicating that only the healthiest metropolitan region will be able to compete effectively either nationally or interna-

13. John D. Kasarda, *Urban Underclass Database* (New York: Social Science Research Council, 1992).

14. John D. Kasarda, "Inner-City Poverty and Economic Access," in *Rediscovering Urban America*, ed. Sommer and Hicks.

15. Neal R. Peirce, Curtis W. Johnson, and John S. Hall, *Citistates: How Urban America Can Prosper in a Competitive World* (Washington, DC: Seven Locks Press, 1993).

16. William R. Barnes and Larry C. Ledebur, *Local Economies: The U.S. Common Market of Local Economic Regions* (Washington, DC: National League of Cities, 1994).

17. Michael A. Stegman and Margery A. Turner, "The Future of Urban America in a Global Economy," *Journal of the American Planning Association*, 62(2):157-64 (1996).

18. Henry G. Cisneros, *Regionalism: The New Geography of Opportunity* (Washington, DC: Department of Housing and Urban Development, 1995).

tionally.[19] This perspective denies the effect of technology and information in changing the role of face-to-face contact. It notes that the continuing consolidation of knowledge-intensive service support activities in these high-end metropolitan economic regions is still taking place. Finally, it supports the monocentric view of a metropolitan region organized around its central city that may not be dominant in terms of population, employment, production, or economic activity but is still dominant culturally, socially, and in terms of critical decision-making functions that keep the regional economy functioning and competitive.

The major difference between the 1980s metropolitan perspective and the 1990s urban policy perspective is space and scale. The new perspective is explicitly urban, with an appreciation for intrametropolitan differences and some concern for functional economic regions as the building blocks of the national economy. The new strategy is also sensitive to the fact that these regions

19. David Rusk, *Cities Without Suburbs* (Washington, DC: Woodrow Wilson Center Press, 1993); Edward W. Hill, Harold L. Wolman, and Coit Cook Ford III, "Can Suburbs Survive Without Their Central Cities? Examining the Suburban Dependence Hypothesis" (Manuscript, Housing and Urban Development Roundtable, Dec. 1994); H. V. Satich et al., "Ties That Bind: Central Cities, Suburbs, and the New Metropolitan Region," *Economic Development Quarterly*, pp. 341-58 (Nov. 1993); Richard Voitch, "City and Suburban Growth: Substitutes or Complements?" *Business Review* (Federal Reserve Bank of Philadelphia), 3:21-33 (Sept.-Oct. 1992); Larry C. Ledebur and William R. Barnes, *Metropolitan Disparities and Economic Growth* (Washington, DC: National League of Cities, 1993).

have different needs and priorities and that one policy does not fit all equally well. This is in contrast to an urban policy that was explicitly sectoral and subordinate to a national economic agenda. What both perspectives have in common is the acceptance of minimal direct intervention by national programs in local areas. Inner-city low-tax Enterprise Zones became Empowerment Zones. There appears also to be an acceptance of privatization and increased local control.

Transportation is such a central part of metropolitan organization that it is almost impossible to understand urban policy without linking it in some way to transportation issues. The movement of people and jobs out of the historic central cities has increased the pressure on the poor and the underclass enormously as access to jobs becomes increasingly difficult. The wholesale economic abandonment of some urban districts has expanded and deepened ghetto conditions. Political fragmentation between the urban core and the periphery and across the periphery means that the transportation infrastructure is one of the few lifelines that metropolitan populations have in common. With the passage of the Intermodal Surface Transportation Efficiency Act of 1992, two issues were recognized. The first is that transportation planning would require metropolitanwide cooperation. Metropolitan planning organizations were authorized and required for that purpose. Second, it was recognized that continued expansion of transportation support through new construction was increasingly doubtful.

With mass transit ridership continuing to fall in most metropolitan areas, with congestion rising and spreading between rush hours, with cars continuing to be the preferred mode of travel, employment continues to move outward, leaving the center cities behind. Further, implementation of information technology in terms of mobile computing and telecommunication as well as telework and distance communications continues to allow even greater decentralization and job migration.

No urban policy is effectively reducing the pattern of urban poverty growth and underclass expansion in metropolitan core cities. Using the 1980 and 1990 Census of Population, Kasarda, applying Ricketts and Sawhill's measures, reports that for central cities in the largest 100 metropolitan areas in general (using their definitions), poverty worsened, extreme poverty worsened, and the underclass expanded, particularly in the largest cities (New York being the major exception).[20] The focus of concern seems to be a combination of functional accessibility, or having the skills to access jobs that are available, and spatial accessibility, or being able to get to jobs that are available. In both cases, our education and economic system is leaving residents of low-income central cities behind.[21]

20. Kasarda, "Inner-City Poverty and Economic Access"; Erol R. Ricketts and Isabel V. Sawhill, "Defining and Measuring the Underclass," *Journal of Policy Analysis and Management*, 7:316-25 (Oct. 1988).

21. John D. Kasarda, "Jobs, Migration and Emerging Urban Mismatches,"in *Urban Change and Poverty*, ed. M.G.H. McGeary and L. E. Lynn, Jr. (Washington, DC: National Academy Press, 1988).

The assumption underlying current urban policy is that metropolitan areas are organized around a historic core city that plays and will continue to play a dominant role in their future. Furthermore, given this thesis, if the core is sick, it will create a disease that will cripple or at least retard the full development of the larger metropolitan economic region. With this diagnosis, the cure is to rebuild central cities of metropolitan regions through new hard and soft infrastructure investments if necessary, even at the expense of investments in the periphery.

At the very least, this perspective implies better evaluation of the hidden costs and subsidies in the present system of decentralized development ranging from transportation to environment and from land-use and density considerations to industrial location. The idea is that if these elements were fully and properly priced, people would change their residential, transportation, and shopping behavior and produce a more rational high-density metropolitan pattern of settlement, effectively manage in-fill, generate a better work-residence spatial match, and lower their commuting costs in terms of time and money.

Suburbanization has been moving with great rapidity, creating a system of decentralization in the midst of increased urbanization. It may be hard for urban intellectuals and city planners to face, but central cities have not been the residential home for most of the U.S. urban population for close to a quarter of a century. Under such circumstances, why would one believe that the center city or the core of the older urbanized area would continue to be dominant as a residence, as a place of work, as a commercial center, or as a retail center? Why would alternative and competing centers, nodes, or edge cities not develop in response to the distribution of population and wealth?

THE WASHINGTON, D.C.,
REGION: A MICROCOSM
OF U.S. METROPOLITAN
DYNAMICS

As a microcosm of the metropolitan pattern of urban reorganization in the late twentieth century, the U.S. national capital region of metropolitan Washington, D.C., is a good example. Similar patterns have been taking shape in New York, Atlanta, Chicago, Dallas, San Francisco, and Los Angeles.

The low-density, decentralized, multinodal metropolitan region is moving quickly to become the American pattern of urban organization. In spite of resistance from city and regional planners and extremely powerful state and provincial regulatory interests, the pattern continues to proliferate, particularly in developed economies. Further, predictions of disastrously long commuting times and mass return to the inner city appear to be overdrawn. This is a pattern of urban spatial organization that is not likely to go away. Policies may modify this pattern at the margins but are not likely to create wholesale restructuring.

Regional organization

The emergence of the new urban region raises a number of important policy questions. Many of these focus on the changing role of actors such as the nation-state, the state or province, local government, and business and community organizations in the economic development process. Others focus on the fact that these are high-cost regional economies and need access to low-cost inputs such as back-office production operations. As these new regional economies emerged, their role expanded and in many cases now supersedes that of local and state/provincial governments in providing leadership and steering for economic development. The steering of development activities and policies has been largely organized in the form of a partnership between the public and private sectors. Universities and other research organizations, such as research laboratories and research parks, also figure prominently in these partnerships.

The U.S. national capital region is a complex of at best loosely confederated counties that belong to the Washington metropolitan region.[22] It is composed of a federal district and several other suburban counties located in the states of Maryland, Virginia, and West Virginia. Most other metropolitan regions are located in one or two states and as a consequence have developed richer regionwide institutional infrastructures, including regionwide community foundations; transportation, hous-

22. Roger R. Stough and Kingsley E. Haynes, "The Vulnerability of the Northern Virginia Region," in *Proceedings of the First Annual Conference on the Future of the Northern Virginia Economy*, ed. R. R. Stough (Fairfax, VA: George Mason University, Institute of Public Policy, Center for Regional Analysis, 1994), pp. 23-33.

ing, social, and like services; planning and management bodies, development policies, and institutions to implement them; and in some cases regionwide governments. Because of the high level of jurisdictional fragmentation in the larger functional region and the "District of Columbia plus the rest of the region" (inside-outside the Beltway) mentality, these institutions have developed in only the most rudimentary fashion for the national capital. However, important building of regional cohesion across the national capital region may be an activity that will most likely evolve slowly and, more important, will evolve even more slowly as long as the level of cohesion in its subregional components remains low.

The northern Virginia subregion, for example, was for the most part dominated by a rural orientation as recently as twenty years ago, when only a few regional institutions existed.

Infrastructure

The use of infrastructure by the private sector to assemble inputs and distribute outputs has been widely appreciated. Further, the ability of private sector organizations to benefit from shared use of infrastructure investments is also well recognized. Similarly, the role of the public sector in directing large, risky investments and allocating their use among competitors may be a contentious issue but certainly is not new. What is less appreciated is the changing meaning of infrastructure and its many roles in regional system dynamics.

Smilor and Wakelin divide infrastructure into hard and soft. Hard

infrastructure includes transportation, telecommunication, research parks and support facilities, and quality-of-life facilities and utilities; soft infrastructure includes human resources, financing, business services, technology transfer, leisure activities, and legal and institutional services. They argue that it is this soft category of infrastructure that will grow at a much accelerated rate and will be essential to future economic growth and technology development and applications.[23]

As noted previously, communication infrastructure includes a variety of information capital (for example, telephones, satellite communications, integrated digital networks, and so forth) and information labor. This sector influences the nature and level of social and political participation and the structure of incentives and organizations in society.

One outcome of these twin trends of deregulation and privatization has been the emergence of what *Fortune* magazine has called the Netplex, more than 1200 telecommunications and information technology firms in the national capital region—most in northern Virginia.[24]

23. Raymond W. Smilor and Michael Wakelin, "Smart Infrastructure and Economic Development," in *The Technopolis Phenomenon*, ed. G. Koznetsky and R. W. Smilor (Austin: University of Texas, IC2 Institute, 1990).

24. Kingsley E. Haynes and Roger R. Stough, "Space, Technology and Edge City: Patterns of Service and Infrastructure Investments: The U.S. National Capital Region," in *Spatial Technologies, Geographic Information, and the Edge City*, ed. Helen Couclelis (Technical Report 96-10, National Center for Geographic Information and Analysis, University of California at Santa Barbara, Dec. 1996).

At the core of the new information infrastructure is the Internet. The investment in this new infrastructure must be measured largely in financial capital spent for services and data. Depending on the yardstick being used, current annual expenditures range from $1.0 billion to $2.8 billion. However, MCI, one of the most aggressive providers of telecommunications and information services, estimates that that figure will rise to as much as $40 billion a year by 1998.

All in all, the infrastructure growth pattern is still built on an optimistic growth perspective and, except for ground transportation, still leads development. However, the development that infrastructure leads is no longer residential but, rather, is employment. Further, fundamental to this expansion is the new high-technology economy that is increasingly located in the edge cities of the metropolitan periphery. To understand this new metropolitan organizational pattern, one needs to understand the technology economy around which it is organized.

PATTERNS OF
TECHNOLOGY
INVESTMENT

Here we will provide a summary of an analysis of the technology sector of the Greater Washington regional economy, but these patterns are typical of other high-growth metropolitan regions as well. The summary is based upon original data collected from a database on technology firms in the region. It was motivated by the recognition that much of the rapid economic growth experienced during the last twenty years was driven by the development of a large cluster of technology-intensive companies. This report summarizes a description and analysis of the size of the companies, their distribution by type of technology, their geographic distribution within the region, economic effects, occupational structure, and educational needs, as well as some of the barriers and opportunities facing the technology sector.

There are 2331 technology firms in the Greater Washington region: 3.0 percent in the District of Columbia; 41.6 percent in Maryland; and 55.4 percent in Virginia. Technology sector employment is 262,337: 1.5 percent in the District of Columbia; 39.1 percent in Maryland; and 59.3 percent in Virginia.

The region's technology firms are most heavily concentrated in computer software and hardware; technical and management consulting and professional services; systems integration; information services and communications; engineering services; defense and aerospace; and biotechnology and biomedicine.

The technology sector of the Greater Washington region plays an important role in the formation and dynamics of the region's economic base. Directly employing 262,337, the technology sector ranks second in size behind retail trade among all sources of private employment. The sector is characterized by above-average earnings and directly generates approximately $21 billion in total industry output—10 percent of the region's total. It also contributes significantly to state and local government finances. Other findings include:

1. Northern Virginia, with 155,675 technology employees, accounts for almost 60 percent of the region's technology workforce, while suburban Maryland's technology sector employs an additional 102,654.

2. Total earnings in the technology sector amount to $9.3 billion and are more dispersed across the region than general employment. Although the sector accounts for only 1.7 percent of all private sector firms, it directly generates 16 percent of all private sector earnings.

3. Economic impact analysis shows that the 262,337 jobs in the technology sector indirectly support an additional 234,733 jobs in other sectors of the regional economy.

Like other sectors of the economy, the technology sector utilizes a large proportion of executive, administrative, and managerial personnel. Together, these occupation classes account for 55,178 positions and 21 percent of the technology labor force. Among the utilized occupations belonging to this class are engineers (16,807 in number); surveyors and architects (8132); computer, math, and operations researchers (7302); and a variety of technicians and technologists (27,117). These workers, combined with executive and managerial positions, account for 50 percent of the technology labor force.

The growth in new technology and its associated jobs reinforces the dispersed peripheral structure of the regional metropolitan economy, and this dispersion is not a function of residential distributions alone. Further, from this pattern it is evident that infrastructure investments are explicit and clearly linked to new economic growth patterns and vice versa.

SOCIETAL CONSIDERATIONS

Parts of the region's economy are in some measure dependent on other parts of the national capital region for labor, markets, and services. The quality of the physical environment is to some extent dependent upon the levels of residuals (airborne and waterborne) generated in other parts of the national capital region and even beyond to include the watersheds of the Potomac and Chesapeake basins. The environmental quality of these larger areas is partially dependent on activities in subparts of the region. Similar arguments could be made in terms of quality of life where factors such as crime, education, entertainment options, and so on are important. In short, it is important to recognize that parts of the region are part of a larger frame of reference, that the frames vary depending upon the purpose or problem being considered, and that the future of the region will depend to some degree on how its relations with these other frames of regional reference are managed.

Patterns of development in the region

There has been a significant divergence in the development paths of the District of Columbia and the northern Virginia and suburban Maryland parts of the region.[25] The population

25. Stephen Fuller, "Federal Spending Trends in Northern Virginia, 1984-1993, and the Growing Importance of Small Business as

of the District decreased from a high of 763,956 in 1960 to 606,900 in 1990; during this period the Maryland and northern Virginia suburban areas grew from 1.2 million to nearly 3.0 million, an increase of 150 percent. While employment levels were similar in 1960 (645,000 in the District; 715,000 in the suburban areas), by 1990 suburban employment was 1.5 million (a 110 percent increase), with the District increasing slightly (not quite 15 percent), to 740,000. Similar changes occurred in personal income, commercial construction, and retail sales.

Beyond these more obvious quantitative indicators, other structural changes occurred. Until the late 1980s, unemployment in the District tended to be at about the national average. Since then, unemployment rates have increasingly exceeded the national average. Over the same period, suburban unemployment rates have decreased relative to those of the District. Crime rates per 100,000 population in the District are nearly twice as high as in northern Virginia or suburban Maryland.[26] District high school dropout rates are also nearly twice as high.[27] The fiscal base of the District is seriously jeopardized with almost daily reports that it will need a bailout, that it will have to make even

more severe cuts in expenditures to balance the budget, or that it will become insolvent.

Using 1991 personal income as an indicator of the size of different sectors, the data show that the whole national capital region may be described as a government and business and technical services center and that manufacturing is relatively unimportant. When the services are examined in more detail, notable differences appear. Business and engineering/management services are much more important in northern Virginia and suburban Maryland; membership organizations and legal services are much more important in the District. Further, direct federal employment, while important throughout the region, is considerably more important in the District and the inner suburbs.

*The doughnut
    metaphor*

The foregoing analysis shows the relative decline of the economy and quality of life in the District. We may illustrate this with a doughnut metaphor, which treats the District as the hole, and northern Virginia and suburban Maryland as the surrounding cake. In adopting the doughnut model, it is an easy next step for some to conclude that the hole is no longer needed, that is, that it is possible for northern Virginia and suburban Maryland to chart development paths essentially independent of the District. In short, in this view, not only is the District considered to be irrelevant, but by continuing to treat it as part of the region, some believe that it will drain resources from the

Sources of Employment Growth," in *Future of the Northern Virginia Economy*, ed. Stough, pp. 68-96.

26. Department of Justice, Federal Bureau of Investigation, *Uniform Crime Reports* (Washington, DC: Government Printing Office, 1985); ibid. (1992).

27. Department of Commerce, Bureau of the Census, *Summary of Social and Economic Indicators* (Washington, DC: Government Printing Office, 1980); ibid. (1990).

future development of its suburbs. The doughnut model is part of the mind-set of more than a few leaders, and it is not a mind-set limited to the Washington, D.C., metropolitan region.

A second reason for the divergence between conditions in the District and the outer parts of the region has been the inability of the historical core to link development on the periphery to its institutions. There is a tendency on the part of core cities even in the best of circumstances—for example, the unified city-county government environment of Indianapolis—not to recognize growth on the periphery, especially when state or local boundaries intervene, until that growth has become quite sizable relative to the core. The fact that economic growth in these areas unfolded very rapidly meant that it was very difficult for the government and nongovernment institutions (such as chambers of commerce) to adjust in time to provide more regionally integrated leadership. Consequently, not only is the District separated from the doughnut, but the parts of the doughnut themselves are highly fragmented, whether one views this from state or local government levels. In short, there is a high level of fragmentation throughout the national capital region, and it exists at many levels. Similar patterns can be seen in the New York, Chicago, and Los Angeles metropolitan regions.

In a recent book, David Rusk examines this pattern throughout the United States. He observes that when the population in the traditional core city area falls by more than 20 percent and when income falls below 70 percent of the median

income of the outlying areas, conditions throughout the whole metropolitan region, which will have already deteriorated, become extremely resistant to change. By "conditions," he means a gamut of problems ranging from crime and education to tax base and growth, to environmental conditions.[28] Rusk's analysis, based on data from 100 United States cities, suggests that outer parts of metropolitan areas need to pay attention to what is happening in the interior and help address deteriorating conditions there. Failure to do so may result in the export or diffusion of conditions in the interior to outlying areas and thus deterioration of conditions there as well.

Despite the rapid development path that has hindered the emergence of a more integrated and cohesive region, some activities aimed at helping the national capital region to build cohesive leadership have been undertaken. The Washington Council of Governments recently executed a consciousness-raising project that included several hundred people participating in a variety of meetings throughout the region. The effort surfaced a wide variety of issues and identified a number of barriers to developing a more cohesive approach to regional problem solving and governance (not necessarily government). The Greater Washington Board of Trade has formed a senior leadership development process now called the "Potomac Conference." The purpose of this group is to develop a more cohesive leadership for addressing regionwide economic, social, and environmental problems. To the group's

28. Rusk, *Cities Without Suburbs.*

credit, it has formed a regionwide program to market the national capital region globally; however, its ability to focus resources on other regionwide issues has been limited. Beyond these two efforts, activity to build a more cohesive approach to problems throughout the national capital region has been insignificant.

Alternative models

Besides the doughnut perspective, some have advanced the concept of a metropolitan area made up of a nonhierarchical network of specialized nodes. Finally, and not in jest, a new perspective of the leapfrogged and abandoned edge cities with external satellite cities has been proposed by Stough.[29] This model maximizes the expanded transportation structure and is dependent on the effective use of new telecommunication technology and the efficient application of intelligent transportation infrastructure.

The social implication of these systems in terms of spatial class and income reorganization for U.S. society in general and urban social systems in particular is well beyond what most groups have been willing to confront.

These decentralized edge-city development patterns are being both led by and reinforced by public and private infrastructure investments. The thought that these patterns will be or even can be turned around in the near future, if ever, seems folly. Further, it is time to recognize that the capital investments to expand and propel continued decentraliza-

tion are being made now. These infrastructure investments are the reproductive capital that will produce the next generation of public and private investment to at least support the present pattern, if not extend it. The national capital regional pattern just described is being repeated across the United States in major growing metropolitan areas, and there are signs of these patterns in European and Asian metropolises as well.

U.S. federal urban policy has begun to recognize the fabric of this pattern as policymakers move their lens of analysis from the metropolitan region to intrametropolitan spatial organization.

CRITIQUE AND CONCLUSION

The difficulty in looking at new patterns is that we often see them through an old lens. It is very difficult to break out of the "old wine in new bottles, or new wine in old bottles" syndrome. We take what we know and try to recant it to make it interesting and palatable, or we take newly recognized phenomena and push it into patterns we have dealt with before. It is our view that the present federal urban policy is doing the latter.

Present sources of federal urban policy perspectives recognize the decentralization discussed in this article. Further, independent sources support the perspective that technology continues to encourage this decentralization.[30] Still other sources

29. Roger R. Stough, "Technology Will Spur Satellite Cities, More Sprawl," *Edge City News* (Jan.-Feb. 1996).

30. Office of Technology Assessment, *The Technology Reshaping of Metropolitan America*, OTA-ETI-643 (Washington, DC: Government Printing Office, 1995).

note that high-level, sophisticated business support services—such as international banking, intellectual property, accounting, and legal services—continue to concentrate in very large metropolitan areas in the United States and elsewhere (such as Melbourne and Sydney in Australia and Paris in France)[31] due in part to better transportation and communication linkages across the system of metropolitan places. This concentration at higher levels in the urban or metropolitan hierarchy is not antithetical to the continued decentralization within metropolitan areas.

The present federal interpretation is that the U.S. metropolitan areas are functional economic regions. Each is made up of a series of economic nodes with the older central city as the heart and core of the intrametropolitan system. In terms of the urban planning, urban geography, and regional economics literature, this is a recognition of B.J.L. Berry's application and adaptation of Christallär and Lösch's central place and localized economies concepts to intrametropolitan organization; to this has been added Sable's concept of integrated research and development regions.[32] Typical of those latter ideas

are the network regions of flexible specialization including the Silicon Valley; Route 128; the Carolina Triangle; Austin, Texas; and the national capital Netplex. Internationally, they incorporate the Third Italy, Baden Würtemburg, and the Cambridge axis in England. The general argument is that nations are composed of economic regions that compete and cooperate both within and across systems of national borders and that these regions are the building blocks of the new global economy.

Countries in general and the United States in particular will do well when these innovative metropolitan research-and-development economies are healthy. This health is dependent on all parts of these functional economic regions doing well. In particular, it is vital that old cores do well because they are central to the rest of the suburbanized metropolitan economy. Hence support of cooperative and enhancement mechanisms for the core city will benefit the metropolitan regional economy and hence regional and then national competitiveness. This is the essential rationalization for today's federal urban policy focused on metropolitan city centers.

Our critique supports this general strategy of helping and supporting intergovernmental linkages to older centers, but its logic is fundamentally different. These differences are im-

31. Alex Schwartz, "Corporate Service Linkages in Large Metropolitan Areas: A Study of New York, Los Angeles and Chicago," *Urban Affairs Quarterly*, pp. 276-96 (1992); Kingsley E. Haynes, Roger R. Stough, and William M. Boyer, "Transportation, Technology and Governance in Edge Cities: Implications for Asian and Pacific Rim Urbanization," in *Proceedings of the Fourth Asian Urbanization Conference*, ed. L.-H.N. Chiang, J. F. Williams, and H. L. Bednarek (East Lansing: Michigan State University, 1996).

32. Brian J. L. Berry, "Cities as Systems Within Systems of Cities," *Papers of the Re-*

gional Science Association, 13:147-63 (1964); Walter Christallär, *Die Zentralen Orte in Suddeutschland* (Jena: Gustav Fischer, 1993); August Lösch, *The Economics of Location* (New Haven, CT: Yale University Press, 1952); Charles Sable, "The Rise of Regional Economies" (Speech delivered to Automobile Manufacturers Group, Detroit, MI, 1987).

portant because they generate a different rationale for support and different priorities and strategies.

The alternative perspective argues that except for a few historical relics such as New York, Boston, and Chicago, central cities in an intra-metropolitan matrix are not more important economically, politically, or financially than other edge-city and inner suburban nodes. Rather, the appropriate model is one of beads in a network, with each bead having both a general local supply function for common goods and services and a set of specialized functions within this metropolitan complex. The older city—the core bead—is no more important than another bead in the complex and often serves a special function for centralized public services, government, and arrangement purposes and for specialized entertainment and some unique commercial functions such as high-level convention traffic. With a networked metropolis as the base, the way to support these older beads is to examine their roles in the larger network and rethink how to expand, extend, and augment those roles. We need to stop thinking of these old centers as "core" in any way. They need to be supported in the same way as any other node undergoing stress will need to be supported in an interdependent metropolitan area. This implies a different attitude toward intergovernmental cooperation, one that is more horizontal and equality oriented across nodes and emphasizes different strategies for economic development and hence a different role and different opportunities for federal urban policy.

The history of U.S. federal urban policy has not been good, but the recent history has been slightly brighter. The future of federal urban policy is dependent on recognizing new urban realities and designing appropriate response mechanisms. This is a challenge and an opportunity.

ANNALS, *AAPSS*, **551**, May 1997

Globalization, Immigration, and Changing Social Relations in U.S. Cities

By GLENDA LAWS

ABSTRACT: The current process of globalization, with deep historical roots, has had a significant impact on social problems in U.S. cities. My focus is the links between globalization, immigration, and urban social relations. At the heart of this linkage is an economic restructuring across societies and in the U.S. city that has potent social consequences for immigrant populations. Such people, induced to migrate by changing economic circumstances, find growing ghettoization, isolation, and cultural antipathies in their new settings. In the new globality, immigrant populations are commonly fingered as the other, the invading and ominous people threatening time-tested social norms and economic principles.

Glenda Laws was an associate professor of geography at the Pennsylvania State University. She was an urban social geographer with an interest in marginalized populations and political struggles around their well-being. Throughout her career, Dr. Laws focused on, among others, the mentally ill, the homeless, the poor, immigrant women, and the elderly. She was interested in social and economic restructuring and, specifically, the spatial implications of restructuring for those marginalized groups in urban areas. Dr. Laws died in June 1996, aged 37.

G LOBALIZATION has a social and cultural impact on the lives of various social groups in several different ways. It is not simply an economic process.

Some people, including investors who have seen their profits grow and workers who have been employed because of expanding business opportunities, have benefited from the growth of global markets, while others have not. Consequently, relations between people living and working in U.S. cities have changed during the latest round of global restructuring. Immigrant groups have been particularly affected. That is because, in many respects, immigrants and immigration levels are directly related to the globalization of the economy. People, for the most part, migrate in search of economic opportunities (for example, work or investments), and as the economy has globalized, people from around the world find that opportunities attractive to them might well cross international boundaries. Once arrived at their destination, however, immigrants often experience various forms of segregation. Before turning to a discussion of some of the ways globalization has contributed to the economic, social, political, and spatial segregation of immigrants, I want to start with several preliminary observations.

First, despite much attention being given to the idea of globalization as if it were a recent phenomenon, it would be naive to suggest that U.S. cities have only recently entered a global political economy. Ever since the first European settlements, cities in North America have been linked, to a greater or lesser degree, to the machinations of a global system. The term "globalization," as it is currently used, suggests that linkages between places around the world are now more numerous and more intense than hitherto and that supranational organizations are assuming an ever greater importance. In the context of economic activity, this involves the growth over the last few decades of multinational corporations, the expansion of international capital markets, and related changes in patterns of international trade. Each of these elements of globalization, however, has a history measured in centuries rather than decades. Because of its long historical antecedents, perhaps it is best to think of the current round of globalization, in its economic, political, and sociocultural guise, as a round of qualitatively different international relations, usefully characterized by Jan Nederveen Pieterse[1] as inherently fluid, indeterminate, and open-ended.

Although these new and multiple forms of global interdependence have implications for localities (for example, U.S. cities and their suburbs), the global and the local, or globalization and localization, do not stand in simple opposition to one another. Rather, they are intimately related and it is not particularly useful to discuss either without the other.

Second, we should note the importance of focusing upon the political and sociocultural dimensions of globalization—in terms of both causes

1. Jan Nederveen Pieterse, "Globalization as Hybridization," in *Global Modernities*, ed. Mike Featherstone, Scott Lash, and Roland Robertson (Thousand Oaks, CA: Sage, 1995), p. 46.

and effects. We witness, for example, the growth of international governing bodies such as the United Nations and the World Bank and of advocacy groups such as Amnesty International and the increasingly important role such organizations play in political decision making and developments in the global economy.[2] Further, in terms of sociocultural relations, globalization involves the migration of people and customs. In some instances, large-scale migrations have resulted in the loss or marginalization of some cultures as some immigrants come to dominate indigenous populations (for example, migrations from the so-called Old to the New World under colonial expansions). In other instances, the immigrants themselves are ostracized and segregated in their new locations. Such, in fact, is the situation in many U.S. cities as the twentieth century draws to a close.

Transformations in the global political economy have had a significant impact on relations between residents of U.S. cities. Since the social problem of residential segregation in U.S. cities has been around for some time, it is certainly not a product of the latest round of globalization. Likewise, it would be difficult to argue with any certainty that poverty among inner-city residents is directly related to globalization or that violence directed at minority groups is an outcome of globalization processes. However, the form and function of segregation under globalization might be changing. We need to ask

what role urban or local segregation plays in a global economy that (seemingly) increasingly looks to supranational organizations. We must, however, bear in mind that if globalization could be used to explain everything, its analytical value for understanding specific manifestations of social problems would need to be questioned. Despite such caveats, I do believe that transformations in the global political economy have had a significant impact on social problems in U.S. cities, and I hope to tease out some of these links in the ensuing discussion. My focus here is on immigrants who have relocated as a result of changing conditions associated with globalization. Although a comprehensive examination of this topic would include consideration of the conditions in the places from which immigrants move, space does not permit coverage here. I will therefore concentrate on the experiences of and attitudes toward immigrants who have settled in the United States. To organize what follows, I begin by reviewing the links between globalization, immigration, and urban social relations. Then, at the risk of oversimplification, I consider some of the economic, social, and political experiences of recent immigrants living in U.S. cities. Finally, I will explore the implications of continued globalization for residents of U.S. cities.

GLOBALIZATION,
IMMIGRATION, AND
URBAN SOCIAL RELATIONS

In the contemporary global political economy, some countries function as labor-exporting nodes, for both long- and short-term migrants, while

2. See Commission on Global Governance, *Our Global Neighborhood* (New York: Oxford University Press, 1995).

others act as labor-importing countries. Saskia Sassen describes "migration as a global labor supply system"[3] that provides workers to both urban and rural labor markets in developed industrialized economies. This implies that both capital and, to a lesser extent, labor are mobile on a global scale. For both capital and labor, a "sentimental attachment to some geographic part of the world is not part of the [global economic] system."[4] Of course, many businesses (especially small firms) and people do find themselves attached, whether by choice or circumstance, to a particular place and, as a result, may find that they are not competitive in the global market. At various spatial scales, whether international, national, or local, some regions lose workers and capital investment while others gain.

Explanations for large-scale movements of workers and their families between nation-states are rooted in long and complex histories that surround the diffusion of capitalism. Colonial expansions prior to World War I depended on such migrations between the Old and New Worlds. With rapid economic growth since World War II, immigrant workers from less developed countries have become an increasingly important component of the labor forces of most developed countries. Sassen describes current trends as follows:

Two features characterize labor migration: the growing use of immigrant labor in the tertiary sector of developed countries and the growing use of foreign and native migrants in the secondary sector of developing countries. . . . Unlike other labor-intensive components of industrialized economies, service jobs cannot easily be exported. Thus, the growing concentration of immigrant labor in the service sector of highly industrialized countries may be pointing to constraints in the historical transformation of the international division of labor, insofar as most service jobs must be performed *in situ*. This growing concentration of immigrant labor in service jobs in developed countries can be viewed as the correlate of the export of [manufacturing] jobs to the Third World.[5]

At the local scale, U.S. cities, along with their counterparts in other developed economies, have played an important role in the global labor market. The hierarchical organization of multinational corporations has designated some cities as headquarters locations that act as sites for leadership, research and development, and interaction with politicians. These command points watch over the global empires of the largest corporations. More routine functions, like manufacturing, have moved offshore, taking with them many relatively well-paid blue-collar jobs.[6] However, the loss of some, indeed many, manufacturing jobs has not seen the eradication of low-wage positions in U.S. cities. Although in-

3. Saskia Sassen, *The Mobility of Labor and Capital: A Study of International Investment and Labor Flow* (New York: Cambridge University Press, 1988), pp. 31-36.

4. Lester C. Thurow, *The Future of Capitalism: How Today's Economic Forces Shape Tomorrow's World* (New York: William Morrow, 1996), p. 115.

5. Sassen, *Mobility of Labor and Capital*, p. 53.

6. Stephen Hymer, *The Multinational Corporation: A Radical Approach*, ed. Robert B. Cohen, Morley Nikosi, and Jaap van Liere, with the assistance of Noel Dennis (New York: Cambridge University Press, 1979).

creasingly challenged by Japan and other Asian economies, the postwar dominance of the U.S. economy has created (and continues to create) incomes and consumption opportunities that require minimally paid positions. The following description of the local social geography and economy of one neighborhood, Lennox, near the Los Angeles international airport captures the links between globalization and the low-wage workforce:

The proximity of [the airport] is not coincidental. Many [immigrants] were drawn by the lure of work in area hotels and restaurants, the low-wage service jobs now largely the domain of immigrants. Indeed Lennox is a kind of late-20th Century company town, housing a Third World servant class of maids, waiters and others whose cheap labor sustains an international transportation and tourism hub.[7]

Left behind, too, are those manufacturing activities that can find a cheap enough labor force within the United States to make them competitive in the international market (as well as those manufacturers who require a relatively skilled labor force that cannot as yet readily be found outside the developed economies). Sweatshops (and other institutionalized forms of low wages), then, represent one way of maintaining competitiveness. In addition, those employed in the headquarters offices of multinational corporations require support staff (such as accounting and legal expertise, clerical assistants, and janitorial services), and this has cre-

ated demands for a whole range of business and personal services. That is, multinational corporations, and the ancillary services that are generated in a region by their presence, are very much dependent on a large, international labor market. The domestic side of that labor market includes a significant number of immigrants.

Of course, this is not an especially new development in the evolution of the U.S. space economy. In the first decade of the twentieth century, nearly 8.8 million people moved from abroad to major U.S. industrial cities. This number translates into a rate of 10.4 immigrants for every 1000 people living in the United States. Both the number and the rate fell off until the post–World War II economic boom, which created renewed demand for immigrant labor. In addition, changes to immigration laws in 1965 resulted in higher levels of migration related to family reunification. The new legislation also led to a change in the countries of origin of migrants, from mainly European sites to regions in Central and South America and Asia. Between 1981 and 1990, 7.34 million immigrants entered at a rate of 3.1 per 1000 population. Between 1991 and 1993, amid growing calls for a slowdown in immigration, the rate had reached 4.8 per 1000, and some 3.71 million immigrants were admitted. In addition, the Bureau of the Census estimates that there may be as many as 4.00 million undocumented immigrants.[8] In 1994, 8.7 percent of the U.S. popu-

7. Patrick J. McDonnell, "Economic Shocks South of Border in Lennox; Jobs: Like Other Immigrant Areas, It Has Inexorable Ties to Mexico," *Los Angeles Times*, 20 June 1995.

8. U.S., Department of Commerce, Bureau of the Census, *Statistical Abstract of the United States: 1995*, 115th ed. (Washington, DC: Department of Commerce, 1995), tabs. 5, 10.

lation was foreign born, the majority of whom live in cities. More than 18 million foreign-born individuals lived in metropolitan areas in 1990, while only 1.3 million resided in nonmetropolitan areas.

Migrants change the character of the places in which they settle. They establish businesses, invest in housing and other aspects of neighborhood infrastructure, celebrate cultural festivals, and bring with them a variety of cultural practices. Sometimes this multicultural aspect of migration is greeted enthusiastically by host communities; more often it is welcomed with ambivalence. However, it takes only the most casual attention to the popular media to realize that there is a groundswell of opposition to continued immigration at what is popularly perceived to be a large scale. Despite this opposition, there remains a persistent demand for both legal and illegal migrant labor. Undocumented immigrants are able to find work in U.S. cities as local manufacturers meet the demand for cheaply produced goods. The products of sweatshops find markets in the United States. And these markets are not only found among struggling small businesses or in the informal economy. Large retailers purchase (knowingly or otherwise) and then sell clothing produced by illegal aliens in Los Angeles sweatshops.[9] Furthermore, affluence in the United States has created a demand among relatively well-off families for housekeepers and garden-

ers, many of whom are immigrants.[10] Rural regions, too, exhibit a "dependence on an imported peasantry."[11]

Domestic labor markets, then, offer opportunities for global migrants, even while simultaneously there is an almost continuous call for immigration reform. Despite such calls, there are, of course, many supporters of liberal immigration policies. Advocacy groups are joined by business interests that see migrant labor as one means of maintaining competitiveness. A recent advertisement on the Internet asked, "Will immigration damage your business?" and argued that a reduction in the number of employment-based immigrants and restrictions on the length of time temporary workers could stay in the country would be problematic for businesses.[12] Tensions between those who support and those who oppose immigration is indicative of how globalization affects relations between urban residents.

Sassen, in a study of "the global city," examines the increasing social polarization evident in New York City, London, and Tokyo as economic restructuring not only widens the income gap between rich and poor but also accentuates the contrasts between the gentrified commercial and residential settings used by the most

9. Frank Swoboda and Margaret Webb Pressler, "US Targets Slave Labor Sweatshop; Back Wages Sought from Clothing Makers," *Washington Post*, 16 Aug. 1995.

10. See, for example, Lynda Natali, "Wealthy Enclaves in O.C. [Orange County] Hide 'Household Slaves,'" *Los Angeles Times*, 1 June 1991.

11. Eric Schlosser, "In the Strawberry Fields," *Atlantic Monthly*, p. 80 (Nov. 1993).

12. Heather Hartung and Pamela A. McKnight, "Will Immigration Reform Damage Your Business?" (Advertisement of Brown, Todd & Heyburn PLLC at http://www.bth-pllc.com/legalpad/immrefrm.html).

privileged urban residents and the sweatshops and crowded houses where poor people work and live.[13] She demonstrates that globalization has invoked not only new economic geographies but also new social geographies. Spatial segregation of different social groups has persisted under globalization even at the same time that it has promoted international, interethnic, and interracial contacts through global migration. Increasing social polarization is a question of social justice, and it begs the questions of how some groups are privileged by social processes and how others might be disadvantaged by those same processes.[14]

In what follows, I will focus primarily on discussions of the economic experiences of immigrants based on their labor force attachment; then I will turn to a consideration of some sociocultural experiences including the assimilation-versus-multiculturalism debate and the violence that sometimes arises from intolerance of cultural difference. I also consider the political powerlessness of immigrants. To illustrate the discussion, I draw upon popular sources, especially reports from newspapers, because these are the sites from which many people gather information to develop their opinions about the merits of, or problems associated with, immigration policy and immigrants.

Economic segregation:
Labor market positions
and experiences

"Economic segregation of immigrants" refers to the fact that many simply do not have access to the same resources as the U.S.-born population. One of the most important determinants of both individual and household resources is the positions that workers hold in labor markets. Occupational and sectoral concentrations mean that some groups of immigrants receive, on average, very low wages. Income levels clearly have implications for opportunities and experiences outside the workplace, such as housing, health care, and leisure. For both advocates and opponents, then, the links between immigration and domestic labor markets are critical.

Opponents suggest that by accepting low wages (because they are often high compared to those that immigrants received in their home countries), immigrants have two important potential impacts on local labor markets. First, wage rates are driven down. Second, immigrants are employed in jobs that would otherwise be filled by unskilled or low-skilled U.S.-born workers. For immigrants who had been in the United States for less than five years in 1990, average wages were almost 32 percent below those of U.S.-born workers.[15] It may

13. Saskia Sassen, *The Global City: New York, London, Tokyo* (Princeton, NJ: Princeton University Press, 1991).

14. See Iris Marion Young, *Justice and the Politics of Difference* (Princeton, NJ: Princeton University Press, 1992).

15. George J. Borjas, "The Economic Benefit of Immigration," *Journal of Economic Perspectives* (1995); Michael Fix, Jeffrey S. Passel, and Wendy Zimmermann, "The Use of SSI and Other Welfare Programs by Immigrants" (Testimony before U.S., Congress, House, Ways and Means Committee, 23 May 1996, copy available from the authors at the Urban Institute, Washington, DC).

seem unclear why immigrants should be castigated for the unfairness of this situation if we assume that employers should pay fair and reasonable wages to all workers, regardless of their immigrant status.

The sweatshop conditions in which many immigrant workers find themselves are also indicative of the intensity of exploitation found in some urban areas. On 2 August 1995, a raid on a factory in El Monte, California, exposed a "workshop that held immigrant workers in 'slave labor' conditions inside a barbed-wire compound and forced them to work seven days a week for as little as 50 cents an hour."[16] In February 1996, the factory's operators pleaded guilty to a number of charges including indentured servitude. In this particular case, the majority of workers were described as "illegal aliens," but a suit filed in April 1996 claimed that the operators were paying legal Latino immigrant workers only $1.63 per hour for as many as 13 hours of work per day in another two factories in Los Angeles.[17] Textile and clothing sweatshops seem to be especially exploitative in their treatment of workers—and, importantly, women. At least part of the explanation for the

atrocious conditions such workers find themselves in must relate to the erosion of organized labor with respect to its important watchdog role. Globalization has seen many textile activities move offshore. There has been a parallel decline in the number of unionized employees. The Garment Workers Unions suffered a serious membership loss from 314,000 members in 1979 down to 133,000 in 1993.[18] Unions need, for the sake of all workers, to ensure that foreign-born workers are paid wages equal to those of U.S.-born employees.

In September 1995, a letter to the editor of the *New York Times* by the president of the National Association of Manufacturers reveals an interesting business perspective on the links between attitudes toward immigration and the structure of labor markets:

American manufacturing no longer has an interest in maintaining a mass influx of unskilled, low-wage immigrants. While a large number of unskilled laborers helped fuel the Industrial Revolution, the technology-driven plants and offices of today's competitive global economy require the expertise of skilled workers. . . .

16. Swoboda and Pressler, "US Targets Slave Labor Sweatshop."

17. See "39 Garment Workers File Suit to Recover $1.8 Million in Wages," *Los Angeles Times*, 5 Apr. 1996. See also Diane E. Lewis, "Sweatshop Workers Get Early Holiday Gift," *Boston Globe*, 10 Dec. 1995; *Sweatshops in New York City, A Local Example of a Nationwide Problem* (Washington, DC: General Accounting Office, 1989); *Garment Industry, Efforts to Address the Prevalence and Conditions of Sweatshops* (Washington, DC: General Accounting Office, 1994).

18. Bureau of the Census, *Statistical Abstract*, tab. 696. There is little doubt that globalization has eroded the power of unions in the United States. Businesses can escape union demands by moving operations to a foreign location. Increasing numbers of part-time and other nonunion jobs have undermined traditional sources of union membership. These trends have seen "unions do a u-turn on immigrant worker issue" as "an emerging generation of California labor leaders envisions poorly paid foreign-born workers—regardless of their immigrant status—as becoming a booming new base of support of U.S. unions." See Stuart Silverstein, "Unions for a U-turn on Immigrant Worker Issue," *Los Angeles Times*, 3 Nov. 1994.

The National Association of Manufacturers is interested in the immigration issue, but only to maintain the employment-based immigration that provides American companies with the essential technical expertise in short supply in the United States. The shortage of available expert workers is a growing concern of American business.[19]

The distinction drawn here between unskilled and expert workers means that Schlosser's "imported peasantry"[20] is less valued than the class of "high-tech itinerants wandering the globe."[21] Interestingly, the representative of the National Association of Manufacturers does not note that the service and agricultural sectors seemingly still rely on low-skilled immigrants. Lobbyists for the agriculture industry, for example, recently sought federal legislation that would have granted visas to 250,000 temporary foreign farm workers.[22] Furthermore, this perspective does not help us understand the persistence of sweatshop forms of manufacturing in those areas that are not so much "technology driven" as they are labor intensive.

Iris Marion Young argues that exploitation in the U.S. wage labor market may be at its most extreme in the case of the menial work performed by members (especially those classified as "minorities") from the so-called new service class.[23] Newspaper reports suggest that migrant workers, sometimes unaware of their legal rights, are especially susceptible to poor treatment. For example, in January 1996, the Service Employees' International Union charged that three immigrant workers were cheated out of wages to which they were entitled by a contractor with the Massachusetts Bay Transportation Authority. The landscape and property management contractor was accused of claiming that "the three full-time workers [were] part-time employees to avoid paying prevailing wages."[24]

Some immigrants simply cannot find a way into the labor market, especially the legal market, and constitute part of the category of people Young describes as suffering from marginalization; they are "people the system of labor cannot or will not use."[25] Exclusion from the labor force then leads to deprivation in a number of areas of everyday life since a life of poverty does not allow individuals to find adequate housing, health care, and other resources for themselves and their families. This situation has been a cause of some of the most heated political debates over the last decade or so. Immigrants are accused of burdening an already overstretched welfare system in calling upon public assistance programs for basic goods and services. Although illegal immigrants are especially vulnerable to such accusations, the anti-

19. Jerry J. Jasinowski, "What U.S. Business Wants From Immigration" (Letter to the editor) *New York Times*, 13 Sept. 1995.
20. Schlosser, "In the Strawberry Fields," p. 30.
21. Leslie Helm, "Creating High-Tech Workshops: US Firms Find Skilled—and Cheap—Programmers Abroad," *Los Angeles Times*, 15 Nov. 1993.
22. The proposal was rejected by the U.S. House of Representatives on 21 Mar. 1996.

23. Young, *Justice and the Politics of Difference*.
24. Diane E. Lewis, "MBTA Contractor Sued by Union over Wages," *Boston Globe*, 12 Jan. 1996.
25. Young, *Justice and the Politics of Difference*, p. 53.

immigrant rhetoric used tends to extend the debate to all foreigners. At times this demands that legal immigrants be denied Social Security and other benefits unless they take out U.S. citizenship.

But is it clear that immigrants are as much of a drain on public assistance as might be thought? According to George Borjas, the relative position of immigrants in the U.S. economy deteriorated between 1970 and 1990. During those two decades, the percentage of immigrants receiving welfare increased from less than 6 percent to just over 9 percent.[26] Importantly, these figures reveal that more than 90 percent of immigrants do not receive welfare. Fix, Passel, and Zimmermann further note that immigrants use welfare programs at about the same rate as U.S.-born residents, although there may be significantly higher usage among particular subsets of immigrants (such as refugees and elderly people).[27] Wages for immigrants have not kept up with those of U.S.-born workers.

Whereas in 1970, immigrants and U.S.-born workers were, on average, receiving almost equal wages, the wage differential in 1990 showed immigrants earning more than 15 percent less than the U.S.-born. Perhaps the growing visibility of the poverty experienced by some segments of the immigrant population over the last two decades might account for some of the opposition to continued migration. The degree to which immigrants might be a drain on a particular pool of resources, however, really depends on the spatial scale of analysis being discussed. Researchers at the Urban Institute in Washington, D.C., argue, for example, that "while immigrants generate a net fiscal surplus, the bulk of the taxes they pay are federal, while the obligations for providing them services remains with local and state governments. Hence, in some communities, immigrants generate a net deficit at the local level."[28] That is, in the overall operation of the U.S. economy, immigrants are a positive force; however, in particular communities and neighborhoods, immigrants might draw upon public resources more heavily than U.S.-born residents do.

Naturally, the restructuring of the U.S. economy, as noted in the letter from the representative of the manufacturers' association cited earlier, has created demands for highly skilled immigrant labor. The latest cohorts of immigrants tend to be more highly educated than either earlier immigrants or U.S.-born residents of comparable age.[29] In 1994, 147,012 employment-based immigrants were admitted to the United States. More than 40,000 of these were classified as priority workers or professionals with advanced degrees.[30] While there is evidence that these workers do relatively well

26. Borjas, "Economic Benefit of Immigration."

27. Fix, Passel, and Zimmermann, "Use of SSI."

28. Michael Fix and Jeffrey S. Passel, "Perspective on Immigration: Balancing the Ledger on Jobs, Taxes," *Los Angeles Times*, 2 Aug. 1994.

29. "Foreign-born Residents Highest Percentage of US Population Since World War II, Census Bureau Reports" (Press release, CB95-155, U.S. Department of Commerce, Bureau of the Census, 25 Aug. 1995).

30. Bureau of the Census, *Statistical Abstract*, tab. 5.

when it comes to wages, in some cases even highly skilled immigrant workers find themselves in exploitative situations. One *Los Angeles Times* report describes the creation of high-technology sweatshops staffed by "skilled—and cheap—programmers" from abroad: "Legions of programmers, many working on dubious visas, are hacking away right now in cheap motel rooms, guarded hideaways and corporate computer centers throughout America." The relationships to globalization are made explicit in the following description:

These new high-tech itinerants wandering the globe in search of work are mirrored by a new breed of work wandering the globe in search of cheap labor. Linked to the United States by satellite and electronic mail often backed by government subsidies, overseas workers are providing quality programming at prices far below what it would cost here.[31]

Despite their very high skill levels, then, foreign programmers often enter the United States (on short-term visas) to be paid less than the prevailing wage. Opponents have criticized the immigrants, saying they lower wages, but at least one anti-immigrant group has placed the blame on the corporations that allow their contractors to pay these low wages. Such a strategy places pressure on U.S. firms to pay immigrant workers at prevailing rates so that they are not as competitive with local workers.

The longer immigrants reside in the United States, the better their wages and labor market position are likely to be. Immigrant labor markets are, however, polarized between the low wages of the unskilled who often

31. Helm, "Creating High-Tech Sweatshops."

find work only through informal contacts, and the highly paid positions held by in-migrating individuals whose professional skills are in high demand. Both segments of the immigrant labor market are the target of efforts to restrict the number of people migrating into this country. But where does that leave immigrants who are outside the labor market, and what, then, are their experiences?

Sociospatial segregation

Accompanying globalization and the influx of migrants has been the growth in anti-immigrant sentiment, evident in any number of sources, including print media, talk radio, and political campaign speeches. By deliberate choice, many of the phrases used here (and elsewhere in this article) come from newspaper reports. It is such popular representations as these that fuel many of the debates about immigration and immigrants. They are the sources from which many people gather information to develop their opinions about the merits of, or problems associated with, immigration policy and immigrants. The extent of the necessity of migrant labor is not clear in the minds of many residents of the United States. Opponents to large-scale immigration complain that because of their supposed heavy use of public services, immigrants, especially (though not exclusively) undocumented workers and their families, are a burden to an economy that already has too large a deficit. At a time when politicians grapple with how to balance budgets at federal, state, and local levels, and when unemployment among some segments of the working-age population is very high, questions are asked about why more people are allowed to enter the country. Advocates of immigration argue that immigrants and their families contribute to both the cultural and economic development of the nation.[32] These debates about the relative merits of legal and illegal migration create tensions not only in federal policy debates but also in communities and neighborhoods where there are large concentrations of immigrants.

One suburban Los Angeles resident told a *Los Angeles Times* reporter, "What we have in Southern California is not assimilation—it's annexation by Mexico."[33] In another case, a man charged with assaulting an immigrant reportedly told an arresting officer in Glendale, California, "All of them should go back where they came from. . . . They take our homes, our jobs, they buy up

everything, and look at me. I was born here. They don't belong here."[34] U.S.-born (and some immigrant) residents argue that there are simply too many immigrants entering the country who have rejected assimilationist models and who favor a multicultural society that preserves cultural differences.

At the center of many debates is the resistance or inability of some immigrants to adopt English as their primary language. In some cases, immigrants, especially older people and recently arrived migrants, have limited English skills, and thus there has been a growing trend for government services to be provided in other languages. For example, to avoid claims of anti-Hispanic bias, the Chicago Housing Authority introduced a range of Spanish-language services.[35] Opposition to this trend has resulted in greater visibility for the English-only movement.[36] Supporters of English-only initiatives—such as Arizonans for Official English, U.S. English, and English First—lobby at various levels of government for legislation that makes it illegal for government services to be provided in another language. By spring 1996,

32. Advocacy groups like the Federation for American Immigration Reform (FAIR) are especially visible opponents of immigration. For details of the arguments against immigration, see Roy Beck, *The Case Against Immigration: The Moral, Economic, Social and Environmental Reasons for Reducing Immigration Back to Traditional Levels* (New York: W.W. Norton, 1996). See also V. Briggs, Jr., *Mass Immigration and the National Labor Market* (Armonk, NY: M.E. Sharpe, 1992); P. Brimelow, "Time to Rethink Immigration?" *National Review*, 22 June 1992, pp. 30-46. For a very brief overview of the benefits of immigration, see Fix and Passel, "Perspective on Immigration." The full study by Fix and Passel is reported in their *Immigration and Immigrants: Setting the Record Straight* (Washington, DC: Urban Institute, 1995).

33. Quoted in Patrick J. McDonnell, "Study Disputes Immigrant Stereotypes, Cites Gains," *Los Angeles Times*, 3 Nov. 1995.

34. Quoted in Ed Bond, "Man Faces Hate Crime Charge in Assault," *Los Angeles Times*, 8 Apr. 1994.

35. "Hispanics and Housing Subsidies" (editorial), *Chicago Tribune*, 24 Apr. 1996.

36. Bill Piatt, *¿Only English? Law and Language Policy in the United States* (Albuquerque: University of New Mexico Press, 1990); Raymond Tatalovich, *Nativism Reborn: The Official English Language Movement and the American States* (Lexington: University Press of Kentucky, 1995); James Crawford, *Hold Your Tongue: Bilingualism and the Politics of English Only* (Reading, MA: Addison-Wesley, 1992).

23 states had adopted some measure that makes English the "official" language, and the Supreme Court agreed to take another look at the issue.[37] Immigrant parents themselves are not always supportive of bilingual education. For example, a group of Latino parents in Los Angeles demanded that their children be placed in English-only classes because they want them to learn the dominant language.[38]

There is clear evidence that proficiency in English makes a difference to the range of job possibilities open to many immigrants. This in turn can affect the types of housing and other social necessities that are available to immigrant workers and their families. For the poorest immigrants, housing is a major problem. *Los Angeles Times* writer David Freed describes "cramped, decaying hovels" that "have slid into filthy disrepair over the years" and that have "crumbling walls and dripping ceilings." These are the homes of some of the least-skilled immigrants from Asia, Mexico, and South America.[39] It is not just housing but also the communities in which immigrants live that face problems when low wages predominate. First-generation immigrants, especially those with low skills and thus low wages, often find themselves in communities where basic infrastructure is deteriorating.

The situation in Washington Heights, a neighborhood of Dominican immigrants in New York City, exemplifies the material hardships faced by immigrant communities in the midst of global affluence:

Washington Heights still has movie theaters and florists and other strong life signs gone from neighborhoods that have succumbed to urban blight, but it also has wall murals that serve as memorials to young men killed in the neighborhood's drug wars. Factory workers see jobs disappearing. Small-business owners are struggling to stay ahead of their rents and debts. Community organizations built on publicly funded programs are groaning under government budget cuts. Neighborhood community centers are threatened with closures and curtailed hours.[40]

Related to the backlash against migrants are hate crimes in which they and their families are subject to violence targeted at individuals and the property they own. Hate crimes are directed at people on the basis of their immigrant status, race, ethnicity, or other attributes ascribed to a social group.[41] Specific statistical data are unreliable because of serious

37. See Joan Biskupic, "English-Only Case to Get Court Review: Arizona Law Covers Government Business," *Washington Post*, 26 Mar. 1996.

38. Amy Pyle, "80 Students Stay out of School in Latino Boycott," *Los Angeles Times*, 14 Feb. 1996.

39. David Freed, "Web of Misery: The 'Bricks': Big Profit in Slum Decay," *Los Angeles Times*, 30 July 1989.

40. Roberto Suro, "They Came to Improve But Just Try to Survive; Poverty Threatens the Community Dominicans Built in New York," *Washington Post*, 19 June 1995.

41. See Los Angeles County Commission on Human Relations, *Hate Crime in Los Angeles County 1992: A Report to the Los Angeles County Board of Supervisors* (Los Angeles: Los Angeles County Commission on Human Relations, 1993); Anna Cekola, "Attack on Vietnamese Immigrant Called a Hate Crime," *Los Angeles Times*, 2 May 1994; Art Barnum, "Vietnamese Church's Scars Are Only Outside," *Chicago Tribune*, 18 Apr. 1994; Bond, "Man Faces Hate Crime Charges"; "Arson Fire Destroys House of an Iraqi-American Family," *New York Times*, 22 Feb. 1991; "Racial and

underreporting not only by the victims but also due to the reluctance of some agencies who are supposed to be reporting to the federal government to do so fully. Because of its racialized nature, violence directed toward immigrants spills over onto U.S. citizens and U.S.-born people who appear to be immigrants. The National Asian Pacific American League Consortium released a report in 1995 that found that often Asian Americans were told to "go home . . . as if they were not Americans."[42] Violence, as many people have noted, is an expression of perceived power relations. Immigrants are often the target of abuse and violence because they are believed to be receiving more than they deserve and at the expense of others. Perpetrators, for example, might believe that immigrants are taking jobs or using up resources to which they themselves are more entitled. This raises questions about perceptions of citizenship and what it means to be a citizen in one place but not in another.

Immigrants and politics: Questions of powerlessness

Powerlessness refers to the lack of control people have over their day-to-day lives. Young argues that the roots of powerlessness lie in positions held in the workforce. Those people with the most privileged and respected positions are more powerful than those who are not in such positions. Thus

Religious Hate Crimes," *Los Angeles Times*, 24 Mar. 1988.

42. Lena H. Sun, "Hate Crimes Against Asian Americans Increase," *Washington Post*, 1 Aug. 1995.

low-skilled immigrants usually end up in jobs in which they have little authority. Higher-skilled immigrants who are admitted on temporary work visas may not have any power to change jobs, regardless of how terrible the working conditions in which they find themselves might be. Social power can, however, be exercised in other areas of life, such as in the electoral process. Immigrants, legal and otherwise, low-skilled or high-skilled, may find that they are relatively powerless in this respect. For example, a highly skilled immigrant engineer living in Silicon Valley may hold a position that is both privileged and much respected. But that same engineer may not be able to vote on legislation that affects the lives of immigrants in the United States. Thus this person is not powerless in the same sense as someone who is denied access to the labor market, but is in other ways—in this case, in terms of voting rights. Clearly, to speak of immigrants and their experiences is not to imply a homogeneous group of people who will all have identical experiences. Immigration, as a social attribute, intersects with many others—and race is perhaps the most critical factor.

There are attempts to extend voting rights to legal immigrants, at least at the local level. Within the Los Angeles Unified School District, criticism developed around a proposal to allow parents, regardless of their citizenship, to vote in school board elections. In Washington, D.C., in 1992, a council member introduced a bill that would allow immigrants to vote in some circumstances. In Takoma Park, Maryland, voting rights for legal immigrants were granted in the early 1990s.[43]

Globalization that encourages migration across international boundaries may well diminish the powerlessness faced by some people. Refugees, for example, who face political persecution in their home country might well find their position improved on being granted residency in a U.S. city. The period during which their case is being heard, however, is one in which their lives are still out of their control. Immigrants as a social group are clearly not totally powerless; they have relatively less power than some other groups.

Cutbacks in the welfare state may well be linked to the increasing integration of the U.S. economy into the global economy and its loss of dominance. The deficit is clearly a result of globalization, and it is linked to all kinds of cutbacks in domestic policy.

CONCLUSION: POLITICAL
AND POLICY IMPLICATIONS

Rhetorical and often inflammatory statements about immigration and immigrants often have little relationship to the reality of the situation. The veracity of claims from both opponents and advocates of immigration is not easily determined. Despite the isolationist rhetoric of some conservative politicians in the United States, it is unlikely that the country can uncouple itself from the global political and economic structures that are now in place. Globalization gives businesses the choice of importing workers or exporting employment and production to other countries. Both create competition for U.S.-born workers living and working at home. Both also encourage, if not rely upon, significant global migration. Thus, despite calls for reform (read "restrictions") of federal immigration policy, it is unlikely that the United States can close its doors to all foreigners—even while immigration to the United States is not as open as some critics would claim.

While globalization is often defined in economic terms, its social consequences are great. This is not to imply that some global economic processes determine local social conditions without any reciprocity. Around the world, concern has been expressed about the extent to which global economic processes might be eradicating some local cultures. However, immigrants to U.S. cities also modify the social and cultural geographies of the places in which they live and work.

Just as more obviously multinational corporations and governments at all levels have developed strategies that simultaneously respond to and promote globalization, so groups of less privileged people also develop such strategies. Globalization has been described as a "new spatial geopolitics."[44] The new urban geopolitics

43. Charisse Jones, "Quezada's Proposal for Non-Citizen Voting Assailed," *Los Angeles Times*, 7 Feb. 1992; Shaun Sutner, "Measures Designed to Enlarge Voter Rolls Stir Debate," *Washington Post*, 21 May 1992; Beth Kaiman, "Deciding Ballot Rights: Takoma Park to Rule on Non-Citizen Vote," *Washington Post* (Maryland weekly—Montgomery sec.), 31 Oct. 1991.

44. Mike Featherstone and Scott Lash, "Globalization, Modernity and the Spatialization of Social Theory: An Introduction," *Global Modernities*, ed. Featherstone, Lash, and Robertson, p. 3.

of U.S. cities pits localities against one another as they engage in bidding wars for foreign investment; social groups against one another as each group attempts to stake out a territory of its own; and businesses and the state against communities.

ANNALS, *AAPSS*, **551**, May 1997

Globalization and Residential Segregation by Race

By VILNA I. BASHI and MARK ALAN HUGHES

ABSTRACT: The United States has long been characterized by racial segregation in residence. As the country moves into a period of increasing global interaction, these questions might be posed: Will globalization effect change in U.S. residence patterns by race? If so, how? If not, why not? To consider these questions, we briefly review segregation in the United States and present data for eight metropolitan areas to illustrate the extent of residential segregation. Next, we examine four leading conceptions of globalization and consider whether these suggest ways in which globalization may affect residential segregation in the United States. We conclude that globalization falls low on a long list of factors related to residential segregation. In particular, we argue that desegregation would require deliberate steps in domestic public policy.

Vilna I. Bashi is a Mellon Postdoctoral Fellow at the University of Pennsylvania's Population Studies Center. Beginning September 1997, she will be an assistant professor in the Department of Sociology at Northwestern University.

Mark Alan Hughes is vice president for policy development at Public/Private Ventures in Philadelphia.

I N this article, we argue a rather simple point, namely, that globalization is likely to be a relatively unimportant factor in either the explanation or the amelioration of residential segregation by race in the United States. While this is somewhat at odds with the general line of argument in this issue of *The Annals*, we invite readers to pause and consider placing segregation into that large category of conditions that reasonable minds would acknowledge to be unaffected in significant ways by globalization.

Lengthy empirical evaluation being beyond the scope of this article, we seek to make this point prima facie. We think it a costly error to assume globalization will have great effect on segregation and be distracted thereby from more proximate explanations and potential solutions.

The article consists of three parts. First, we present the basic conditions of residential segregation by race in the United States through a brief review of recent literature and an examination of residence patterns in the eight largest U.S. metropolitan areas. These settlements are important in their own right, since they capture much of the total U.S. population affected by segregation and represent the places most salient to the issues raised by globalization. The finding here is that residential segregation by race appears to be pervasive in U.S. settlements and appears to be invariant with respect to hypothesized impacts of globalization or to the extent to which a city has become global.

Second, we review various approaches to globalization as a theoretical approach to settlements and social changes related to settlements. Though there is some basis for a theoretical stretch in this literature to accommodate segregation, we find little in the leading conceptual frameworks of globalization to suggest a close connection to residential segregation. While many theorists specify and some scholars observe a relationship between globalization and increasing income inequality and while the relationship between such changes and racial income disparities is important, the leading students of racial segregation point to segregation's extent and maintenance far beyond what can be explained by differences in income.

In the third and final section, we turn to the administrative geography of federal public housing assistance as an example of an alternative, more proximate explanation. We briefly examine the administrative rules that govern housing assistance and the boundaries that interact with these rules in two of the United States' global cities: New York and Los Angeles. We argue that with segregation mechanisms like these, one need not look to globalization to find an explanation and potential solutions for racial segregation.

RACIAL SEGREGATION
IN THE LARGEST U.S.
METROPOLITAN AREAS

In their book *American Apartheid*, Douglas Massey and Nancy Denton retell the history of residential segregation in the United States, lay out the social forces that are brought to bear in creating the patterns that we now see, and explain why segregation persists despite the repeal of laws that allowed the practice to continue. No group in the United States has ever been segregated for the length of time and to the same degree that African Americans have. It is not just places to live that are at stake— segregation concentrates poverty and its correlates, and isolates black people from opportunity in many ways.[1]

While surveys show that blacks prefer to live in mixed neighborhoods, whites tend to move after a small number of blacks enter a neighborhood. Segregation persists because the U.S. settlement structure ensures that there is always some all-white neighborhood to which displeased whites can move. Such neighborhoods could not survive if there were not social mechanisms in place to ensure their maintenance. Massey and Denton show that in 1980, 16 metropolitan areas were hypersegregated,[2] or segregated on four of the five dimensions they calculated to measure segregation. Thus they report that one-third of all African Americans in the United States live under conditions of intense racial segregation. By 1990, 20 metropolitan areas were hypersegregated (14

of the 16 from 1980, plus 6 newly hypersegregated areas).[3]

In the 1990s, most residences and, often, most workplaces are now located beyond big-city boundaries in a new kind of suburbia that we are still struggling to understand.[4] To illustrate one aspect of this new metropolitan form, we examine segregation in the eight largest metropolitan areas in the United States: New York, Los Angeles, Chicago, Washington-Baltimore, San Francisco–Oakland, Philadelphia, Detroit, and Dallas–Fort Worth. Together, these eight metropolitan areas account for one-quarter of the total population of the United States. Over this period, while population shifts have occurred, segregated residence patterns remain intact.

Of these eight metropolitan areas, all but metropolitan Detroit gained in total population during the 1980s. Note that although metropolitan New York is still the largest settlement in the United States, by far the largest increase in population occurred in metropolitan Los Angeles (3 million in Los Angeles versus one-

1. Douglas S. Massey and Nancy A. Denton, *American Apartheid: Segregation and the Making of the Underclass* (Cambridge, MA: Harvard University Press, 1993).

2. The authors use five dimensions for measuring the extent of segregation: unevenness of distribution, racial isolation, neighborhood clustering to form enclaves, concentration versus sparseness of settlements, and spatial centralization around the urban core. Hypersegregation means that an area is "very highly segregated on at least four of the five dimensions at once." Massey and Denton, *American Apartheid*, p. 74.

3. Nancy A. Denton, "Are African-Americans Still Hypersegregated?" in *Residential Apartheid: The American Legacy*, ed. R. D. Bullard, J. E. Grigsby, and C. Lee (Los Angeles: University of California Press, 1994), pp. 49-81.

4. For a thoughtful discussion of the issues, see Anthony Downs, "The Need for a New Vision of U.S. Metropolitan Areas" (Goldman Sachs Real Estate Discussion Paper, 1989). For an introduction to the research debates, see William Frey and Alden Speare, "U.S. Metropolitan Area Population Growth: 1960-1990" (Research report no. 91-212, Population Studies Center, University of Michigan, May 1991). For a more popular introduction, see Joel Garreau, *Edge City: Life on the New Frontier* (New York: Doubleday, 1991).

half million between 1980 and 1990 in each of the other consolidated metropolitan statistical areas [CMSAs]). The four largest gains in population occurred in the newer Sunbelt metropolitan areas of Los Angeles, Dallas–Fort Worth, San Francisco–Oakland, and the metropolitan area of Washington-Baltimore.

Yet, some parts of the metropolis gained while others lost. In four of the eight areas, the central cities lost population during the 1980s. Perhaps the most dramatic shift was in metropolitan Washington-Baltimore, where the central cities lost population even though the CMSA as a whole gained nearly a million new residents. Metropolitan Chicago had the largest decline in central city population during the 1980s, losing over a quarter of a million persons. Even the central cities with the largest population growth during the 1980s—Los Angeles, San Francisco–Oakland, and Dallas–Fort Worth—captured only about one-third of their respective metropolitan growth. The older regions of the Northeast and Midwest have declining central cities and growing suburbs (the exception, again, is New York). The newer metropolitan areas of the West and South have growing cities and faster-growing suburbs. By 1990, this postwar process of rapid population suburbanization had gone so far that suburban residents outnumbered city residents in all eight metropolitan areas and in the nation as a whole.

It is important to note—and this is our main focus here—that this process of suburbanization has not been uniform. The most extreme example is the continuing segregation of Afri-can Americans in central cities. In general, African Americans are more segregated than any other ethnic group, and they remain equally segregated in all income levels. Furthermore, segregation has not declined as black incomes and education have risen.[5]

In Figure 1, we consider this segregation at the very gross scale of city and suburbs. The figure shows the percentage of the population in central cities and suburbs that was African American in 1990. In metropolitan Chicago, for example, the central cities were 36.3 percent black and the suburbs were 5.6 percent black. That is, the percentage of the city population that was black in metropolitan Chicago was about six and a half times the percentage of the suburban population that was black. Note that, with no racial segregation, the percentages in the cities and suburbs would be the same. Since metropolitan Chicago as a whole was 19.2 percent black in 1990, the cities in the region had about twice and the suburbs had about one-quarter as many African Americans as they would have had with no racial segregation.

In every one of these metropolitan areas, the percentage of the central city population that was African American was at least twice as high as the suburban percentage, and in several it was over four times as high. Note that the columns are arranged

5. This has been well established in an influential series of writings by Douglas S. Massey and his coauthors. These include Douglas S. Massey and Nancy A. Denton, "Trends in the Residential Segregation of Blacks, Hispanics, and Asians," in *American Sociological Review*, 52:802-25 (1987); Massey and Denton, *American Apartheid*.

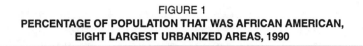

FIGURE 1
**PERCENTAGE OF POPULATION THAT WAS AFRICAN AMERICAN,
EIGHT LARGEST URBANIZED AREAS, 1990**

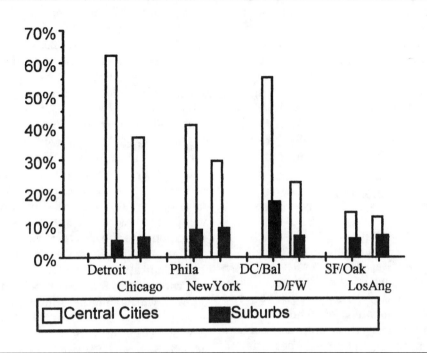

in order of their ratio of city and suburban percentages of population that were black, from most divergent on the left to least divergent on the right. Even in metropolitan areas with large suburban African American populations, the pattern of black city, white suburbs remains very strong.[6] For example, the Baltimore-Washington CMSA has the nation's largest suburban black population,

788,000 in 1990. This is over three times the size of Chicago's suburban black population. Still, suburban Baltimore-Washington had only about two-thirds as many suburban blacks as it would if there were no racial concentration. (Of course, this level of analysis neglects the fact that a majority of the CMSA's suburban blacks reside in a single county of the region, Prince George's, Maryland. As this shows, suburbanization alone is a poor indicator of integration.)

6. Non-Hispanic whites are a majority in the suburbs of all eight metropolitan areas. In fact, the suburbs are more than 80 percent white in all the metropolitan areas except Los Angeles, San Francisco–Oakland, and Washington-Baltimore.

As Massey and Denton extensively show, and as our far-from-exhaustive examination of the eight largest metropolitan areas illustrates, segregation by race in the United States is pervasive and ongoing. We have illustrated the extent to which central cities remain disproportionately black. As seen in Figure 1, segregation appears to be prevalent in all major urban areas of the United States. This is the case even in cities like New York and Los Angeles, which have internationally focused local economies and greater influxes of foreign-born people—arguably signs of a more global orientation.

GLOBALIZATION AND RESIDENTIAL SEGREGATION

We have just looked briefly at the state of residential segregation in the United States. In order now to assess the impact of globalization on residential segregation, we first have to define globalization. The definitions we use may then serve as markers from which to trace the potential effects of globalization on residential segregation.

For this purpose, in this second part of this article, we employ four alternative and distinct definitions of globalization,[7] provided to us by four authors: Lester Thurow, Paul Krugman, Saskia Sassen, and Malcolm Waters.

Thurow on globalization

Thurow's *Head to Head* characterizes the global economy as the arena for fierce economic competition

7. There are others. The four we have chosen are radically different from one another and, together, provide what we believe might be the broadest base by which globalization's impact might be assessed.

between three economies: those of the United States, Japan, and the European Community.[8] The winner of the competition is the one who will control the largest market, for that is the country or region that will become the richest, while all others fight to gain market access. He asserts that the global future will show "the house of Europe" to be the internationally competitive winner.

Thurow's global economy is centered around capitalism. He reports that history has shown other competing systems to have failed, and to date the key to all international development has been by economic integration into the Western capitalist system via access to Western markets. Capitalism is the global future, but capitalism's future is not secure. Thurow warns that the United States is not in a position to win the global competition, mainly because its "Anglo-Saxon capitalism" has an individualistic mode of operating— where it is every man for himself, workers have no firm loyalty, and workers are seen by firms as merely a factor of production to be used at the lowest cost for only as long as needed. By contrast, Germany and Japan both have "communitarian" brands of capitalism which emphasize worker-firm commitments.

Thurow speaks more about the meaning of nation and ethnicity under globalism in *The Future of Capitalism*. Ethnicity in the global era,

8. Lester C. Thurow, *Head to Head: The Coming Economic Battle Among Japan, Europe, and America* (New York: Warner Books, 1992). See also idem, *The Future of Capitalism: How Today's Economic Forces Shape Tomorrow's World* (New York: William Morrow, 1996).

to Thurow, basically means ethnic factionalism.

Where homogenous ethnic groups exist in different parts of the same country, large states are breaking up or threatening to break up—as in Canada and India. . . .

In the United States the same demands show up not as geographic separatism but in demands for special ethnic quotas and privileges. Every American can now claim to belong to some minority group that deserves special treatment. Special groups (such as environmentalists, the handicapped) now dominate the political process. A deaf Miss America is criticized by other deaf Americans for speaking rather than using the sign language that makes her handicap obvious. All want to be distinguished from the white male majority and given a guaranteed legal "minority" position. In response the white male "majority" (an actual minority) wants all of those special privileges cleansed from the land. . . .

. . . living peacefully together has become harder.[9]

Thus Thurow suggests that ethnic factionalism is the means by which social demands will be addressed in a global society. These demands can only be made greater in a global economy where economic inequality is expected to increase. Thurow predicts increased inequality to result from an increased scarcity of low-wage jobs under global competition.

In a global economy where goods can be sourced in low-wage Third World countries, the effective supply of unskilled workers has expanded enormously. As a consequence, wages must fall for unskilled workers in rich countries. Quite simply, supply and demand require it. In

a global economy a worker has two things to offer—skills, or the willingness to work for low wages. Since products can be built anywhere, the unskilled who work in rich societies must work for the wages of the equally unskilled who live in poor societies. If they won't work for such wages, unskilled jobs simply move to poor countries.[10]

Certainly, the lower half of the economic distribution in the United States will suffer decreased earnings under globalization, according to Thurow. (He states that in the long run the upper half of the distribution may, too, suffer job losses, since they will no longer be needed to manage jobs that have been sent overseas. Again, overall, the United States as a whole will be the loser.) This increased inequality will, according to Massey and Denton, mean an increased concentration of poverty in communities that are predominantly poor and African American, along with the attendant negative social consequences: crime, drugs, and the like.[11]

Krugman on globalization

If globalization is defined as "international competitiveness," then Krugman says that globalization is more a chimera than a reality.[12] He suggests that those, like Thurow, who state that the United States' economy is in danger of "losing the war" in the global competition are misattributing our economy's short-

9. Thurow, *Future of Capitalism*, pp. 239-40.

10. Thurow, *Head to Head*, p. 52.

11. Massey and Denton, *American Apartheid.*

12. This section is based on Paul Krugman, *Pop Internationalism* (Cambridge: MIT Press, 1996).

comings to a global economy. Krugman writes:

Consider this statement: "Modern technologies of transportation and communication make it possible to produce anything anywhere. This technological shrinking of the world has only been reinforced by the fall of communism, which has made the Third World safe for multinational corporations. As a result, a massive redeployment of capital and technology from the high-wage countries of the West to low-wage developing nations is now occurring. This redeployment of capital along with the flood of low-cost imports is destroying the well-paying manufacturing jobs that used to support a large middle class in the United States and Europe. In short, globalization favors Western capital, but is devastating to Western labor."

Convincing as this may sound, the statement is specious. In fact, I made it up to illustrate a view of the world that passes for sophistication among many policy intellectuals but is almost completely refuted by the available evidence.[13]

Krugman denounces arguments that consider nations to be like corporations in competition with one another. The people putting forth such arguments, Krugman says, write as if there is such a thing as absolute advantage. They, then, obviously do not understand the Ricardian comparative advantage, which states that it is advantageous for nations to trade, even if one nation is better than its potential partners at producing all goods that might be traded. The best outcome is to have each nation produce the goods that it is best at producing, that is, where it has comparative advantage. International trade does not have winners and losers.

Krugman explains that "declining wages and rising unemployment are not things that might happen once globalization really gets going; they are trends that have been in progress for 20 years," mainly as a result of technological change biased in favor of high-skilled workers.[14] The key result here, as was the case under Thurow's globalization, is increased inequality of earnings (at least just short of the very long run), which derives from the benefits accrued to the highly skilled because of the higher demand for their labor—although this is not because of international competitiveness, which Krugman believes is "a largely meaningless concept."[15] As Krugman writes, "We have found that increased wage inequality, like the decline of manufacturing and the slowdown in real income growth, is overwhelmingly the consequence of domestic causes."[16]

Sassen on globalization

Recent changes in the international economy, according to Sassen, are evident in the shift to a geographically dispersed but globally integrated economy, which has led to important changes in the organization of labor and urban life throughout the world.[17] This process of glo-

13. Ibid., p. 193.

14. Ibid., p. 195.
15. Ibid., p. 17.
16. Ibid., p. 45.
17. Saskia Sassen, *The Mobility of Labor and Capital: A Study in International Investment and Labor Flow* (New York: Cambridge University Press, 1988). See also idem, *The Global City: New York, London, Tokyo* (Princeton, NJ: Princeton University Press, 1991).

balization focuses not on the nation-state but on cities (some of which are more important to the global economy than others) and on the restructuring of labor (where both high-skilled and lower-skilled services become more important to global cities, and manufacturing production and consumer services become more geographically dispersed throughout the world).

Sassen argues that the dynamic and highly mobile nature of capital investment that marks the current age is distinctly related to the international movement of labor. This relationship is marked by the disruptive nature of capital investment in the developing world, which creates pools of labor that are not readily absorbed domestically, thus making international migration both an option and a strategy for those whose labor is not demanded in the new investment areas.

This global relationship between labor and capital has caused the emergence of a few major cities as new strategic command centers for the global economy. As globalization develops, these global cities—like New York, London, and Tokyo—develop specialized producer service industries—for example, legal and financial services, among others—that help manage the regionally scattered enterprises that compose the modern transnational corporation. Thus finance, manufacturing, and clerical activities become internationalized, while global cities become homes for concentrations of producer service activities. Immigrants, displaced by capital investment in their countries of origin, are drawn to these global

cities and are incorporated into a growing and parallel service sector—this one based on low-skill personal services like domestic work. Thus global cities emerge, and urban native-born labor and immigrant labor are reorganized to suit the demands of the new economy.

Unlike the case when manufacturing production dominated the economy and led to an expanding middle class, Sassen says that

> today growth is based on an industrial complex that leads . . . to an increasing dispersion in the income structure and in the bidding power of firms and households. There is social and economic polarization, particularly strong in major cities which concentrate a large proportion of the new growth industries and create a vast direct and indirect demand for low-profit services and low-wage jobs.[18]

For example, there is a continuing occupational stratification by race and nationality—blacks, Hispanics, and immigrant minorities replace whites in old low-wage jobs and move into new low-wage jobs in New York and London. Furthermore,

> a new class alignment is being shaped, and global cities have emerged as one of the main arenas for this development: They contain both the most vigorous economic sectors and the sharpest income polarization. The concrete expression of the new class alignment in the structures of everyday life is well captured in the massive expansion of a new high-income stratum alongside growing urban poverty.[19]

Thus, according to Sassen, economic inequality of income and lifestyle is

18. Sassen, *Global City*, pp. 300-307.
19. Ibid., p. 337.

the emerging trend for global cities, which are the centers for the emerging global economy. Declining traditional industrial sectors result from worldwide dispersal of manufacturing production operations, thus the less-than-global city loses its former role as production center. Jobs still exist in declining sectors, and low-skilled, low-paying service sector jobs are increasingly available, although the latter are less desirable (and thus prime sectors for the hiring of immigrant labor).

Waters on globalization

Waters takes a very different approach to studying globalization.[20] Rather than tracing globalizing trends, Waters first constructs a definition of the concept and then searches the economy, polity, and culture to find evidence that the concept exists. Waters defines globalization as *"a social process in which the constraints of geography on social and cultural arrangements recede and in which people become increasingly aware that they are receding."*[21]

Krugman actually agrees with Waters on one important point: "It is a late 20th-century conceit that we invented the global economy just yesterday."[22] But while Krugman suggests that America's urban producers were aware of competition from foreign producers perhaps at least 100 years ago, Waters argues that the concept began to develop in the fif-

teenth century, with European exploration and expansion around the globe.

Social exchanges link social organization with territories, and different types of exchanges accomplish different types of territorial arrangements: material exchanges localize; political exchanges internationalize; and symbolic exchanges globalize.[23] To Waters, the advancement of a globalizing culture—mainly due, in this most recent era, to advanced communication systems—is the most certain sign that globalization is taking place. Globalization advances with capitalist development. It deterritorializes (that is, places less emphasis on national borders) and incorporates societies in a Western system of modernization.

Culturally, globalization makes pluralism evident, allows for the reconstitution of nations into states of recognizable (ethnic) minorities, brings international migrants to the capitalist center, and introduces new ethnic identities—through electronic images and tourism—to the periphery. Waters suggests that this is what has happened with the term "black," which allowed for the formation of international coalitions among the peoples who found themselves under that label.

In summary the effect of globalization on ethnicity is to revive it and to differentiate it from politics and economics. It enables the view that all ethnic identities are legitimate and not merely those successful ones that managed to establish states in the nineteenth century. In some instances this means the disruption of

---

20. Malcolm Waters, *Globalization* (New York: Routledge, 1995).

21. Ibid., p. 3 (italics in original).

22. Krugman, *Pop Internationalism*, p. 207.

23. Waters, *Globalization*, p. 9.

confederations of nations (e.g., Canada, Czechoslovakia, UK, USSR, Yugoslavia). However, all political entities are coming to be regarded as legitimately, even positively multicultural.[24]

Waters, of all the authors on globalization examined here, seems to be the most optimistic about the future of tolerance. However, there is an important difference between accepting the idea of multiculturalism—"cosmopolitania," or acceptance of different ethnic groups—and the acceptance of people of different races.[25] Races and ethnic groups are not the same. Racial enmity is very different from ethnic intolerance. Waters seems to suggest that globalization will bring about greater tolerance of all kinds as ethnicity, along with other social concepts, becomes "de-territorialized." But the term "black"—a color, not a culture—has been "de-territorialized" for some time. This is why racism against blacks allowed the trade in black slaves from many different parts of Africa to many other parts of the world for some time during the period when, according to Waters, globalization was operative in the socioeconomic arena.

Each of the authors we examine here suggests very different global scenarios; one even states that globalization (if synonymous with international competitiveness) does not exist. None suggests that a change in racial attitudes is coming. (Although Waters sees multiculturalism in our future, he does not address the issues

of race and racism. Thurow, instead, predicts increased ethnic and racial factionalism.) Worse yet, Sassen and Thurow both suggest that the future may hold increased inequality of income, the burden of which in the United States disproportionately falls upon the nonwhite. For Massey, that future is here.[26]

But let us briefly visit with the possible effects of inequality on segregation. We know that, for the African American community in particular, residential segregation in all levels of earnings is consistently higher than for every other group. Thus neither income nor earnings explain segregation levels. For residential desegregation to occur under increased economic inequality, white disdain for living among nonwhite groups will have to overcome class-based negative attitudes as well as racial prejudice. That is, in a scenario of increased inequality, whites will have to agree not only that people of color should live among them but that low-income persons should live among those who have money, even if the low-income persons are nonwhite. We already have hypersegregated cities even with the repeal of legislation mandating their existence. Under the scenario of a global future of increased inequality, therefore, we may see a piling on of additional inequality-driven segregation above the race-driven segregation that is fundamental to U.S. settlements. But this strikes us as a potential sideshow in the face of existing

24. Ibid., p. 161.

25. Vilna Bashi and Antonio McDaniel, "A Theory of Immigration and Racial Stratification," *Journal of Black Studies* (in press).

26. Douglas Massey, "The Age of Extremes: Concentrated Affluence and Poverty in the Twenty First Century," *Demography* (in press).

high levels of segregation unrelated to income inequality alone.

A MORE PROXIMATE EXPLANATION OF RESIDENTIAL SEGREGATION

In this section, we discuss housing assistance programs designed to aid the stability and socioeconomic mobility of low-income households and, in practice, to aid African Americans in particular. The geography of housing assistance programs has a largely unexamined effect upon program administration and outcomes. We use the term "fragmentation" to refer to the extent to which an administrative geography divides a metropolitan area. We discuss the fragmentation of public housing assistance to illustrate the importance of policy in shoring up residential segregation practices. In the end, we hope the reader might see the potential for public policy to aid in remedying segregation in our communities, and why the solutions to—or at least the responsibility for—this problem lie in our hands today.[27]

Public housing and section 8 housing assistance payments are by far the largest federal housing programs for the disadvantaged. In fiscal year 1993, Low-Rent Public Housing provided 1.4 million units at a federal

expenditure of $6.2 million. Section 8 low-income housing assistance supported 2.8 million units with $11.2 million in federal funds.[28]

Expenditures on these programs are distributed, via U.S. Department of Housing and Urban Development (HUD) field offices, to allocation areas that are based on municipalities, counties, or a group of municipalities or counties. Each allocation area is intended to be the smallest practical area of sufficient size to support at least one feasible program or project. An entire central city may be set aside as a separate allocation area. The goal of the allocation process is the equitable distribution of federal housing assistance in accordance with the relative housing needs—population, poverty, overcrowding, substandard housing, and so on—in each allocation area within the field office jurisdiction. The functioning body of an allocation area is the public housing authority (PHA). PHAs develop and manage public housing as well as administer section 8 housing assistance payments.

Public housing

As HUD and federal policy generally move away from the construction of traditional public housing developments toward funding other projects, the main issue for policy becomes access to a metropolitan area's existing stock of public housing units. On this topic, the salient administrative rules are those governing waiting lists.

27. For a more complete discussion of administrative geography, see Mark Alan Hughes and Sally A. Hart, *Safety Net or Safety Maze: The Administrative Geography of Federal Assistance in the Ten Largest Metropolitan Areas* (Philadelphia, PA: Public/Private Ventures; Washington, DC: Department of Housing and Urban Development, Office of Policy Development and Research, 1996).

28. U.S. General Accounting Office, *Welfare Programs: Opportunities to Consolidate and Increase Program Efficiencies* (GAO/HEHS-95-139), 31 May, 1995, p. 34.

Each PHA is required to maintain its own waiting list for the stock of public housing units located within its geographical jurisdiction. Waiting lists are "unconsolidated," meaning that a family must fill out a separate application for the PHA of each allocation area in which it seeks a unit. Thus metropolitan-wide public housing opportunities are complicated directly by the simple number of PHA allocation areas in a metropolitan area. Currently, it is at the discretion of the local PHA to take application by mail; most suburban PHAs will accept applications only in person. An applicant may then have to travel several times to the PHA office to acquire an application, to get answers to any questions regarding the application (there is no required standard application), and to submit the application for processing. This must be done for every PHA allocation area in which the family seeks a housing opportunity. Thus both the number and the location of the PHAs and their offices matter.

In addition to managing its own waiting list, each PHA is allowed to grant preferences in the order in which families are drawn from the list and placed in housing units. PHAs are allowed to give priority to residents of their own jurisdiction, although they may not weight this priority by length of residence. HUD requires that applicants who work in a PHA jurisdiction must be prioritized as equivalent to a resident of the jurisdiction. Two factors, however, limit the degree to which this rule actually promotes access. First, it extends the preference status only to applicants who have already found a job in the PHA's territory, limiting the utility of housing mobility as an instrument for finding a job and creating something of a catch-22 for those seeking opportunities for mobility. Second, it limits the waiting-list equality only to that particular PHA. The more fragmented a metropolitan labor market, the more likely that a suburban housing search by an applicant employed within the jurisdiction of one suburban PHA will land the applicant in the jurisdiction of another suburban PHA—one in which his or her work status will not be relevant.

Section 8

Housing assistance payments provide subsidies that participating households can apply to private market rental housing. In brief, a participant pays 30 percent of his or her income in rent and the section 8 assistance pays the difference up to a capped market rent based on household size. The participants are responsible for finding this housing and are free to do so in any area where the PHA determines that it is not legally barred from entering into contracts. This makes housing assistance payments a far more portable alternative than public housing. PHAs are encouraged to promote choice of housing opportunities by cooperating with other PHAs, and HUD gives preference to PHAs that provide families with the broadest geographical choice of units. Under current practice, however, participants have somewhat limited access to housing in PHA allocation areas outside the one in which they currently live.

There are two forms of section 8 housing assistance—certificates and vouchers—and these are applied very differently. PHAs may make arrangements between themselves to accept each other's housing certificates. If an agreement does not exist, however, then a participating family that moves out of its original PHA jurisdiction retains its assistance only if the destination PHA admits the family to the latter's section 8 program. Under the voucher program, any PHA must admit a family with a voucher from another PHA as if the family were part of its own program. The sending PHA must reimburse the receiving PHA for the full cost of the voucher and for 80 percent of the administrative costs. The sending PHA, however, may in some cases deny the request to move.

While vouchers are indeed a fairly portable alternative, the waiting lists are very long: 150,000 in New York and 40,000 in Los Angeles, where the list is officially closed until 2001. For the present, public housing waiting lists and lack of PHA coordination in section 8 housing remain administrative rules that interact with administrative boundaries in ways that may limit access to metropolitan-wide opportunities.

Let us briefly consider the administrative boundaries to which these rules apply. We can devise various measures of geographic fragmentation. The simplest measure of fragmentation is the extent to which the number of PHAs per urban area exceeds one. By this standard, all the urbanized areas are clearly fragmented. Importantly, we should remember that the total number of PHAs represents the number of applications, waiting lists, and parties to inter-PHA agreements needed to maximize a participant's access to employment throughout the metropolitan labor market.

Alternatively, we can look at fragmentation by changing the base unit against which the number of PHAs is compared. Table 1 summarizes the administrative geography of federal housing assistance to the disadvantaged in the eight largest urbanized areas. Three other measures of fragmentation are given in the last three columns: (1) the total number of PHAs in the urbanized area, (2) the number of PHAs in the urbanized area per 1 million housing units, and (3) the average land area of PHA jurisdictions outside the large cities. Figure 2 displays the actual boundaries of all PHA jurisdictions serving one of the largest urbanized areas in the United States, Los Angeles. The fragmentation evident in the table and the map indicates a significant level of fragmentation in the administrative geography of federal housing assistance. Seen in terms of separate applications, preferential waiting lists, required interagency agreements, and so on, the map suggests the extent to which a PHA geography is imposed on metropolitan housing markets and, in particular, on suburban opportunities for employment, education, and so on that are mediated by housing markets.

The Clinton administration is cognizant of the problems created by

TABLE 1
PUBLIC HOUSING AUTHORITIES, EIGHT LARGEST URBANIZED AREAS, 1995

Urbanized Area	Housing Units	Land Area (square miles)	PHAs	PHAs per Million Units	Suburban Land Area per PHA
New York	6,252,000	2966	101	16	27
Detroit	1,463,067	1119	31	21	32
Los Angeles	4,069,916	1966	29	7	54
Philadelphia	1,678,549	1164	19	11	57
San Francisco–Oakland	1,478,575	874	12	8	77
Washington, D.C.	1,359,716	945	12	9	80
Chicago	2,645,656	1585	15	6	97
Dallas–Fort Worth	1,369,138	1443	8	6	143

FIGURE 2
LOS ANGELES URBANIZED AREA, PUBLIC HOUSING AUTHORITIES, 1995

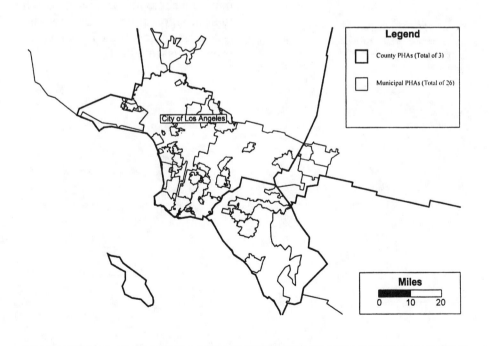

fragmentation and has moved toward policy instruments that are less constrained by administrative geography.[29] But we must also note that HUD's reform plans have been stymied by budget concerns and by the failure to reauthorize the Housing Act. Whether the progress in addressing the problems of fragmentation will remain in view during the coming years is very much in doubt. How much easier to point to worldwide forces than to fix administrative rules and boundaries closer to home.

CONCLUSION

Globalization, whatever it may be, does not affect everything, and it will probably have no significant direct impact upon residential segregation in the United States. As the first part of this article indicated, segregation is fairly complete and systematic. It has a basis in the attitudes of whites who largely prefer not to live with blacks, and it is perpetuated by a social system that protects the interests of those who hold these attitudes.

Explanation is where the mind comes to rest. Minds of great stamina may reach globalization in the search for an explanation of continuing patterns of racial segregation in the United States. But we find sufficient explanation in far more proximate causes: white racial attitudes, public policy mechanisms, and so on. On the topic of segregation, the real problem is less one of sustained explanation than of sustained action.

29. U.S. Department of Housing and Urban Development, *HUD Reinvention: From Blueprint to Action* (Mar. 1995).

ANNALS, *AAPSS*, **551**, May 1997

Urban Housing in an
Era of Global Capital

By DAVID W. BARTELT

ABSTRACT: U.S. cities have become increasingly bound into a global system in the decades since World War II. Of primary importance for urban housing are the implications of this system for the flow of residential capital, and the effects of a global labor market on U.S. wages and incomes. Globalization has overlaid issues of liquidity and new forms of financial investment on an already difficult housing situation for older manufacturing cities. Using Philadelphia as an example, issues of abandonment, affordability, and homelessness are discussed as they reflect the effects of a global urban system. The conclusion seeks to reorient discussions of local housing policy in this global context.

David W. Bartelt is professor of geography and urban studies at Temple University. His areas of interests are in community development policy, especially in regard to housing, economic development, and public education. He is the coauthor of Philadelphia: Neighborhoods, Division and Conflict in a Postindustrial City; North Philadelphia: An Atlas and Resource Guide; *and* Housing Philadelphia. *He is currently establishing a program linking human capital and investment capital policies in Philadelphia.*

121

TO consider the impact of globalization on American cities and their housing is to change the terms of the conceptual framework by which housing is traditionally viewed. The transformation of postwar American economic hegemony into a global network of land, labor, and capital is well established.[1] The rapid and dramatic changes in the organization of work, the consequent shifts in the traditional relationship of work to residence, and a reorientation of residential finance have called into question the role of the house as both a symbolic and an economic anchor for urban neighborhoods.

Introducing a global perspective to the analysis of cities and their housing transforms the basic conceptual framework of disciplinary and market-based analyses of urban housing. Traditional models of housing issues are cast in terms of supply and demand linked to a spatially ordered economic opportunity structure, or ecology. Introducing the globalization of world urban systems suggests that contemporary housing problems, and the uneven nature of housing problems across U.S. cities, must be recast in terms of labor migration and capital flows on a transnational scale.

Urban development remains a hostage to urban fortune,[2] but driven less by local entrepreneurs than by transnational systems and organizations. Cities, like their neighborhoods, are themselves investment sites, their future driven by their place in a global economy. The built environment generally, and housing in particular, appear to be increasingly responsive to the roles that cities play as production sites, wholesale and retail marketplaces, and corporate or political headquarters within a transnational economy.

Globalization both embodies the expansionist mode of the capitalist world economy and calls our attention to the triumph of the market over premodern and modern constraints of space and time. Cybernetic models of production control are woven into trading programs and commodity calculations such that irreducible minima of downtime are sought, and the targeted return on labor, raw materials, and plant costs is ratcheted upward.[3] From a production perspective, outsourcing and just-in-time technologies minimize the capital investment of all participants in the process by dividing the steps of production, disaggregating the total costs of production, and passing them down and along the production chain.[4]

This article examines the ways in which urban housing can be placed within a global context. The focus of this work is on Philadelphia and its

1. Paul L. Knox, "World Cities in a World System," in *World Cities in a World System*, ed. Paul L. Knox and Peter J. Taylor (New York: Cambridge University Press, 1995), pp. 3-20; Michael Timberlake, "The World System Perspective and Urbanization," in *Urbanization and the World Economy*, ed. Michael Timberlake (Orlando, FL: Academic Press, 1985), pp. 3-24.

2. John Logan and Harvey Molotch, *Urban Fortunes* (Berkeley: University of California Press, 1987).

3. Scott Lash and John Urry, *The End of Organized Capitalism* (Madison: University of Wisconsin Press, 1987), pp. 4-7, 201-7.

4. David Harvey, *The Limits to Capital* (Chicago: University of Chicago Press, 1982), pp. 373-412. See also idem, *The Condition of Postmodernity* (Cambridge, MA: Basil Blackwell, 1990), pp. 173-200.

environs, a metropolitan area that has changed from an overcrowded manufacturing center to a partially abandoned, postindustrial city in the global economy.[5] The effects of these changes on the city's housing dynamics and community structure are considered, with a closing discussion of the implications of addressing housing issues in a global environment.

HOUSING AND CITIES IN A GLOBAL CONTEXT

The nexus of globalization and urban housing lies in the significant shifts in the nature of urban social and spatial structures that have accompanied the emerging global scope of the world economy and its transnational system of cities. Urban housing is a central element of urban sociospatial structures, and it is a major component of people's lives in every city. In the context of globalization, housing problems are multileveled: as the immediate issues present in the social relationships between landlord and tenant, mortgagee and mortgagor, or shelter dwellers and homeless service provider, but also as the expression of capital and labor flows that are global in scope.

Housing is a commodity that has long been noted to have unusual qualities for an item that is traded in a market. It is durable, costly, often appreciates in value, and constitutes

5. In this article, I will be referring to cities as if they were a social unit, not a politically bounded entity—essentially as metropolitan areas, but without the formality of the county-based Census Bureau definition. This will be the case except for situations where the context of the discussion indicates that direct city-to-suburban comparisons are being made.

its own market—it is (usually) not produced and taken to a market but is set in a fixed location in which it competes with similar, although not identical, commodities. It is costly, so much so that ownership involves (typically) entering into a long-term mortgage loan, with mortgages themselves being instruments in the workings of financial markets. Similarly, tenants find themselves indirectly participating in this market through the proportion of their rent that addresses the debt service of the landlord.

In short, housing is the antithesis of the quickly exhausted, nondurable, easily replaceable commodity items on which much of the current manufacturing economy is dependent. Further, once built, the durability of housing stamps an identity on a particular landscape, as does all of the built environment, creating an inertia of sorts that contrasts with the central images of industries moving overseas and money markets engaging in large-scale transactions in micro-seconds, 24 hours a day, inherent in the very concept of globalization.[6]

The stability of place implied by the American house in an urban neighborhood of similar units is drawn in stark contrast to the flows of capital and production that give life to the city itself. The changing panoply of jobs, income, and opportunities defines the historically rooted ecology of the built environment.

6. H. J. Blommenstein, "Structural Changes in Financial Markets: Overview of Trends and Prospects," in *The New Financial Landscape* (Paris: Organization for Economic Cooperation and Development, 1995), pp. 9-10.

Neighborhoods become islands in the flows of capital in and through the city.[7] Yesterday's cart paths become either today's highways or its dark alleys; warehouses are either leveled or become the new landscape of opportunistic residential real estate investors for a new class of urban residents; fields become malls, developments, or industrial parks; and neighborhoods face uncertain futures as the urban life built around agglomerated industrial combinations gives way to distributed, attenuated, and dispersed locales.

To link globalization to urban housing is thus to grapple with the relationship between a constant in urban analyses (the distribution and quality of housing across an urban landscape) with a process that cities experience differentially—the effects of the globalization process on the ecological changes experienced by cities and on the financing of housing production and purchase. Globalization is a concept that is here taken to be the way in which components of capital and labor flows in the modern world economy are mediated through existing urban locales.

Two central assumptions about housing are important to recognize: first, that financing needed to construct, and sell, housing as a commodity must be available; and second, that urban growth and, by extension, the housing market are fueled by the development of urban jobs.[8] It is here that the intersection of globalization and urban housing is reached. The globalization of the world economy is, in the end, the development of a transnational production process. Cheaper labor is pursued, and higher-cost production sites, eschewed. As a corollary, labor flows to production sites and bids to obtain scarce jobs, effectively lowering wage levels and labor costs.[9] Concomitantly, the internationalization of financial mechanisms and capital formation drives the trading system at this global scale.

GLOBALIZATION OF CAPITAL
AND LABOR IN THE U.S. CITY

Implicit in the foregoing formulation is a dialectic between the local and the global that frames the impacts of globalization on any one city and its housing. The narrative of development of any particular city and its environs is best told as the history of how a city, or even a system of cities, reacts to the reality that the city per se is no longer dominant in capturing the flows of trade, capital, and population. Instead, cities begin to react to a set of globally framed decisions about production, investment, and the terms of trade.[10]

7. David Bartelt et al., "Islands in the Stream: Neighborhoods and the Political Economy of the City," in *Neighborhood and Community Environments*, ed. Irwin Altman and Abraham Wandersman (New York: Plenum, 1987), pp. 163-89.

8. Additionally, household formation rates due to single parenting, delayed parenting, and divorce introduce variation into the level of housing demand in a given area.

9. Saskia Sassen, "On Concentration and Centrality in the Global City," in *World Cities*, ed. Knox and Taylor, pp. 63-79; idem, *Cities in a World Economy* (Thousand Oaks, CA: Sage, 1994).

10. Robert A. Beauregard, "Theorizing the Global-Local Connection," in *World Cities*, ed. Knox and Taylor, pp. 232-48.

This is a change in the level and terminology of explanation for urban phenomena, from internal, *structured* hierarchies of opportunities, privilege, and wealth to external *processes* of labor and capital flows. Cities, as such, are understood or argued to be nodes in the networks of worldwide development. It is not that their internal structure disappears or is no longer of importance, but the extent to which it hinders or facilitates the participation of a city in a global context is of increased and often greater significance in settling the fate of a city.

Housing is responsive to the influx and exodus of labor forces in two ways. As the size of a metropolitan population waxes and wanes in response to economic opportunities that are present within its environs, housing stocks will respond. They further respond to shifts in the location of jobs, from the core of an urban area to its suburban periphery and from one region to another. The spatial shifts in the American economy from the Rustbelt to the Sunbelt reflect this kind of movement, and it has been cited in Great Britain as a key force in the emptying out of both housing and factory dwellings.[11]

The global labor process contains a further implication for the housing market. Implicit in the notion of global competition over jobs is the suppressive effect of that competition

on wages overall, especially in economies that had developed a high-wage sector in manufacturing. A significant body of literature has documented the decreasing share of the income distribution held by the lowest half of the economy and, in several instances, the possibility of a slump in the lower middle-income groups that had been the backbone of a manufacturing economy's wage distribution.[12] The growth of a low-wage economy almost inevitably implies an increased problem of housing affordability for the very poor, and a growing problem for the providers of low-income housing, for example, landlords.[13]

Population mobility and income distributions are instrumental in affecting the demand for housing. The primary way in which both the supply and the demand sides of the residential housing market are affected by the globalization process is through the redefined nature of capital flows. Capital has long been recognized as having at least a dualistic character to it, both fixed and mobile. Capital investments in plants, trans-

11. J. Anderson, S. Duncan, and R. Hudson, "Uneven Development, Redundant Spaces? An Introduction," in *Redundant Spaces in Cities and Regions*, ed. J. Anderson, S. Duncan, and R. Hudson (London: Academic Press, 1983), pp. 1-16; Anne Markusen et al., *The Rise of the Gunbelt* (New York: Oxford University Press, 1991).

12. Barry Bluestone and Bennett Harrison, *The Deindustrialization of America* (New York: Basic Books, 1991); idem, *The Great American Job Machine: The Proliferation of Low-Wage Employment in the U.S. Economy* (Washington, DC: Congress, Joint Economic Committee, 1986); Carolyn Adams et al., *Philadelphia: Neighborhoods, Division, and Conflict in a Postindustrial City* (Philadelphia: Temple University Press, 1991), pp. 44-65.

13. Michael Stone, *Shelter Poverty* (Philadelphia: Temple University Press, 1993), pp. 45-52, 144-53; David W. Bartelt and Anne B. Shlay, *Housing Philadelphia: Low and Moderate Income Home Ownership—Opportunities and Constraints* (Philadelphia: Temple University, Institute for Public Policy Studies, 1995), pp. 15-18.

portation, and other forms of technology are relatively fixed, while the operations of the market that generate new capital for both investor returns and reinvestment into plants, money markets, and the like are more liquid in nature.

In the global economy, financial institutions have increased opportunities for alternative investment sites in a wide variety of locations and in a wide variety of venues. Banks and financial entities make decisions about to whom to lend and where to invest but, equally significant, in which sector to invest. One dimension of this decision is facing the problem of "long-term investments in a short-term world."[14]

The consequences for the urban housing market are several, I would argue. First, an increasing number of banks have developed specialized profit centers within their structure to address mortgage lending markets, either as separate mortgage departments or as separate entities within a bank's conglomerate structure.[15] Second, the consequences of bank deregulation, begun during the Reagan era, have included several merger waves that have driven banks to reduce costs wherever possible.[16] This has meant, among other things, a significant number of branch closings, centralization of mortgage lending offices (in many cases), and the end of many traditional community-based banking efforts.[17] In short, globalization has forced cities and their neighborhoods to compete with the Third World for investment capital at the very time that they are experiencing significant outflows of traditional city-building jobs—jobs in manufacturing and wholesale trade in particular.

Because housing finance involves a relatively long-term risk, housing itself is a commodity in tension. Financial institutions balance the intersection of long-term, relatively immobile capital sunk into the built environment and their preference for a more liquid form of investment. The impact of a global investment environment, plus a deregulated environment, pushes financial investments toward liquidity and away from long-term investments as a defense against rapidly shifting economic tides.

Three sources of empirical information support this argument. First, data collected by the Department of Housing and Urban Development (HUD) suggest that the relative investment in the housing sector within the U.S. economy has declined over the past three decades. Housing investment as a proportion of the nation's gross domestic product (GDP) has declined by roughly 30 percent in the years 1960-95, from a 5.7 percent share in 1960 to 4.0 percent in 1995.[18] These data reflect the degree to

14. Martin Mayer, *The Money Bazaars* (New York: Dutton, 1984), p. 253.

15. Peter S. Rose, *The Changing Structure of American Banking* (New York: Columbia University Press, 1987), pp. 3-33.

16. Edward C. Ettin, "The Evolution of the North American Banking System," in *New Financial Landscape*, pp. 183-85.

17. Richard D. Crawford and William W. Sihler, *The Troubled Money Business* (New York: Harper, 1991), pp. 57-63.

18. Department of Housing and Urban Development, Office of Policy Development and Research, *U.S. Housing Market Conditions, 1st Quarter, 1996* (Washington, DC: Department of Housing and Urban Development, 1996), p. 72.

which housing investment has shrunk relative to other expenditures in the economy. While residential investment dollars rose by a factor of 10 (from $28.1 billion to $289.8 billion), the GDP rose even more dramatically, from $494.2 billion to $7,245.0 billion, an increase that is 15-fold. The decline in the share of the GDP is relatively constant over the years and suggests a long-term decline in the economic importance of housing in the domestic economy.

More direct evidence of the link of housing capital to the globalization process is reflected in data collected by the International Monetary Fund (IMF) on both commercial banks and the thrift industry (savings banks and savings and loan institutions) annually from 1965 to 1994.[19] The IMF summary data indicate three basic trends: (1) the relative growth of external investment and asset development by commercial banks shows a clear temporal trend toward a global investment posture; (2) both banks and thrift institutions moved toward a strategy emphasizing liquidity as a general strategy of risk management; and (3) there has been a decided move of financial assets from the thrift sector to the commercial banking sector among U.S. financial institutions.

A direct indication of increased foreign involvement is the degree to which foreign assets are a part of the commercial banking community's asset base. While this has varied over the years, these assets have more than doubled in the years between

1965 and 1994. Similarly, there has been a constant growth in the proportion of bank borrowing attracted from overseas (treated in financial reports as liabilities—dollars "borrowed" from international sources). Thrift institutions have not been permitted to engage in foreign lending asset development.

However, both thrifts and commercial banks show evidence of moving toward a more liquid position. Thrift institutions, which had had almost all of their deposits restricted to time and savings accounts under earlier regulatory strictures, have moved increasingly away from the 90 percent level of 1965, to roughly two-thirds of their collective worth (66.1 percent). Both demand deposits (checking accounts) and money market instruments have become a more significant component of their liability structure.

Commercial banks, on the other hand, have moved away from the demand deposit business, in relative terms, increasing their activity in bond, money market, and foreign activity, as noted earlier. Strikingly, while thrifts have had to maintain a relatively constant reserve ratio against their liabilities, commercial banks back their liabilities with less than 2 percent of assets in cash reserves.[20]

19. International Monetary Fund, *International Financial Statistical Yearbook* (New York: International Monetary Fund, 1995), pp. 776-77.

20. Ibid. It should be noted that the distinction made here between banks and thrifts increasingly promises to become an anachronism. Federal regulators have been more and more willing to merge thrift institutions with commercial banks as a consequence of the crisis within the savings and loan industry—galvanized by rapid deregulation and the attempts, sometime fraudulent, of savings-and-loans to become full bank participants in financial markets.

Globalization of finance capital has thus created a potential problem for the supply side of the housing industry, but particularly for urban housing. The banking industry faces a clear locational issue undergirding its contemporary investment policies: the speed with which money can be made versus the long-term character of the mortgage loan.

It now takes eleven seconds to post a bank transaction from one part of the world to any other part of the globe. Money is information in motion, and the advent of a global communications network has created a single global capital market in which money is transferred around the world at virtually the speed of light.[21]

This tension is also reflected in the changing source of mortgages. As banks and thrift institutions have become more diverse and increasingly sensitive to global capital shifts, they have moved away from the home mortgage origination process. According to HUD data, there has been a significant movement of mortgage originations away from banks and thrifts to mortgage companies. For commercial banks, the dollar share of mortgage originations has fluctuated over the years since 1970, ranging from 19 percent to 24 percent of all mortgages (except for a brief period around 1990, when commercial banks took on a significant part of the portfolios of failed savings and loan associations). However, the market share for thrift institutions, the traditional source of home mortgages, has dropped precipitously, from 47.5

percent of originations in 1970 to under 19.0 percent in 1995.[22]

Specialized mortgage companies, operating either as part of a bank's conglomerate structure or as independent entities, grew significantly, as they increased their market share from 25 percent in 1970 to over 55 percent in 1995. These entities moved from the margin to the mainstream as they increasingly reflected the desire to avoid long-term investment vehicles by banks. Having immediate access to the banking community but having some degree of independence, they structurally insulated banks and thrifts from some of the risks linked to long-term loans.

Housing, as a competitor for investment in capital markets, competes with a market ideal of an immediate-turnaround, high-return instrument—an ideal that is very often present within a set of global investment options. In a global context, mortgages require too much in the way of information and transaction costs for banks, given that personal income and property resale value constitute the major offset to risk. It is safer for the modern banking institution to engage in direct lending to established mortgage companies, and to divest itself of mortgage originations in the secondary market, than it is to remain the lender of first resort.

PHILADELPHIA

Philadelphia is a city in the North American urban network that has played a significant part in that network's development, while its own

---

21. Crawford and Sihler, *Troubled Money*, p. 13.

22. Office of Policy Development and Research, *Housing Market Conditions*, p. 67.

particular political and economic strengths (and weaknesses) have been an inescapable component of its experiences in a transnational urban system. Put simply, Philadelphia's importance as both a political and economic center in the United States reached a peak during the industrial era prior to World War II. Its strength was its diversity of products within the manufacturing sector; its weakness was the relatively strong dependence on the manufacturing sector as a whole as its primary employment base through 1960. The local manufacturing economy stressed both heavy industries (shipbuilding, machine tools, and so forth) and consumer goods (especially textiles, but also printing and publishing). Strong warehousing, retail, and service sectors complemented these aspects of the local economy.

After World War II, Philadelphia experienced a dramatic series of social and economic changes. Immediately after the war, roughly half of the jobs within the city of Philadelphia were in the manufacturing sector. For the region as a whole, the proportion was closer to 60 percent.[23] By 1986, this had slipped to less than 25 percent for both city and suburb, and more recent estimates are that less than 15 percent of the region's jobs are in the manufacturing sector.[24]

Areas that were within the city boundaries but were residentially undeveloped (both working farms, in the northeastern section of the city, and areas bordering swamplands, in the southwest) were the sites of "suburban" development within the city.

23. Adams et al., *Philadelphia*, pp. 36-40.
24. Ibid.

Fueled by the same factors that fueled other cities' suburban growth spurts (pent-up demand after World War II and the depression, Federal Housing Administration and Veterans Administration mortgages, highways that opened up the suburbs, and the racial antipathy of whites toward African American communities[25]), Philadelphia's suburbs, within and without the city, expanded dramatically during the 1950s and 1960s, while continuing to grow, albeit less dramatically, through the 1970s and 1980s.

The city of Philadelphia's population peaked after the 1950 decade, at more than 2.0 million people. In 1970, however, the city's population showed its first decennial census decline, from 2.0 million people in 1960 to 1.9 million. By 1980, the population had dropped still further, to about 1.7 million, and by 1990, it had dropped to 1.5 million. At the same time, the region had increased from a level of about 3.5 million people in 1950 to nearly 5.0 million in 1990.[26]

The city's housing stock had both increased—by roughly 25 percent, to some 700,000 units by 1970[27]—and changed in character. Newer housing was oriented toward single-family living on larger building lots, while

25. Kenneth Jackson, *Crabgrass Frontier* (New York: Oxford University Press, 1985); Douglas S. Massey and Nancy A. Denton, *American Apartheid: Segregation and the Making of the Underclass* (Cambridge, MA: Harvard University Press, 1993).

26. Adams et al., *Philadelphia*, p. 17; Department of Commerce, Census Bureau, *Census of Population and Housing: Metropolitan Area Characteristics, Philadelphia MSA* (Washington, DC: Government Printing Office, 1993).

27. Adams et al., *Philadelphia*, pp. 66-83.

older, inadequate housing stock was removed from some of the oldest areas of the city in the first applications of urban renewal.[28] The row-house architecture of Philadelphia's older, manufacturing communities was strongly echoed in the brick-front duplexes and quad units of its suburbs within the cities, but with lawns and garages (in the rear, under the house) clearly indicating a symbolic commitment to the suburban lifestyle.

The spatial distribution of these changes across the region was uneven. Clearly, Philadelphia has lost its traditional role as the central element driving the surrounding region. If we consider the population and employment shares of Philadelphia and its surrounding counties, the city's have clearly dropped. In 1950, Philadelphia had over half of the regional population and over two-thirds of its jobs within the region's boundaries. In 1990, each of these shares had shrunk to less than one-third.[29]

In the housing arena, a similar pattern of uneven development emerges across the region. As the metropolitan area around Philadelphia expanded and the city's population declined, the housing stock did likewise but less rapidly. In the period since 1950, Philadelphia has declined in population by about 25 percent, and its housing stock has shrunk, from its high of 700,000 occupied units in 1970 to 610,000 in

1990.[30] Meanwhile, the region's housing stock has almost doubled, from slightly over 1.0 million units in 1950 to 1.9 million in 1990.

It would be a mistake to account for these shifts in people, jobs, and homes as solely the by-product of the region's suburbanization. Three parallel and mutually supporting processes have taken place, each of which can be traced to the increased salience of globalization in the day-to-day life of the city. First, the urban economy has both decentralized and become multinucleated in the Philadelphia region, breaking apart the close links between the city's manufacturing base and many of its neighborhoods.[31] This spatial dispersion has yielded a local version of a global process: the competition of localities within a region for a slice of the metropolitan pie.

Second, the economic role of the central city, apart from competing for locational advantage, has become more focused on a mixture of both "command and control" functions in the global economy, with increases in business services, the health and pharmaceutical industries, and tourism.[32] Philadelphia has been forced to

30. Department of Commerce, Census Bureau, *Metropolitan Area*; Bartelt and Shlay, *Housing Philadelphia*, p. 4.

31. Theodore Hershberg et al., "A Tale of Three Cities: Blacks and Immigrants in Philadelphia: 1850-1880, 1930 and 1970," *The Annals* of the American Academy of Political and Social Science, 441:55-81 (Jan. 1979); Adams et al. *Philadelphia*, pp. 75-77.

32. Greater Philadelphia First, *An Economic Development Strategy for the Greater Philadelphia Region* (Philadelphia: Greater Philadelphia First, 1995); Anita A. Summers and Thomas F. Luce, *Economic Development Within the Philadelphia Metropolitan Area*

28. Ibid., pp. 107-13.

29. Ibid., p. 17; Department of Commerce, Census Bureau, *Metropolitan Area*; Department of Commerce, *County Business Patterns, 1990* (Washington, DC: Government Printing Office, 1992).

compete more directly with other cities in other regions of the country—and the world. Third, the dynamics of housing economics and Philadelphia's fragmented neighborhood politics have fostered racial antipathy as a critical factor in residential choices.[33]

Put simply, Philadelphia has lost population over the decades since 1960 as its large factories and warehouses have become less and less viable as production sites in a new global economy. Philadelphia's diverse economy, while it shielded the city from the economic downturns that affected single-industry cities like Detroit and Pittsburgh, also has made it difficult to develop a coherent economic or neighborhood development initiative to counter these efforts. The local politics of the city, always neighborhood oriented, became much more turf oriented and less involved with citywide issues, as different neighborhoods, economic sectors, and political movements fought over their "rights" to a slice of a shrinking pie.[34]

Abandonment

These patterns are nowhere more clearly reflected in the housing arena than in the case of abandoned housing. The decline in the number of occupied housing units in Philadelphia has meant that significant numbers of dwellings either have become uninhabitable or have been demolished—usually in that order. A de-

cade ago, the pattern of abandonment was linked to three factors: the collapse of the manufacturing economy (the slow decline of the urban villages surrounding older factories in the city); the intertwining of private sector investment patterns and public policy in the development and perpetuation of racial ghettoes; and speculative investments in neighborhoods where housing was held "fallow" in the expectation of gentrification.[35] Today's policy debates recognize the decline of gentrification activity and have begun to discuss alternative uses for abandoned properties and empty lots.[36]

Recent estimates have led the more jaundiced veterans of housing struggles to conclude that Philadelphia's one growth industry is in abandoned houses. According to Philadelphia's Office of Housing and Community Development, some 29,000 residential structures are currently abandoned. About 19,000 of these are so seriously deteriorated that attempts to rehabilitate them would require upwards of $110,000 per unit and would take over $2 billion to accomplish. Another 6000

35. David Bartelt and George Leon, "Differential Decline: The Neighborhood Context of Abandonment," *Housing and Society*, 13(2):81-106 (1981); David W. Bartelt, "Housing the 'Underclass,'" in *The Underclass Question: Lessons from History*, ed. Michael Katz (Princeton, NJ: Princeton University Press, 1993), pp. 118-57.

36. Philadelphia City Planning Commission, *Vacant Land in Philadelphia* (Philadelphia: Philadelphia City Planning Commission, 1995); Pennsylvania Horticultural Society, *Urban Vacant Land: Issues and Recommendations* (Philadelphia: Pennsylvania Horticultural Society, 1995).

(Philadelphia: University of Pennsylvania Press, 1987).

33. Adams et al., *Philadelphia*, pp. 93-98.
34. Ibid., pp. 124-53.

buildings would require a moderate level of rehabilitation, costing an estimated $45,000 per unit, or about $270 million. The remaining 3000 abandoned dwellings are regarded as being in "move-in" condition and would not be seen as qualifying for a public subsidy.[37]

Realistically, of course, it is doubtful that an effective demand exists for such housing. To absorb the costs of renovation and rehabilitation of this housing would be to suppose far greater pressures for existing housing than appears to be the case. Further, in the period since the mid-1970s, when the problem of residential abandonment first became apparent in Philadelphia, the level of abandonment has fluctuated, from a low of 19,000 achieved in the early 1980s to a high of 29,000, which occurred in the late 1970s and in current estimates.[38] While population and job losses have driven the overall shrinkage of the population and the housing stock, it is also apparent that different levels of demolition have had an impact. In the current set of estimates, it is assumed that the number of abandoned dwellings will not grow if the city is able to demolish an estimated 1000 buildings a year—as an estimated 10,000 structures are predicted to enter the abandonment stream in the next decade.[39]

Affordability

Additionally, a closer look at the internal dynamics of the region's housing reveals a growing set of market-related problems. Of particular note are the problems of rental housing affordability and an increasing gap between city and suburban housing values that effectively fuels further out-migration by the economically viable.[40]

Philadelphia's tenants are especially vulnerable to housing costs. Over 50 percent of the city's tenants paid more than 30 percent of their income in rent in 1989, and most renters have income levels below the poverty line.[41] Effectively, this reflection of the deteriorated income distribution in Philadelphia both fuels the abandonment problem and isolates the city's renters from the ownership market. Landlords with a low-income clientele find it increasingly difficult to generate a rate of return on their properties such that they are a desirable investment. As maintenance costs and taxes increase over time, the issue of profitability forces many property owners into deferred maintenance and delinquent tax payments, precursors to eventual abandonment.[42]

High housing costs may drive many renters to consider the possibility of home ownership, but several impediments remain within the market. While housing within Philadel-

37. Office of Housing and Community Development, *Vacant Property Descriptions: A Reinvestment Strategy* (Philadelphia: Office of Housing and Community Development, 1995).

38. George Leon, "Residential Abandonment: Ghosttowns, Ghettoes and Goldcoasts" (Diss., Temple University, 1985).

39. Office of Housing and Community Development, *Vacant Property*, p. 20.

40. Bartelt and Shlay, *Housing Philadelphia*, pp. 15-20.

41. Ibid., p. 16.

42. George Sternlieb, *The Tenement Landlord* (New Brunswick, NJ: Rutgers University Press, 1975).

phia remains comparatively affordable to that of the suburbs (the 1989 median value in the city was slightly more than $49,000; for the suburbs, it was almost $120,000), lenders are hesitant about lending to single-parent, single-income households with weak credit histories and with uneven employment records.

In short, while the postwar mortgage supported the development of middle-class and upper-middle-class suburban communities, it was largely predicated on a high-wage labor force purchasing new housing in neighborhoods and communities that were not perceived as risky. Even today, the primary program to generate "below-market" mortgages in Philadelphia—the Delaware Valley Mortgage Plan—stipulates that no more than two properties on a facing block segment can be vacant if a loan is to be made. This effectively locks out many neighborhoods from the limited access to available mortgage credit.

Homelessness

If abandoned buildings imply a surplus of housing units, it is seemingly paradoxical that the city of Philadelphia also experiences significant levels of homelessness. In 1989, it was estimated that the city was the site of between 35,000 and 45,000 episodes of homelessness a year.[43] In 1995, the extent of homelessness, while improved slightly, was still sig-

nificant.[44] The vast majority of people entering the city's shelter system came not from any one neighborhood but from a variety of locations around the city—overwhelmingly from African American communities with older housing stock. Given the information on high housing costs and the fact that Philadelphia's African American community has experienced double-digit unemployment levels through two economic revivals (both in the 1980s and in the past three years), these results are not surprising.[45]

Homelessness is often cited as a problem proceeding from personal pathology. The research on Philadelphia, as well as many national surveys, suggests that this is too simple a response.[46] As the global economy has disrupted the local economic base, the lack of jobs for many in the community outstrips the fiscal resources at hand, for either public assistance or job creation. This is complicated by stagnant housing values in the city (diminishing the base for property taxes) and the rapid growth

43. Phyllis T. Ryan, Ira L. Goldstein, and David W. Bartelt, *How Can This Be: Homelessness in Pennsylvania* (Philadelphia: Coalition for the Homeless in Pennsylvania, 1989).

44. Dennis P. Culhane, Chang-Moo Lee, and Susan M. Wachter, "Where the Homeless Come From: A Study of the Prior Address Distribution of Families Admitted to Homeless Shelters in New York City and Philadelphia" (Working paper, Fannie Mae Office of Housing Research, 1996).

45. It is vital to recognize that the direct causes of homelessness span the range of addiction, mental illness, poverty, spousal abuse, and life skills, to name the major factors cited in the aforementioned studies. The intersection of poverty with the remaining factors is striking.

46. Anne B. Shlay and Peter H. Rossi, "Social Science Research and Contemporary Studies of Homelessness," *Annual Review of Sociology*, 18:129-60 (1992).

in mental health and detoxification treatment costs.

Philadelphia's future

When a city loses its position within the global hierarchy of urban regions, both a community linked to the new economy and a remnant community, linked to past social arrangements, coexist, albeit gingerly. Retired workers, those who never made it into the labor market during the last manufacturing uptick, and those who are held to the region by kinship or other social ties are locked into their homes as financial capital for home mortgages dwindles in availability. As the city becomes more and more threatened by abandonment, it becomes less and less valued as an investment site.

Home owners, culturally and economically valued, experience a form of economic entrapment, as the risk of divestment becomes too great for those with limited assets. Landlords with low-income tenants in poor neighborhoods find that funding maintenance for their buildings is more difficult to achieve, and a cynical endgame scenario of tax delinquency, sheriff's sales, crack houses, and, at times, arson becomes the fate of many neighborhoods. Globalization has contributed to these realities by altering the fundamental urban processes of job development and residential capital formation. Perhaps more significantly, the globalization of capital makes it virtually impossible for cities experiencing declines in population and increased demand for human services to confront these problems with a significant resource base.

These parallels of abandonment and homelessness are an expression of both the specific situation of an older industrial city thinning out its redundant spaces and a more general set of trends redefining the contemporary city and its residential landscape.[47] While its abandoned dwellings reflect many of the same market, political, and cultural forces noted by Jakle and Wilson in their evocative phrase "derelict landscapes," Philadelphia's housing also represents an appositional case, a flip side, if you will, to the growing form of urban development that Garreau has termed the "edge city."[48] Disinvestment and the devaluation of inner-city housing are implicitly the consequences of investment choices made in favor of housing and other markets elsewhere.[49]

This argument is presented not as one that suggests that the political will to address urban problems—or even just Philadelphia's—is somehow lacking or that we have a suburbanized culture that precludes rediscovering and resettling the city. Rather, the traditional model of the central city as the primary source of attraction (the center of gravity, as it were) has given way to the polynucleated metropolis, in which the city's investments in its built past—its housing, its factories, its streets, its rail lines, its retail strips—are arti-

47. Anderson et al., eds., *Redundant Spaces*.

48. John A. Jakle and David Wilson, *Derelict Landscapes: The Wasting of America's Built Environment* (Savage, MD: Rowan & Littlefield, 1992); Joel Garreau, *Edge City* (New York: Anchor Doubleday, 1991).

49. Neil Smith, *Uneven Development* (Cambridge, MA: Basil Blackwell, 1984).

facts of a past set of social and economic arrangements that no longer fit the contemporary world of small production units and just-in-time production. In the new world urban economy, cities are distributional sites more than production locations. Their economic value is linked to services and command and control functions in a locationally ubiquitous economy, rather than realizing local investments and economic development from the export of goods to other markets.

URBAN HOUSING IN A GLOBAL POLITICAL ECONOMY

Globalization's effects on urban housing can thus be traced to three factors. First, the rapidly changing nature of housing finance, and the banking industry generally, is a direct result of the globalization of capital investment overlaid on a very conservative approach to housing investment. Over the long run, global tendencies toward liquidity of investments may call into question the basic model of late-twentieth-century housing consumption—home ownership—as a potential source of immobility and dysfunctionality in a global system.

Second, the increased mobility of labor pools, in at least a regional sense of global economies, has changed the ethnic, demographic, and economic realities of many urban areas, such that both established cities and newer nodes of global development have qualitatively different types of housing problems from those of cities that are more peripheral to the global economy. These differen-

tials in the urban experience suggest that we should expect to find differences in housing values, tenure choices, and community formation across these varieties of urban form.

Third, and more indirect, is the inability, fiscally and politically, of political structures at local levels to cope with housing issues in a globally driven economic environment. The relationship between neighborhoods left behind by global economic development and those better integrated into such development will occupy center stage. Meanwhile, local government will continue to grapple with the tensions of satisfying the demands of the new economy, while confronting the fear of a transnationally generated ghost town.

Finally, I am struck by the ways in which the entire discussion of housing and community development policy has changed in the face of the new globalization. The theoretical mission of capitalism—to limit the effects of space and time on production and commodification and, indeed, to press these physical absolutes into the service of the market process—is no longer theoretical but real. Against this background, the traditional role of a national housing policy as the basis of urban community development must be recognized as policy history, oriented toward a post-depression world of U.S. economic hegemony rather than a global political economy.[50] With the new housing realities of the global urban network, the issue then becomes how to ad-

50. R. Allen Hays, *The Federal Government and Urban Housing*, 2d ed. (Albany, NY: SUNY Press, 1995), pp. 277-95.

dress the housing needs of cities left behind by these changes.

Given the forces identified in this discussion, the only resolution that appears close at hand is the reworking of the ecologists' slogan of the past two decades, "Think globally, act locally."[51] In practical terms, this will amount to developing redistributive processes that take globalization seriously: to develop processes that intersect the global flows of labor and capital and redirect a fraction of these flows to existing cities, at the same time as community-based institutions develop internal models of circulation that retain the use of these resources for extensive periods of time. In essence, the time has come to reenergize local economic development, combining economic and community development.[52]

51. Michael P. Smith, "The Disappearance of World Cities and the Globalization of Local Politics," in *World Cities*, ed. Knox and Taylor, pp. 249-66.

52. Julia Ann Parzen and Michael Hall Kieschnick, *Credit Where It's Due: Development Banking for Communities* (Philadelphia: Temple University Press, 1992).

ANNALS, *AAPSS*, **551**, May 1997

Shifting Terrains: Mapping Education Within a Global Landscape

By GREG DIMITRIADIS and GEORGE KAMBERELIS

ABSTRACT: In this article, the authors draw on critical social theory and educational theory and research to review and deconstruct educational discourses that have become common in this era of mass globalization. Key issues embedded within these discourses include addressing the educational needs of children from marginalized social and cultural groups, preparing students for the information-based jobs of the future, restructuring schools to fit with the reterritorialization of urban and suburban spaces, and gauging the effects of mass media on stereotypical notions of youths, schools, and schooling. The authors deploy Arjun Appadurai's model of ever shifting and interrelated global flows to bring into relief how various aspects of globalization both enable and constrain different kinds of social, spatial, and economic mobility for today's youths. They conclude by suggesting new ways to understand the complex and paradoxical effects of globalization on education and schooling.

Greg Dimitriadis is currently a doctoral student in the Department of Speech Communication at the University of Illinois at Urbana-Champaign.

George Kamberelis is an assistant professor of speech communication and curriculum and instruction at the University of Illinois at Urbana-Champaign. He teaches and conducts research on language and literacy socialization, multicultural education, and classroom discourse.

NOTE: The authors contributed equally to this article and are listed alphabetically.

L IKE all forms of "official knowledge,"[1] educational practice, research, and policy are mediated by
complex cultural and political economies, involving (at least) local, state,
and federal governments, the academy, various corporate interest
groups, and dominant media. One
needs, thus, to cast a broad theoretical net when attempting to understand how educational practices, research agendas, and policies are
produced, distributed, and received.[2]
Such a net must be both flexible and
resilient as these political and cultural economies are both stable and
dynamic, reflecting the particular
paradoxes emerging in this era of
mass globalization. Two complex and
often contradictory dimensions of
globalization—shifting labor demands (resulting from the restructuring of the world economy) and the
increased recognition of the educational rights of marginalized groups
(for example, people of color, migrant
peoples, and women)—are especially
relevant as they have exerted particular pressure on emerging educational agendas.

Within the economic sphere,
postindustrial capitalism has ush-
ered in rapid and dramatic structural
changes with concomitant changes in
work and consumer cultures.[3] Most

notable among these changes has
been the emergence of information-
based economies and service economies, as well as the globalization of
consumerism, corporate capitalism,
and popular culture.[4] These changes
have had different effects on different
groups of people in emerging international labor markets. New elites, as
well as new underclasses, have developed, often in complementary yet discontinuous ways. Indeed, we live in a
time when both industrial and
postindustrial forms of labor practices can exist side by side at the very
same work sites, such as fast-food
restaurants. These seeming disjunctures between industrial and dein-
dustrial ideologies and practices
have had a considerable impact on
schools and schooling, where educational agendas and ideologies are
now in flux.

The debate around marginalized
peoples is key here as well. Virtually
all Western countries have increasingly become concerned with the legal and political enfranchisement of
cultural and linguistic minorities. According to Edward Said, these
changes are more than the mere surface effects of "political correctness."
Rather, they mark the efforts of colonial powers to interrogate and revise
imperial histories and institutions.[5]
These powers (which had previously

1. Michael Apple, *Official Knowledge:
Democratic Education in a Conservative Age*
(New York: Routledge, 1993).

2. See, for example, Michael Apple, *Teachers and Texts* (New York: Routledge & Kegan
Paul, 1985); Norman Fairclough, *Discourse
and Social Change* (Cambridge: Polity Press,
1992).

3. Scott Lash and John Urry, *The End of
Organized Capitalism* (Madison: University of
Wisconsin Press, 1989).

4. See, for example, Peter McLaren, *Critical Pedagogy and Predatory Culture: Opposi-
tional Politics in a Postmodern Era* (New York:
Routledge, 1995); Colin Lankshear, "Curriculum as Literacy: Reading and Writing in 'New
Times,'" in *The Insistence on the Letter: Literacy Studies and Curriculum Theorizing*, ed. B.
Green (London: Falmer, 1993), pp. 154-74.

5. Edward Said, *Culture and Imperialism*
(New York: Alfred A. Knopf, 1993).

viewed themselves in monocultural and assimilationist terms) have had to respond to material changes in society brought about by migration, multiculturalism, multilingualism, shifting labor markets, and economic redistribution. Education has been one of the social institutions most affected by these responses, as is evident in all manner of educational reform from bilingual instruction to multicultural curricula to broader agendas for education in the workplace. Yet such changes have also spawned more reactionary and conservative agendas as well, such as the English-only movement, cultural literacy, and legislation such as Proposition 187 in California, which is designed to exclude "undocumented" residents from schools and other public services. Importantly, most of these undocumented residents are Chicanos, the fastest-growing subpopulation in the state. Like the emerging economic landscape, the emerging cultural landscape is often realized in paradoxical and discontinuous ways.

Globalization and its effects have, indeed, forced us to think about educational issues through a complex and interdependent set of cultural, political, economic, and representational lenses. Taking a brief look at the relations between information technology and education brings these often paradoxical and contradictory processes into relief. Responding to the ever changing landscape of capitalist nation-states, for example, information technology corporations like AT&T and Apple have increasingly drawn on the rhetoric of education to market their products. Their advertisements promise a utopia, a shrinking world where information is available at the touch of a finger and exotic peoples can be accessed with a click of a mouse. These images are replete with wonder, enchantment, and awe. They promise a generation of young people capable of dealing with both the challenges and the possibilities of a radically shrinking world, a world increasingly constituted by and through rapidly developing technological apparatuses. Such images do not, however, speak to the profound pains that many young people suffer (and will suffer) because of these same companies, as evidenced broadly by recent layoffs at AT&T. These disjunctures suggest that a responsible appraisal of the effects of globalization must theorize links between seemingly disparate phenomena, recognizing that such connections are no longer entirely stable since totalizing explanatory narratives have been called into question.[6]

The work of Arjun Appadurai is helpful here because he demands that globalization be viewed in terms of interactions and flows between various cultural, social, economic, technological, and representational phenomena without assuming that connections between these phenomena are simple, natural, or immutable. According to Appadurai, "the new global cultural economy has to be seen as a complex, overlapping, disjunctive order, which cannot any longer be understood in terms of ex-

6. Jean-Francois Lyotard, *The Postmodern Condition: A Report on Knowledge* (Minneapolis: University of Minnesota Press, 1979).

isting center-periphery models (even those which might account for multiple centers and peripheries)."[7]

APPADURAI'S FRAMEWORK

The vocabulary that Appadurai develops to explore such "disjunctures" is a vocabulary of "scapes." He defines "scapes" as interdependent dimensions of global flow, and he proposes five key ones: ethnoscapes (people), technoscapes (information), finanscapes (capital), mediascapes (images or representations), and ideoscapes (ideologies). Importantly, flows between these scapes are not simply a matter of monolithic Western domination, but uneven and shifting movements in which the ideas of center and periphery are no longer valid. These scapes intersect in myriad ways, which are relatively stable yet allow some room for surprise and for the articulation of the not yet imagined.

Using Appadurai's notion of scapes, we want to reexamine various dimensions of the debates going on in education today that revolve around multiculturalism, democratization, social justice, and the relations between education and our increasingly globalized society. To do so, we will examine Appadurai's scapes in two ways: for the utopian potential they often seem to index, as well as the crucial social problems such indexing practices tend to gloss or conceal. After exploring each of these scapes, we will envisage some possible connections that can be drawn between them. The process of drawing such connections will allow us to generate an emergent vocabulary for understanding the complexities of education in a radically changing world.

Ethnoscapes

We begin with ethnoscapes, which are landscapes "of persons who constitute the shifting world in which we live." These are ever shifting configurations of various and increasingly mobile people: "tourists, immigrants, refugees, exiles, guestworkers," and so on.[8] Because education has had to come to terms with these globally shifting and changing populations, multicultural education has become an increasingly important issue, especially in dense urban areas.[9] Shifting population demographics have called traditional kinds of curriculum and learning into question. Researchers, practitioners, and special interest groups alike have called for more culturally relevant education, more multicultural education, more bilingual education, and more user-friendly learning settings. Approaches generated from these demands, however, have tended to be of the "we are the world" sort, emphasizing the easy and world-expanding sharing of different perspectives. Little, if any, attention has been paid to power differentials between the various groups that are represented and served by these approaches.

8. Ibid., p. 7.
9. For a treatment of key debates around education and changing demographics, see the recent special issue of *Education and Urban Society*, 25(3) (May 1993).

7. Arjun Appadurai, "Disjuncture and Difference in the Global Cultural Economy," *Public Culture*, 2(2):6 (1990).

Additionally, multicultural education programs are often articulated with various forms of dialogic pedagogy and other perspective-sharing tools such as cooperative learning and collaborative inquiry. Such approaches are embedded in a rhetoric that constructs globalization in terms of a shrinking world where multiple and different perspectives interact peacefully and productively within an increasingly small global village. By making mutual understanding a consummate value, these questions and issues gloss the radical particularity of cultures. As Jean Dennee notes, "Having a global perspective means that one is aware that one's view of the world is not universally shared. A high level of awareness takes into account *empathy*, the capacity to see oneself in the other person's situation."[10] Because the key questions and issues of difference are reduced to personal ones, differences are viewed in a relativistic way. Although these "we are the world" approaches to multicultural education allow for a momentary tantalization by all that is different, they allow no room for real social or political engagement because they gloss over the particularity of cultures, focusing instead on the ways in which we are really all the same underneath.

Because the effects of shifting population demographics are often myriad and contradictory, adopting a global perspective is not always easy. The increasing diversity of our urban centers, the increasing plethora of different peoples—with their differ-

ent voices and perspectives—has a more insidious side, but one that is seldom brought clearly into view. In addition to bringing different peoples together, the shrinking of the world has helped to foster new kinds of violence. A central tension is at work here. While urban centers are reflecting new kinds of diversity, the various demands and effects of citizenship—including geographic ones—are still exceedingly pressing. Enabled by the overlap of various cultural spaces, new kinds of individual and collective unrest (riots, assassinations, racist attacks, and so on) have become increasingly and exceedingly apparent. In this regard, James Holston and Arjun Appadurai note, "If the city is a special site for [the] formations and reformations of citizens, it can also be a special war zone, a space in which these processes find expression in collective violence."[11]

The "we are the world" approaches to cultural pluralism cannot account for such social and political confrontations. Rather, we must also look to the ways in which people are stuck in cities, limited by the imposition of increasingly shrinking resources. The violence in Los Angeles after the Rodney King verdict is instructive here. As Lawrence Grossberg notes, such violence was very much related to the overlapping and often conflicting mappings of the different cultural spaces that are occupied by groups with different kinds of mobility.[12]

10. Jean Dennee, "Developing a Global Perspective Through Cooperative Learning," *Clearing House*, 66(6):367 (July-Aug. 1993).

11. James Holston and Arjun Appadurai, "Cities and Citizenship," *Public Culture*, 8(2):200 (Winter 1996).

12. Lawrence Grossberg, "Cultural Studies and/in New Worlds," in *Race, Identity, and Representation in Education*, ed. C. McCarthy and W. Crichlow (New York: Routledge, 1993), pp. 102-3.

Grossberg's spatial treatment of identity is helpful, especially in light of King's comments at the now famous mid-"riot" press conference. While King's comment, "Can we all get along?" is the one usually remembered from this conference, he also commented that "we're all stuck here for awhile."[13] The kind of immobility indexed by this comment is the flip side of the ideal of shifting and mobile populaces, the utopian potential of liberal pluralism. Although it is directly intertwined with such violence, such immobility is often ignored, which is problematic because immobility is so central to the lives of many young people, especially those living in poor urban areas.

Appadurai does not seem to account for this sense of being stuck very well. His conception of globalization directs one toward flows and movements but does little to account for the fact that access to flows and movements is not evenly distributed. Doreen Massey provides a countering balance to Appadurai's work by introducing the notion of "power geometry" into the condition of globalization.[14] In her discussions of power geometries, Massey makes it clear that social categories such as class, race, gender, sexual preference, age, occupation, and so on are among the many factors that greatly restrict one's ability to participate in global movement. She reminds us, for example, of the inner-city resident confined to the ravages of day-to-day living on a woefully inadequate minimum wage, or the African American child who must walk through a virtual war zone to get to school only to be strip-searched once he gets there, or the elderly person confined to a nursing home, or the urban dweller simply waiting for a bus that never comes due to local transportation cutbacks. Most important, Massey explains how one group's mobility often contributes to another group's stasis or isolation. A husband's work-related migrations, for example, are implicated in his wife's confinement and isolation. Similarly, a single-mother's full-time employment is implicated in the latch-key status of her children.

Appreciating the tension between global mobility and local immobility is crucial for understanding our increasingly multicultural schools. Indeed, in the face of declining opportunities and dreams, many of our country's children and adolescents have articulated their sense of being stuck, both in their overt testimonies to researchers[15] and through their radical allegiances to the local countercultures of their immediate neighborhoods or surroundings. Many of our schools have responded to such immobility by increasing security, making our schools de facto police stations, and making heroes out of figures like Joe Clark, the former principal of East Side High School in New York who patrolled the hallways with a bullhorn and a baseball bat

13. Robert Gooding-Williams, "Introduction: On Being Stuck," in *Reading Rodney King/Reading Urban Uprising*, ed. R. Gooding-Williams (New York: Routledge, 1993), p. 3.

14. Doreen Massey, *Space, Place, and Gender* (Minneapolis: University of Minnesota Press, 1994), p. 149.

15. See, for example, Anonymous et al., "Youth Speak Out," *Harvard Educational Review*, 65(2):258-81 (Summer 1995); Donna Deyhle, "Navaho Youth and Anglo Racism: Cultural Integrity and Resistance," *Harvard Educational Review*, 65(3):403-44 (Fall 1995).

and who was lauded by then U.S. Secretary of Education William Bennett for creating a "mecca of education."[16]

To summarize, the changing ethnoscape of American society has elicited responses for education reform from all points of the political spectrum. Yet most of these responses have articulated visions for multicultural education that are grounded in utopian rhetorics and that gloss the problems of local immobility that accompany global mobility. To address more effectively the central problems of education in a global cultural economy would seem to require paying more attention to the differential distribution of power within the current American ethnoscape, the effects of this differential distribution, and the contestation of those effects.

Technoscapes

Appadurai's second scape is the technoscape, or "the global configuration, . . . ever fluid, of technology, and of the fact that technology, both high and low, both mechanical and informational, now moves at high speeds across various kinds of previously impervious boundaries."[17] Indeed, we have entered an information age, a time when physical labor is being elbowed out by technology in an increasingly competitive global sphere. Schools—in their efforts to prepare citizen-workers for their societal roles and functions—have tried to respond to these economic shifts. Corporations have intervened in such efforts, forging coalitions with schools to help them prepare students for the demands of international competition. In fact, education is becoming increasingly linked with business interests as institutions are embracing—often as a last resort—the promise of technology in an uncritical fashion.

A key example here is AT&T's Learning Circles (part of the AT&T Learning Network). According to Margaret Riel, "a Learning Circle is a small number of classrooms that interact electronically to accomplish a shared goal. Each classroom in a Learning Circle is a team that contributes to the overall end product [of any project]. Connecting students from different geographic, social, and cultural regions creates a rich diversity of knowledge, skills, and abilities not found in single classrooms."[18] Learning Circles foreground many of the skills that students will need to develop for information-age success, including small-group work, collaboration, and interdependence. Yet the discourse of AT&T's Learning Circles betrays a disjunctive mingling of Progressive Era educational rhetoric and postindustrial rhetoric. Learning Circles capitalize on liberal-humanistic discourse about shared ideals to promote an almost unbridled faith in technology to overcome cultural, social, political, and economic differences. Yet Riel stresses that the manipulation of information allows participants to be faceless, to focus on tasks instead of on personalities or cultures. She notes that the Learning Circles' "human and technical sup-

16. Jonathan Kozol, *Savage Inequalities: Children in America's Schools* (New York: HarperCollins, 1991), p. 162.

17. Appadurai, "Disjuncture and Difference," p. 8.

18. Margaret Riel, "Making Connections from Urban Schools," *Education and Urban Society*, 24(4):478-79 (Aug. 1992).

port systems," which help students with their work, are invisible to other participants, making it "easier for diverse groups to work together."[19]

There is something terribly wrong with this picture. Making various "support systems" invisible as individuals reach out to share perspectives and solve problems divorced from social and political contexts also functions to blur or mask questions of power and its effects. For example, what role has AT&T played in creating the global cultural economy that schools must now prepare students to face? Shifting technoscapes have made companies globally competitive and able to access the cheapest labor possible on a global scale. This labor is, paradoxically, often demobilized by such processes. Riel optimistically notes that "physical walls, special needs, socio-economic barriers, and geographic distances are not absolute boundaries."[20] Yet such constraints, most especially socioeconomic and geographic ones, are becoming more profound for those in increasingly segregated and economically depressed inner cities. Global economic processes, enabled through such technologies, have also created a plethora of minimum-wage service sector jobs for those stuck in these areas. These constraints are real and cannot be wished away by evoking the utopian potential of technology and its ability to constitute virtual communities. Such rhetoric hides some of the most pressing questions facing educators today—basic questions about equity and access.

While providing technological support to education, programs and projects like AT&T's Learning Circles (and others, like Whittle's Channel One)[21] also divert attention from corporate investments in a radically shifting economic terrain. One effect of this diversion is that companies can draw students into a constructed set of cultural and economic circumstances as if these circumstances were both neutral and inevitable. In a critique of the inclusion of technology in the National Curriculum of Wales and England, Naz Rassool notes that "the continuing neutral treatment of technology as a subject within the National Curriculum framework neatly avoids addressing those impacts of technology that include dominant power interests."[22] Although education's engagement with technoscapes through the appropriation and use of information technologies has indeed yielded positive outcomes for some students, these technologies have typically been constructed as deceptively neutral. Most efforts to integrate technology into the curriculum have neither acknowledged nor appreciated the ways in which these same technologies are part of a larger hegemonic project that is restructuring the economies in and through which these students will structure their lives. Technology, and (concurrently) the bottom-line interests of multinational corporations (as they are inflected through technology), are

19. Ibid., p. 487.
20. Ibid.

21. Apple, *Official Knowledge*, p. 100.
22. Naz Rassool, "Post-Fordism? Technology and New Forms of Control," *British Journal of the Sociology of Education*, 14(3):242 (1993).

naturalized, thus appearing as immutable dimensions of reality. In turn, people feel increasingly disenfranchised, powerless to contest these seemingly immanent forces. The heightened political apathy of students on campuses across the nation is only one example of how this particular ideology has affected popular consciousness.

Finanscapes

The third kind of scape Appadurai outlines is the finanscape, which is closely related to the technoscape and involves the disposition of global capital, a "rapid and difficult landscape to follow . . . as currency markets, national stock exchanges, and commodity speculations move megamonies through national turnstiles at blinding speed, with vast absolute implications for small differences in percentage points and time units."[23] Indeed, money is moving at faster and faster speeds and increasingly entwining local economies within global flows of capital. In the United States, for example, shifting finanscapes have eroded the middle class, dividing the country between the haves (those able to be mobile in this shifting economy) and the have-nots (those who are unable). One effect of this erosion is that cities are becoming increasingly segregated from suburbs, forcing education to deal with new and tougher issues of social and economic justice. For example, basic issues such as segregation and desegregation are resurfacing, though they are inflected through

economic concerns deemed immutable. Specifically, the relation between local property taxes and school funding has emerged as a key issue here, as evidenced, for example, in a recent *Time* magazine cover story, "The End of Integration."[24]

Indeed, it is important to emphasize that the problem of segregated schools can no longer be viewed along social justice lines alone. It is also an economic issue, with many suburban schools in wealthy communities spending two or three times as much per student on education as neighboring urban schools.[25] Because segregation has traditionally been viewed along racial lines, however, economic questions have tended to be effaced or ignored in favor of legal discourses about human rights. Issues of inclusion—usually keyed in pluralistic terms—have taken precedence over the hard economic questions and issues that really underlie much of the debate. Many education theorists have been complicit here, as they no longer engage economic issues as clearly as they might, focusing almost exclusively on questions of cultural and racial identity. Yet these latter issues "risk throwing out the class baby with the economistic bathwater,"[26] which is highly problematic given the current economic situation, where corporate mergers are commonplace, where companies are exceedingly mobile and can access labor anywhere in the world, where mas-

23. Appadurai, "Disjuncture and Difference," p. 8.

24. James Kunen, "The End of Integration," *Time,* 29 Apr. 1996, pp. 38-45.

25. Kozol, *Savage Inequalities.*

26. David Livingstone, "Searching for Missing Links: Neo-Marxist Theories of Education," *British Journal of the Sociology of Education,* 6(1):65 (1995).

sive layoffs are common, and where unions have lost much of their power. Although these are fundamental, and exceedingly stark, economic realities, many theorists are not addressing them as such, thus rendering finanscapes as ethnoscapes to a large extent. Only by refusing to elide any and all relevant discourses can we work against rigid and partial explanations or solutions, whether economic, cultural, geographic, or social.

Mediascapes

Appadurai's fourth kind of scape is the mediascape. "Mediascapes refer both to the distribution of the electronic capabilities to produce and disseminate information (newspapers, magazines, television stations and film production studios), which are now available to a growing number of private and public interests throughout the world, and to the images of the world created by these media."[27] As a primary arm of social and cultural reproduction, education has been profoundly affected by the ways mediascapes have defined common cultural sense today. As noted previously, the massive economic shifts that have accompanied deindustrialization and globalization have forced certain geographic or spatial shifts. Notable among these is the rigid split between suburbs and inner cities. Electronic media have emerged as a primary channel of communication between these two sites. For example, the new cinema of young African Americans has emerged as a particularly salient

channel for dialogue across this geographic divide. Urban reality has been related and disseminated in unprecedented ways through films such as *Menace II Society*[28] and *Boyz 'N the Hood.*[29] These films have opened up spaces where realities that have typically been silenced can be voiced, spaces where mainstream educators might begin to explore realities that challenge their assumptions.

It is important to note, however, that such communication is profoundly constrained by ideological imperatives and is often realized in paradoxical ways. The work of Cameron McCarthy is helpful here. He has suggested that film and television media "address and position viewers at the 'center' of a cultural map in which suburban, middle-class values 'triumph' over practices that drift away from mainstream social norms."[30] Indeed, McCarthy sees films such as *Menace II Society* as complicit in the reinforcement of middle-class values and norms.

Such films thus reproduce certain stereotypical, or presumably commonsense, notions about the inner city and, in turn, fuel a panicked rhetoric about public schools as battle zones. In reproducing such supposedly commonsense notions about the split between suburbs and inner

27. Appadurai, "Disjuncture and Difference," p. 9.

28. *Menace II Society*, directed by Allen Hughes and Albert Hughes, New Line Cinema, 1993.

29. *Boyz 'N the Hood*, directed by John Singleton, Columbia Pictures, 1991.

30. Cameron McCarthy, "Reading the American Popular: Suburban Resentment and the Representation of the Inner City in Contemporary Film and T.V." (Manuscript, University of Illinois at Urbana-Champaign, 1995), p. 2.

cities, these films make this split appear immutable, and they construct inner cities, inner-city schools, and inner-city youths as the natural Other to "normal" citizenship practices and American life. In sum, such films are successful in opening up a certain reality to those who live outside of it. However, following McCarthy, we must question if this reality really challenges mainstream commonsense notions or simply reinforces them. This seems a central question for those engaging the complexity of global mediascapes and their relation to education today.

Prevalent educational discourse about skills acquisition and national standards is also imbricated in contemporary mediascapes. Because, as the story goes, schools are battle zones, they can no longer teach students the skills they need to be successful in the workplace and in life. One of the most sustained treatments of this issue is embodied in the film *Lean on Me*,[31] which was based on the figure of Joe Clark (mentioned earlier). As the film opens, the camera pans an inner-city school while the Guns and Roses song "Welcome to the Jungle" plays over almost parodic images of extreme violence and near anarchy. The principal who cleans up this school stresses that his students do not have the basic skills necessary to pass exams and to succeed in society. Their immediate environment is implicitly cited as the cause that inhibits student learning. In Hollywood fashion, the principal launches a campaign of terror to rid the school of its negative elements,

thus reinscribing profoundly conservative notions about what the problem really is. According to McCarthy, the primary function of such representations is to further naturalize already dominant middle-class values. A primary side effect of this function is the abandonment and further marginalization of those who are already have-nots.

As Appadurai notes, the term "mediascapes" refers both to images and to those who control the circulation of those images. With increasing corporate shifts in production and distribution, there seem to be fewer and fewer available social and cultural spaces within which young people can define themselves. Even an art form like rap music, which is often deemed more real than other forms of popular art, is imbricated in dominant cultural imperatives.[32] The production and distribution of such art forms have become increasingly consolidated, with multinational corporations determining more and more what will and what will not be circulated in the public sphere. One effect of this is that there seems to be less and less room for agency or self-definition in many media outlets today, a point that Henry Giroux underscores in "Hollywood, Race, and the Demonization of Youth: The 'Kids' Are Not 'Alright.' "[33] Here he looks at the film *Kids*[34] as existing within a cer-

31. *Lean on Me*, directed by John G. Alvidsen, Warner Bros., 1989.

32. Greg Dimitriadis, "Hip Hop: From Live Performance to Mediated Narrative," *Popular Music*, 15(2):179-94 (1996).

33. Henry Giroux, "Hollywood, Race, and the Demonization of Youth: The 'Kids' Are Not 'Alright,' " *Educational Researcher*, 25(2):31-35 (Mar. 1996).

34. *Kids*, directed by Larry Clark, Shining Excalibur Pictures, 1995.

tain economy of "realistic" representation, which robs kids of agency, perverting them, making them bodies without ideas or voices, consumed for adult pleasure. In contrast, he suggests that the more "homegrown" film *Harlem Diary*[35] allows young people to explore the complexities and contradictions of their lives and to define themselves through the use of relatively cheap video technology. In this film, pedagogy is linked implicitly with a "representational politics [that] expands and deepens the democratic possibilities for producing films that resist rather than reinforce the current racist and demonizing portrayals of subordinate youth."[36] Here pedagogical imperatives are realized as these young people produce complex representations of themselves that challenge dominant and ubiquitous ones. As we think about future educational reform, we must both resist stereotypical representations of youths and open ourselves up to these more challenging ones.

Ideoscapes

Appadurai's final scapes are what he calls ideoscapes. "Ideoscapes are also concatenations of images, but they are often directly political and frequently have to do with the ideologies of states and the counter-ideologies of movements explicitly oriented to capturing state power or a piece of it."[37] In the contemporary American situation, ideoscapes draw upon political ideologies inspired by the Enlightenment to justify themselves. However, Appadurai notes that as Enlightenment-inspired master narratives have spread out across the globe, their internal coherence has loosened, and they have been reconfigured in fundamental ways.

Indeed, education today is marked by a radical confluence of multiple and often conflicting ideologies. Perhaps most notably, a strong conservative ideology about education has taken hold in the United States. This ideology constructs nationalistic, capitalistic interests as natural and immutable, focuses on the acquisition of mobile skills above all else, and promotes agendas such as cultural literacy, national goals, and school choice.

A second powerful ideology of contemporary education is the liberal-pluralist ideology spawned during the progressive education era and recently revived in response to changing population demographics. This ideology promotes the assumptions that we all are really the same underneath, that the goal of education is to share our different perspectives, and that by doing so we will all move toward greater understanding, tolerance, and goodness. It is an ideology that renders the tough questions of difference, distribution, and mobility in terms of equity and not in terms of social justice.

A third ideology circulating within current educational debates is that of critical pedagogy. The roots of this ideology are typically traced to the work of Paulo Freire in Latin America and Jonathan Kozol in the United

35. *Harlem Diary*, directed by Jonathan Stacks, Gabriel Films, 1996.

36. Giroux, "Hollywood, Race, and the Demonization of Youth," p. 35.

37. Appadurai, "Disjuncture and Difference," p. 9.

States.[38] Proponents of critical pedagogy advocate much more emancipatory agendas than proponents of the conservative and liberal-humanist ideologies previously discussed. These agendas are rooted in a resolute belief in democratic potential and the role of education in realizing that potential. Quite often, critical pedagogues have looked to literacy as a practice through which students and citizens can define themselves and their worlds in purposeful and politically transformative ways.

These seem to be the primary ideologies competing within debates about education and schooling in this postindustrial era. Partly as a function of this competition, the concept of education itself is being questioned. This is evidenced in the multiple and contradictory "reform" efforts currently in practice. Some reform efforts have embraced radical political agendas and tried to enact emancipatory visions. Good examples of this thrust are the Central Park East schools in New York City established and run by Deborah Meier and based on principles of democratic citizenship, dialogue, and mutual respect.[39] In contrast, more conservative reform efforts have sought to reinscribe traditional nationalist values in order to return to educational basics and to beef up national standards of educational excellence. Cultural literacy programs and Education 2000 are good examples of this drive. These disjunctures strongly suggest that we are no longer sure what education is all about, how best to prepare students for the uncertain futures they face, or how to link questions of equity with those of social justice.

CONCLUSION

We have presented Appadurai's five scapes—ethnoscapes, technoscapes, finanscapes, mediascapes, and ideoscapes—and we have examined them in relation to various educational issues and debates. A second dimension of Appadurai's organizing framework is its insistence on articulating maps by drawing lines of connection between seemingly unrelated or barely related phenomena. We will conclude by beginning to construct such maps with respect to education in a global cultural economy. Following Deleuze and Guattari,[40] our argument rests on the distinction between a tracing and a map. A tracing is a reproduction of the world that is based on models of deep structure and a faith in their discovery and interpretation. Tracings are based on phenomenological experience that is assumed to be essential, stable, and universal. Defined thus, most ethnographies are tracings of social formations.

Unlike tracings, maps are based on rhizomatic or essentially unpredictable articulations of material reality. Deleuze and Guattari suggest that the creation of maps (as opposed to tracings) provides more sophisticated understandings of the development, maintenance, and rearticula-

38. C. H. Knoblauch and Lil Brannon, *Critical Teaching and the Idea of Literacy* (Portsmouth, NH: Boyton/Cook, 1993).

39. Deborah Meier, *The Power of Their Ideas* (Boston: Beacon Press, 1995).

40. Gilles Deleuze and Felix Guattari, *A Thousand Plateaus: Capitalism and Schizophrenia* (Minneapolis: University of Minnesota Press, 1987).

tion of social institutions such as education. In drawing maps, the theorist works at the surface, creating possible realities by producing new articulations of disparate phenomena and connecting the exteriority of objects to whatever forces or directions seem potentially related to them. As such, maps exceed both individual and collective experiences of what seems naturally real. Deleuze and Guattari suggest that after constructing maps, one may then place more apparently stable tracings back onto them, interrogating breaks and fissures where one finds them.

We believe that using Appadurai's scapes as topological markers for constructing maps of education within a global landscape has considerable explanatory power. Such a practice allows us glimpses of some partial or potential realities not normally visible through the lenses of deep-structure models. For example, what pedagogical insight might derive from mapping connections between global flows of capital and flows of images? When looking at cultural products such as music and film, we are quite often locked into textual readings and iconic treatments of primary actors or movers. What could be gained by paying more attention to how the various flows of money in and between major international distribution companies help forge the landscape upon which such images are articulated and come to make common cultural sense? And how might these commonsense notions either enable or constrain the ideoscapes that help fuel school funding debates? Or how might the confluence of these global flows all relate to

geography, to the constitution of the physical terrain on which the production, distribution, and consumption of these images all occur? Questions of space, particularly as they relate to the growing rift between suburbs and inner cities, are inseparable from the ways that debates about school segregation, property tax distribution, multicultural curricula, and school restructuring efforts are realized today. It is therefore crucial to understand in considerable detail the particular configurations and confluences of these various scapes if we are to deepen our understanding of how education is constructed and practiced. When we fail to do so, we end up asking questions that have already been asked and indexing discourses with which we are already familiar. No matter what our answers are to these questions, we ultimately end up reinforcing our commonsense notions about the world instead of challenging them. In short, we end up stuck in received rhetorical spaces.

To conclude, we have provided but one very glib example of how to draw complex maps of the intersecting forces affecting education in an ever shifting global cultural economy. We think that this approach is particularly promising because it allows us to forge less obvious connections without assuming that they are either immutable or a priori productive. Other kinds of connections can—and should—be drawn. Only by doing so can we hope to understand, and perhaps solve, some of the most vexing problems facing education as we head into the profoundly uncertain twenty-first century.

ANNALS, *AAPSS*, **551**, May 1997

The Iron Lotus: Los Angeles and Postmodern Urbanism

By MICHAEL DEAR and STEVEN FLUSTY

ABSTRACT: In this article, we examine the landscapes of Los Angeles for evidence of a postmodern urbanism. We begin by contrasting the principles of the Chicago school's modernist industrial metropolis with the putatively postmodern Los Angeles school. We then examine the range of contemporary Southern California urbanisms and interpret this evidence as defining the problematic of a distinctively postmodern urbanism embedded within an emergent global capitalism.

Michael Dear is director of the Southern California Studies Center and professor of geography at the University of Southern California in Los Angeles.

Steven Flusty is a native Angeleno and a doctoral student at the School of Urban Planning and Development, University of Southern California, where he specializes in the material culture of everyday globalization.

This latest mutation in space—postmodern hyperspace—has finally succeeded in transcending the capacities of the human body to locate itself, to organize its immediate surroundings perceptually, and cognitively to map its position in a mappable external world.

Fredric Jameson[1]

One of the most enervating aspects of recent debates on the postmodern condition is the notion of a radical break from past trends in political, economic, and sociocultural life. In looking at Los Angeles, we follow Jacques Derrida's invocation that those interested in assessing contemporary change must first "rehearse the break," intimating that only by assuming that a radical break has already occurred will we be able to recognize it.[2] Our approach is cartographic, in that we do not anticipate arriving at closure in this argument. Instead, we provide a road map of an analytical terrain, apprehending the structure of a problematic rather than solving any particular puzzle.

CHICAGO VERSUS LOS ANGELES

It has been a traditional axiom of classical writing about the city that urban structures are the domain of reason.

Jonathan Raban[3]

One of the most persistent models of urban spatial structure is the zo-

nal, or concentric ring, theory, advanced in the 1920s and 1930s at the University of Chicago by Ernest W. Burgess and his associates.[4] Assuming a uniform land surface, access to a single-centered city, free competition for space, and development taking place outward from its central area, Burgess concluded that the city would form a series of concentric zones. The main ecological metaphors invoked were invasion and succession: populations, as their status and assimilation progressed, filtered outward from older residences surrounding a central business district to newer, outlying zones.

Others observed that cities tend to grow in a star-shaped form along major highways, with contrasting land uses filling the interstices between, giving rise to a sector theory of urban structure. Homer Hoyt observed that once variations arise in land uses near the city center, they tend to be perpetuated as the city expands outward.[5] Distinctive sectors are thus likely to grow out from the central business district, usually adjacent to major highways. Hoyt emphasized how "non-rational" factors could alter urban form, as when advertising and promotion influenced the direction of speculative development.

1. Fredric Jameson, *Postmodernism, or the Cultural Logic of Late Capitalism* (Durham, NC: Duke University Press, 1991), p. 44.

2. Jacques Derrida, quoted in Christopher Norris, *Deconstruction: Theory and Practice* (London: Methune, 1982), p. 127.

3. Jonathan Raban, *Soft City* (New York: E. P. Dutton, 1974), p. 157.

4. Ernest W. Burgess, "The Growth of the City," in *The City: Suggestions of Investigation of Human Behavior in the Urban Environment*, by R. E. Park, E. W. Burgess, and R. D. McKenzie (Chicago: University of Chicago Press, 1925).

5. Homer Hoyt, *The Structure and Growth of Residential Neighbourhoods in American Cities* (Washington, DC: Federal Housing Administration, 1939); idem, *One Hundred Years of Land Values in Chicago* (Chicago: University of Chicago Press, 1933).

Real-world urbanism was further engaged by the multiple nuclei theory. In 1945, Chauncy Harris and Edward Ullman proposed that cities have a cellular structure, with distinctive land-use types developing around growth nuclei within the metropolis.[6] They replaced the single-center assumption with multiple nuclei of specialized land uses resulting from (1) accessibility-induced variations in the land rent surface and (2) the mutual forces of repulsion and attraction exerted by adjacent land uses. Harris and Ullman also allowed that the internal structure of the city owes much to the peculiarities of individual sites, detailed social and economic forces, the influence of history, and international influences.

Despite the availability of different versions of urban spatial dynamics, it was the Chicago model that effectively dominated urban studies for most of the twentieth century. Then, during the 1980s, a group of loosely associated theorists and activists based in Southern California suggested that changes in the urban fabric of Los Angeles were symptomatic of broader sociogeographic transformations throughout the United States. One early expression of this emergent Los Angeles school[7]

was the 1986 appearance of a special issue of the journal *Society and Space*, devoted to understanding Los Angeles.[8] In prefatory remarks, Allen Scott and Edward Soja referred to Los Angeles as the "capital of the twentieth century," invoking Walter Benjamin's reference to Paris as the capital of the nineteenth.

By 1993, Marco Cenzatti had written that for the Los Angeles school's practitioners, "Los Angeles comes into the picture not just as a blueprint or a finished paradigm of the new dynamics, but as a laboratory which is itself an integral component of the production of new modes of analysis of the urban."[9] Cenzatti claimed that a focus on restructuring is common to all adherents of the school.[10] The confluence of global changes in economic organization, political structures, and sociocultural practices characterizing the end of the twentieth century makes the restructuring paradigm a seductive leitmotiv for seemingly anarchic contemporary changes. These include deindustrialization and reindustrialization, the emerging information economy, the decline of nation-states and the rise of new nationalisms, the Pacific Rim's new prominence, and so on. The variety and volume of such

6. Chauncy D. Harris and Edward L. Ullman, "The Nature of Cities," *The Annals* of the American Academy of Political and Social Science, 242:7-17 (Nov. 1945).

7. The term "school" is problematic, but we here follow Jennifer Pratt and use the term to refer to "a collection of individuals working in the same environment who at the time and through their own retrospective constructions of their identity and the impartations of intellectual historians are defined as representing a distinct approach to a scholarly endeavor." Quoted in Gary Alan Fine, "A Second Chicago

School? The Development of Postwar American Sociology," in *A Second Chicago School?* ed. G. A. Fine (Chicago: University of Chicago Press, 1995), p. 2.

8. *Society and Space, Environment and Planning D*, 4(3):249-390 (1986).

9. Marco Cenzatti, *Los Angeles and the L.A. School: Postmodernism and Urban Studies* (Los Angeles: Los Angeles Forum for Architecture and Urban Design, 1993).

10. Ibid.

changes almost requires developing alternative, multiple theoretical frameworks that overlap and coexist as explanations of the burgeoning world order. Such a vision is consistent with the project of postmodernism, and it is no coincidence that Los Angeles is regarded by many as the prototypical postmodern city.

WAYS OF SEEING:
SOUTHERN CALIFORNIA
URBANISMS

The problem offered by Los Angeles is a little out of the ordinary.

C. M. Robinson, 1907[11]

What does a postmodern urbanism look like? Edward Relph describes postmodern urbanism as a self-consciously selective revival of elements of older styles.[12] He observes how the fortuitous coincidence of gentrification, heritage conservation, architecture, urban design, and participatory planning created a new eclecticism in urban form, which replaced the singleminded modernist vision of an urban landscape filled with great skyscrapers, megastructures, and machines. Relph underscores the importance of place as the key to understanding social process, urging us to notice "time edges"— lines of hard discontinuity in the segregated metropolis where new confronts old.[13] The palette of urbanisms emerging from these discontinuities

is thick and complicated, as our taxonomy of Southern California's recent urban developments will show.

Edge cities

Joel Garreau argues for the central significance of Los Angeles in understanding contemporary U.S. metropolitan growth. He asserts that "every single American city that *is* growing, is growing in the fashion of Los Angeles," referring to Los Angeles as the "great-granddaddy" of edge cities.[14] For Garreau, edge cities represent the crucible of America's urban future.[15] Located at the intersection of an urban beltway and a hub-and-spoke lateral road, the edge city results from the dominance of the automobile and the associated need for parking; the communications revolution; and the large-scale entry of women into the labor market.[16] These preconditions give rise to a "third wave" of urbanization: the edge cities (previous phases were suburbanization and the malling of America). Garreau identifies three edge-city types: uptowns, or peripheral pre-automobile settlements that have subsequently been absorbed by urban sprawl; boomers, or the classic edge cities, located at freeway intersections; and greenfields, the state of the art, "occurring at the intersection of several thousand acres of farmland and one developer's monumental ego."[17]

Lacking established community, social relations in the edge city are

---

11. C. M. Robinson, "The City Beautiful" (Report to the mayor, City Council, and members of the Municipal Art Commission, Los Angeles, 1907), p. 4.

12. Edward C. Relph, *The Modern Urban Landscape* (Baltimore, MD: Johns Hopkins University Press, 1987), p. 213.

13. Ibid., p. 261.

14. Joel Garreau, *Edge City: Life on the New Frontier* (New York: Doubleday, 1991), p. 3.

15. Ibid., p. 8.

16. Ibid., p. 112.

17. Ibid., p. 116.

determined not by propinquity but via telephone, fax, and private mail service. Lacking a preestablished body politic, edge cities are administered by "shadow governments," that is, plutocratic alternatives to normal politics, accountable to wealth (as opposed to number of voters) and subject to few constitutional constraints.[18]

Privatopia

The privatopian "common-interest development" (or CID) is the quintessential edge-city residential form.[19] Privately governed by homeowner associations, and sustained by proscriptive constitutions of covenants, conditions, and restrictions formalizing CID behavioral and aesthetic norms, privatopia is driven by an ideology of "hostile privatism,"[20] which provokes a culture of nonparticipation. McKenzie warns that far from being a benign or inconsequential trend, CIDs already define a new norm for the mass production of housing in the United States. The "secession of the successful" into privatopia produces altered concepts of citizenship, in which "one's duties consist of satisfying one's obligations to private property."[21] Conservative sociologist Charles Murray applauds this trend:

I am trying to envision what happens when 10 or 20 percent of the population has enough income to bypass the social institutions it doesn't like in ways that

only the top fraction of 1 percent used to be able to do. . . . The Left has been complaining for years that the rich have too much power. They ain't seen nothing yet.[22]

The heteropolitan
theme park

Los Angeles is often invoked as the place where the American (suburban) dream is most easily realized. Its oft-claimed qualities of boundless freedom and benign climate have generated a design dreamscape fostered by a spirit of experimentation, risk taking, and hope.[23] Charles Jencks sees in this improvisational architecture of transience, energy, and unplanned vulgarity a hetero-architecture demonstrating the "great virtue, and pleasure, to be had in mixing categories, transgressing boundaries, inverting customs and adopting the marginal usage." Jencks attributes Los Angeles' hetero-architecture to the city's ethnic pluralism, expressed as "a combination of enclaves with high identity, and multienclaves with mixed identity"[24] and creating opportunities "to accept the different voices that create a city, suppress none of them, and make from their interaction some kind of greater dialogue."[25]

Dreamscapes are marketable as commodified landscapes designed to satisfy fantasies of urban living. Mi-

22. Ibid., pp. 204-5.
23. Thomas S. Hines, "Machines in the Garden: Notes Toward a History of Modern Los Angeles Architecture, 1900-1990." in *Sex, Death and God in L.A.*, ed. David Reid (New York: Pantheon Books, 1992), p. 313.

18. Ibid., p. 187.
19. Evan McKenzie, *Privatopia: Homeowner Associations and the Rise of Residential Private Government* (New Haven, CT: Yale University Press, 1994).
20. Ibid., p. 19.
21. Ibid., p. 196.

24. Charles Jencks, *Heteropolis: Los Angeles, the Riots and the Strange Beauty of Hetero-Architecture* (New York: St. Martin's Press, 1993), p. 32.
25. Ibid., p. 75.

chael Sorkin describes these variegated cityscapes as "theme parks," places of simulation without end, characterized by aspatiality plus technological and physical surveillance and control.[26] Sorkin insists that because "the 800 telephone number and the piece of plastic have made time and space obsolete," these instruments of "artificial adjacency" have eviscerated the traditional politics of propinquity.[27] Sorkin argues that in today's "recombinant city," the social orders legible in such earlier urban forms as agoras or piazzas have been obscured and/or deliberately mutilated. The phone and modem have rendered street life irrelevant, and the new city threatens an "unimagined sameness" characterized by the loosening of ties to specific spaces; rising levels of surveillance, manipulation, and segregation; and the city as a theme park. This new electronically mediated suburb is not missing any particular building or place but the spaces between them, that is, the connections that make sense of urban form.[28]

City as simulacrum

In extremis, California dreamscapes become simulacra. Edward Soja identifies Orange County as a massive simulation of what a city should be: "a structural fake, an enormous advertisement, yet functionally the finest multipurpose facility of its kind in the country." He terms this

assemblage "exopolis," the city without, and asserts that something new is being born there—based on but different from the hyperrealities of more conventional theme parks such as Disneyland.[29] The exopolis is a simulacrum, an exact copy of an original that never existed, where image and reality are spectacularly confused. In this "politically numbed" society, conventional politics are dysfunctional. Orange County becomes a "scamscape," notable as the home of massive mail fraud operations, savings and loan debacles, and county government bankruptcy.[30]

Geographies of restructuring

The exopolis is one of numerous restructurings that Soja employs to link Southern California's emergent urban forms with underlying social processes. Others include flexcities, associated with post-Fordism's deindustrialization and the emergent information economy; and the cosmopolis, the globalization of Los Angeles, in both its world city status and its ongoing multicultural diversification.

These three geographies produce an additional set, comprising the splintered labyrinth, the extreme forms of social, economic, and political polarization characteristic of the postmodern city; the carceral city, the new "incendiary urban geography" amalgamated of violence and police surveillance; and "simcities," Soja's term for new ways of seeing the city

26. Michael Sorkin, ed., *Variations on a Theme Park: The New American City and the End of Public Space* (New York: Hill & Wang, 1992).

27. Ibid., p. xi.

28. Ibid., p. xii.

29. Edward Soja, "Inside Exopolis: Scenes from Orange County," in *Variations on a Theme Park*, ed. Sorkin, p. 101.

30. Ibid., p. 120.

emerging from studying Los Angeles—a kind of "epistemological restructuring" foregrounding postmodern perspectives.[31]

Fordist versus post-Fordist urbanism

One crucial shift underlying restructuring is that from Fordist to post-Fordist industrial organizations. Allen Scott has portrayed the burgeoning Southern California urbanism as a consequence of this deep-seated structural change in the political economy of capitalist industrialism. He argues that there have been two major phases of urbanization in the United States. The first related to an era of Fordist mass production, coalescing in the paradigmatic cities of industrial capitalism—Detroit, Chicago, Pittsburgh, and so on—around industries that were based upon mass production à la Henry Ford. The second phase is associated with the decline of the Fordist era and the rise of post-Fordist "flexible production" based on small-size, small-batch production units integrated into clusters of economic activity. Such clusters have two manifestations: labor-intensive craft forms (in Los Angeles, typically clothing and jewelry) and high technology (especially the defense and aerospace industries). Scott asserts

these so-called technopoles as the principal geographical loci of Southern California's contemporary urbanization process.[32]

Globalization

Consideration of the changing nature of industrial production ultimately encompasses the globalization of capitalist enterprise. Mike Davis claims that if Los Angeles is in any sense paradigmatic, it is because it condenses the intended and unintended spatial consequences of post-Fordism.[33] These include the rise of new globalized circuits of capital and luxury-good consumption and the decline of the mass-consumption, high-wage industrial economy. Davis insists that there is no simple master-logic of restructuring, focusing instead on two key localized macro-processes: overaccumulation in Southern California of bank and real estate capital, principally from the East Asian trade surplus; and the reflux of low-wage manufacturing and labor-intensive service industries following upon immigration from Mexico and Central America. Through such connections, what happened yesterday in Asia and Central America will have an effect in Los Angeles today.[34]

31. Edward Soja, "Los Angeles 1965-1992: The Six Geographies of Urban Restructuring," in *The City: Los Angeles and Urban Theory at the End of the Twentieth Century*, ed. A. J. Scott and E. Soja (Berkeley: University of California Press, forthcoming).

32. Allen J. Scott, *Metropolis: From the Division of Labor to Urban Form* (Berkeley: University of California Press, 1988), idem, *Technopolis: High-Technology Industry and Regional Development in Southern California* (Berkeley: University of California Press, 1993).

33. Mike Davis, "Chinatown Revisited? The Internationalization of Downtown Los Angeles," in *Sex, Death and God in L.A.*, ed. Reid, p. 21.

34. Ibid., p. 26.

Fortified city

The socioeconomic polarization implicit in these models of restructuring points to a dystopian side of Southern California's urbanism. Davis notes how Southern Californians' obsession with security has transformed the region into a fortress.[35] This shift is acutely manifested in the physical form of the city, which is divided into fortified cells of affluence and places of terror where police battle the criminalized poor. Such phenomena place Los Angeles "on the hard edge of postmodernity."[36] They include the destruction of public space, the creation of forbidden cities sealed against the poor, mean streets where the homeless are deliberately contained, high-tech policing methods that have led to an invisible Haussmannization of Los Angeles, and crowd control through sociospatial segregation.

Interdictory space

Steven Flusty has observed how the various types of defensible space have spread across Los Angeles like a canopy of suppression and surveillance. His taxonomy of "interdictory" spaces includes stealthy space, concealed by intervening objects or grade changes; slippery space, rendered unreachable by missing or obfuscated approaches; crusty space, made inaccessible by deliberate obstructions such as walls and checkpoints; prickly space, which cannot be comfortably occupied; and jittery space, which cannot be utilized unobserved.[37] Flusty notes how combinations of interdictory spaces are being introduced "into every facet of the urban environment, generating distinctly unfriendly mutant typologies," of which he identifies five: blockhomes, bunker-style residences with few apertures connecting to the world outside; luxury laagers, gated affluent communities; pocket ghettos, low-income housing ghettos retrofitted with street barricades and the like; strongpoints of sale, commercial facilities that have undergone analogous fortification; and world citadels, self-contained, defensible office towers, often located in clusters.[38]

POSTMODERN URBANISM

[We] are today at the beginning of a truly new economic era. It has transformed both the work people do and the places where they live, in ways which, a mere twenty years ago would have seemed unimaginable. . . . Thanks to these economic changes, place has changed its meaning.

Richard Sennett[39]

Let us imagine that our urbanists could talk with each other to resolve their differences and reconcile their terminologies. We consider that the thrust of their evidence amounts to a schematic that is powerful yet inevi-

35. Mike Davis, "Fortress Los Angeles: The Militarization of Urban Space," in *Variations on a Theme Park*, ed. Sorkin.

36. Ibid., p. 155.

37. Steven Flusty, *Building Paranoia: The Proliferation of Interdictory Space and the Erosion of Spatial Justice* (West Hollywood, CA: Los Angeles Forum for Architecture and Urban Design, 1994), pp. 16-17.

38. Ibid., pp. 21-33.

39. Richard Sennett, "Something in the City," *Times Literary Supplement*, 22 Sept. 1995, p. 13.

tably incomplete, given our objectives in this article. The schematic broadly proposes a proto-postmodern urban process that is driven by a global restructuring and balkanized by a series of interdictory networks; the populations within the consequent geographies are socially heterogeneous and economically polarized; they are educated and persuaded to the consumption of dreamscapes or are consigned to carceral cities. The built environment that is reflective of these processes consists of edge cities, privatopias, and so on.

Recognizing that we may have done serious damage to some commentators' intentions, we now proceed to a reconstruction of their evidence, focusing on the interaction between four spheres: production, consumption, ecology, and coercion. Our promiscuous use of neologisms in what follows is quite deliberate since, after all, we are rehearsing a radical break.

We begin with the assumption that the very occupation and utilization of space, as well as the production and distribution of commodities, depend upon an anthropocentric reconfiguration of natural processes and products. As the scope and scale of globally integrated consumption increases, institutional action converts complex ecologies into monocultural factors of production by simplifying nature into a *global latifundium*. This process includes both a homogenizing intervention, as with California agriculture's reliance upon vast expanses of a single crop, and a forceful interdiction to sustain that intervention, as with aerial spraying of

pesticide over the Los Angeles basin to eradicate the fruit flies attracted to vast expanses of certain single crops. *Holsteinization* is an analogous process of monoculturing people as consumers in order to facilitate the harvesting of their desires. A *praedatorian guard* provides the forceful interdiction discouraging resistance at all levels.

The global latifundium's contemporary form is distinguished by the underlying regime of *flexism*, a pattern of econocultural production and consumption characterized by near-instantaneous delivery and rapid redirectability of resource flows. Flexism's fluidity results from cheaper and faster systems communications, globalization of capital markets, and concomitant flexibly specialized just-in-time production processes, permitting mobile capital and commodity flows to outmaneuver geographically fixed labor markets and bounded nation-states. Capital thus evades long-term commitment to place, further separating localities from control over production and capital accumulation.

These exchange asymmetries produce a *new world bipolar disorder*. This is a globally bifurcated social structure in which those overseeing the global latifundium enjoy concentrated power, while those dependent upon others' command-and-control decisions are pitted against one another and forced to accept shrinking compensation for ever increasing efforts. Of these two groups, the *cybergeoisie* reside in the big house of the global latifundium, providing indispensable command-and-control functions. The cybergeoisie enjoy socioeconomic security with comparatively long time horizons in decision making. Consequently, the typical cybergeoisie anxieties tend toward unforeseen social disruptions, such as market fluctuations and crime.

Protosurps, on the other hand, are the sharecroppers of the global latifundium, providing flexibilized labor on a just-in-time basis. Protosurps include temporary laborers, fire-at-will service workers, and more or less formal vendors. Protosurps are called upon to provide services designed so as to be performed by anyone and are, not surprisingly, subjected to high degrees of uncertainty and relatively short time horizons.

With the subordination of localities to continually shifting global imperatives, the spatial logic of Fordism has given way to a new, more dissonant international geographical order. Identical assembly lines for the production of the same brand of automobile, managed and supplied with parts from distant continents, sit amid fields growing the same strain of strawberry or broccoli for export; adjacent to industrial slums sprout luxury condominiums, indistinguishable in form and occupancy from (and often in direct communication with) luxury condominiums near squatter encampments on the other side of the world. What in close-up resembles a fragmentary, collaged polyculture appears, from a longer perspective, as geographically disjoint but ageographically integrated monocultures—shuffled sames set amid persistent local variation.

This contingent mosaic of monocultures underscores the futility of discussions about *the* city. More holistically, the dispersed net of megalopoles may be viewed as a single integrated urban system, or *Citistat*. Citistat, the collective world city, has emerged from the competing metropolitan webs of the colonial era to become the geographically diffuse hub of an omnipresent periphery, drawing labor and material from readily substitutable locations in that periphery. Citistat is both geographically corporeal and ageographically ethereal, in the sense that communication systems create a virtual space coordinating activities in physical space. Both realms reinforce each other while (re)producing the new world bipolar disorder.

Materially, Citistat consists of *commudities*, centers of command and control, and the *mulches* of the *in-beyond*. Virtually, Citistat comprises *cyburbia*, the collection of complex state-of-the-art interactive data services (generally reliant upon costly and technologically complex interfaces), and *cyberia*, an electronic outland of rudimentary communication systems, interwoven and conditioned preceptorally by the *disinformation sewer highway* (DSH).

Commudities are commodified communities satisfying—and profiting from—the habitat preferences of the cybergeoisie. They consist of carefully manicured residential and commercial ecologies managed through privatopian self-administration and maintained against deviance by a repertoire of prohibitions. Commonly located some distance from restless populations undergoing conversion to protosurpdom, individual commudities are increasingly teleintegrated to form cyburbia,[40] the high-profile tollways of Citistāt's virtual twin. Teleintegration is already de rigueur for the *citidels*, commercial commudities consisting of high-rise corporate towers from which the control of production and distribution in the global latifundium is exercised. Despite personal and institutional globalization, the secured separateness of commudities serves as a barrier to communications not vectored by the DSH, a process that results in a comparatively holsteinized population.

The in-beyond comprises mulches, that is, communities predicated upon ethnocultural similarity and operating as repositories of cheap, on-call labor. This pastiche of affinity clusters possesses a cultural diversity and porosity rendering it a hotbed of *wild memetic contagion* (see below). The in-beyond's global connectivity is less glamorous than that of the commudities, but nevertheless it is extensive. Intermittent phone contact and remittances through cyberia,[41] the potholed public streets of Citistāt's electronic shadow, are augmented by extensive networks of snail mail, personal migration, and the hand-to-hand passage of mediated communications (for example, cassette tapes). Such contacts occasionally diffuse into commudities.

Political relations in this postmodern globality tend toward polyanarchy, a politics of respect for—or at least grudging tolerance of—difference emerging from interactions and accommodations between mulches, between commudities, and, less frequently, between mulch and commudity. Polyanarchy's more pervasive form is *pollyannarchy*, polyanarchy's neutered evil twin, implicit in the multiculturalists' assertion that "everything would be O.K. if we could just get along." Pollyannarchy demobilizes challenges to the controlling beneficiaries of the new world bipolar disorder, as evidenced by the continuing spectacle of electoral politics or by Los Angeles' unity campaign run by corporate sponsors following the 1992 uprising.

The continual collisions resulting from increased immigration and severe social differentiation induced by flexism also promote wild memetic contagion.[42] This is a process by which the culture of an individual or group influences that of another previously unexposed individual or group. Memetic contagion is evidenced in Los Angeles by such hybridized agents as Salvadoreno Santeros (spiritual communities) or blue-bandanna'd Thai Crips (gang members). The inevitable tension between the anarchic diversification born of memetic contagion and the not-quite-hegemonic manipulations of the holsteinization process may prove to be the central cultural contradiction of flexism.

Wired throughout the body of Citistāt is the DSH, the mass infotainmercial media owned by roughly two dozen cybergeois institutions. The

40. The word "cyburbia" was coined by Fred Dewey in Fred Dewey and Ralph Rugoff, "The Floating World," in *The Wild Palms Reader*, ed. Roger Trilling and Stuart Swezey (New York: St. Martin's Press, 1993).

41. Cf. Daniel Rushkoff, *Cyberia: Life in the Trenches of Cyberspace* (New York: HarperCollins, 1995).

42. Richard Dawkins, *The Selfish Gene* (New York: Oxford University Press, 1976), pp. 203-15.

DSH disseminates holsteinizing ideologies and incentives while inflating
the symbolic value of commodities. At
the same time, it serves as the highly
filtered sensory organ through which
commudities and mulches experience the world beyond their unmedi-
ated daily experiences. The DSH disseminates engineered memetic
contagion, encouraging participation
in a global latifundium represented
as both inevitable and desirable.
However, since the DSH is a broad-
band distributor of communications
designed primarily to deliver con-
sumersheds to advertisers, the ultimate interpretation of messages carried by the DSH is difficult to
predetermine. Thus the DSH inad-
vertently becomes a vector for wild
memetic contagion, including the
conversion of cybergeois youths to
wannabe gangstas via the dissemi-
nation of hip-hop culture across commudity boundaries.

The new world bipolar disorder's
power asymmetries may become so
apparent that even the DSH becomes
incapable of obscuring them, thus
leaving protosurps disinclined to
adhere to the social contract. This
instability creates the potential for
violence, pitting Citistat and cybergeoisie against the protosurp
mulches, and leading inevitably to a
demand for the suppression of protosurp intractability. The praedatorian
guard thus emerges as the strongest
remaining vestige of the state. This
public-private partnership of merce-
nary sentries, police expeditionary
forces, and their technological exten-
sions (video cameras, helicopters,
criminological data uplinks, and so
forth) watches over the commudities

and minimizes disruptiveness in occupied mulches. The praedatorian
guard is thus the mechanism of control through coercion, even at the international level where asymmetri-
cal trade relations are reinforced by
the U.S. military. It may be only a
matter of time before the local and
national praedatorians are adminis-
tratively and functionally merged.

CONCLUSION: THE SPATIAL
LOGIC OF KENO KAPITALISM

. . . and the realization dawned here that
crime might be the new form that politics
was taking in this unpredictable era.

Alma Guillermoprieto[43]

Nowhere is the essential anarchy
of the globally flexible, resolutely
capitalist postmodern political economy more evident than in Los Angeles' urban development process.
"Keno kapitalism" is the synoptic
term we use to describe the spatial
manifestations of the postmodern urban condition. Urbanization is occurring on a quasi-random field of opportunities; capital touches down almost
by chance on a parcel of land, ignor-
ing the opportunities on adjacent
lots, thus sparking the development
process. The relationship between
development of one parcel and nonde-
velopment of another is a disjointed,
seemingly unrelated affair. While not
truly a random process, the traditional agglomeration economies
guiding urban development in the
past no longer apply. Conventional
city form, Chicago-style, is sacrificed
in favor of a noncontiguous collage of

43. Alma Guillermoprieto, "Whodunnit?"
New Yorker, 25 Sept. 1995, p. 44.

parcelized, consumption-oriented landscapes devoid of conventional centers yet wired into electronic propinquity and nominally unified by the mythologies of the DSH. Los Angeles is the mature form of this acutely fragmented and specialized postmodern urban aggregate, a partitioned gaming board subject to perverse laws and peculiarly discrete, disjointed urban outcomes. Las Vegas may be regarded as a youthful analogue. Given the pervasive presence of crime, corruption, and violence in the global city (and geopolitically, as the nation-state gives way to mafias and micronationalisms), the gaming analogy seems especially appropriate.

ANNALS, *AAPSS*, **551**, May 1997

Globalization to a Latin Beat:
The Miami Growth Machine

By JAN NIJMAN

ABSTRACT: Miami's globalization is accompanied by a restructuring of the city's political economy and the emergence of a powerful growth machine. After the shock caused by massive Latino immigration wore off, the old business elite combined forces with the new Hispanic (Cuban) elite and capitalized on Miami's international economic opportunities. Miami's experience illustrates the materialist imperatives of globalization and its unplanned social consequences. The benefits of economic growth are not equally distributed, and there are notable discrepancies along ethnic lines. The growth machine generates local narratives that emphasize the values of multiculturalism, but Miami's civic society has become fragmented and fragile. As an extreme example of a globalized city, Miami offers a glimpse of the fate of urban civilization in the global era.

Jan Nijman is an associate professor of geography and director of the International Studies Program at the University of Miami. His main research interest is in the geography of international relations. His previous publications on Miami deal with the city's position in the international urban hierarchy and with social polarization as a consequence of economic internationalization.

164

THE local government of Dade County, in which Miami is located, has a special maintenance squad to "clean up dead chickens, goats and other items found each morning on the grounds of the County Courthouse. The remains are the product of rituals performed by relatives and friends of some Caribbean born defendants in need of a little extra help with their legal problems," usually regarding immigration. Such sacrifices are said to be quite common in parts of the city where recent immigrants are concentrated.[1]

Arguably, Miami is the most foreign of any large metropolitan area in the United States. Its exotic qualities often invoke images of glamour and splendor, but at times there is also a sense of alienation from mainstream America. This city[2] is above all a showcase of the forces of globalization, and of the complexity of those forces. Miami defies most conventional thinking about cities and urban development in the United States. This is true not only with regard to its unique ethnic relations (the topic of most studies of Miami) but also with regard to the city's political economy, which has thus far received very little attention.

Twice in a recent six-month period, the national edition of the *New York Times* was accompanied by a special advertising supplement for Miami.[3] The covers of these glossy magazines feature photographs of slick real estate developers who are the main financiers of this expensive advertising blitz. The purpose is to lure affluent northerners to Miami: "It's time for New York and the rest of America to discover what international visitors already know."[4] It is indeed hard to think of another city the size of Miami that can market itself as a foreign city inside the United States.

Due to its Latin American connections, Miami has grown impressively, both economically and demographically, and many observers would argue that Miami as a city has prospered accordingly. As we shall see, Miami's internationalization also facilitated the emergence of a peculiar kind of socioeconomic and political establishment and a forceful growth machine. Miami's designation as the "capital of the Americas" has proven a powerful sales pitch to the rest of the world as well as locally.

The purpose of this article is to get to some of the fundamental undercurrents that were instrumental in the re-creation of this city. It links the process of globalization to internal machinations by Miami's business elites, but it also focuses on the socioeconomic and political consequences of globalization and on the role of Miami's civic culture.

It is by no means easy to go beyond the well-known stereotypes of this city. The lack of transparency of Miami's inner workings is reflected in Joel Garreau's characterization of Miami as the "intrigue capital of the hemisphere": "Secrecy punctuated by tall tales envelops aspect after aspect of Miami. A reporter attempting to

1. "In Miami, Sacrifices Are Extralegal Help," *New York Times*, 10 Apr. 1995.

2. This article focuses on Miami's metropolitan area. The terms "city" and "metropolitan area" are used interchangeably.

3. *New York Times*, 15 Dec. 1995; ibid., 2 June 1996.

4. *New York Times*, advertising supp., 15 Dec. 1995, p. 43.

get at a description of the internal workings of the place is tempted to throw up his hands."[5] Garreau attributes this lack of transparency to sensitivities surrounding Cuba politics and Miami's role as a haven for debased political groups in Central America, as well as to the importance of the drug trade and immense amounts of illegal money circulating in Miami.

Many cities have highly internationalized landscapes while they are not considered primary world-cities.[6] Miami fits this description, along with cities such as Amsterdam, Rio de Janeiro, and Milan. But Miami is an extreme case. According to some measures, such as immigration, Miami is the most internationalized metropolitan area in the country. The effects of globalization on Miami have been massive, and unprecedented in urban America.

The consequences of globalization are not necessarily all good or all bad. To be sure, it is difficult to pass a comprehensive value judgment on the consequences of globalization (consequences for whom?). In addition, Miami's postmodern appearance allows a variety of interpretations of the true character of this city. It is possible, nonetheless, to discuss some of the implications of globalization in more or less objective terms, especially with regard to the restructuring of Miami's establishment and the ways in which it embraced the alleged virtues of globalization.

MIAMI AS CAPITAL OF THE CARIBBEAN

In about forty years, not a long time in the life span of cities, Miami transformed from a quiet resort town at the periphery of the United States to a dynamic metropolis in the center of a growing economic region comprising North and South America and the Caribbean. Between 1960 and 1990, the population of Dade County more than doubled, to approximately 2 million people, and the urban economy grew accordingly. By 1996, Dade County's economy was worth $56 billion, exceeding the gross national product of Colombia, one of its main trading partners.[7]

Miami's transformation and growth are based on the convergence of two developments: the arrival of very large numbers of Latin American immigrants and the globalization of the world economy. The latter facilitated the intensification of finance and trade flows across political borders, allowing for the emergence of international economic regions, such as the one in which Miami plays a prominent part. Massive immigration, in turn, gave Miami a definitive advantage in terms of human resources and as a node in the globalizing world economy.

In 1960, on the eve of Miami's transformation, Latins made up 5 percent of the metropolitan populace.

5. Joel Garreau, *The Nine Nations of America* (Boston: Houghton Mifflin, 1981), p. 174.

6. For an elaborate argument about the command function of so-called world cities, see Saskia Sassen, *The Global City: New York, London, Tokyo* (Princeton, NJ: Princeton University Press, 1991).

7. Metro Dade, *Hispanics in Dade County, 1990* (Miami, FL: Office of Latin Affairs, Metropolitan Dade County Planning Department, 1994); "Dade's Economy Eclipses Output of Some Nations," *Miami Herald*, 16 June 1996.

Today, they represent more than half of the city's 2 million people, and approximately 66 percent of all Latins are Cuban. Just as spectacular was the drop in the share of the Anglos (or, more accurately, non-Hispanic whites), from 80 to about 30 percent. The proportion of non-Hispanic blacks increased slightly, to around 20 percent. According to the 1990 census, almost half of Miami's population was born abroad, and over 60 percent speak a language in addition to English at home.

Local parlance has it that "had it not been for the Cubans, Miami would have been a dead duck."[8] Miami's rise to prominence is often attributed to its becoming a multicultural city. The presence of large numbers of relatively skilled and educated bilingual Latinos makes Miami an attractive location for companies that do business in Latin America. Hence, the influx of immigrants was accompanied by a rapid internationalization of Miami's economy.

By now, Miami handles more than a third of all U.S. trade with Latin America and over half of all U.S. trade with the Caribbean and Central America. Trade continues to increase rapidly, and recent years have witnessed the fastest rates of growth ever.[9] Of 352 multinational companies with offices in Miami, 70 percent were established after 1980, and the number of new establishments has

continued to grow over time.[10] Miami has become the third foreign banking center in the United States (after New York and Los Angeles) in terms of the number of foreign banking offices.[11]

Thus Miami has become the main gateway to Latin America and the Caribbean, out-competing cities such as Houston, Los Angeles, New York, and New Orleans. A recent acknowledgment of Miami's impressive economic achievements came with a book by Harvard professor Rosabeth Moss Kantor entitled *World Class*, which identified Miami as the prime example of a world-class trading city in the United States.[12] Kantor attributes Miami's success to the city's "cultural connections," namely, the presence of binational communities. It is also the product, however, of the deliberate growth strategies of Miami's business elite. The next section focuses on the ways in which the city's establishment capitalized on the opportunities of globalization.

THE MIAMI GROWTH MACHINE

Miami's economic transformation did not just come about by chance, at least not entirely. Against the backdrop of the broader historical currents mentioned previously, its economic development is the product of

8. The words of one local observer in Alejandro Portes and Alex Stepick, *City on the Edge: The Transformation of Miami* (Berkeley: University of California Press, 1993), p. 144.

9. Beacon Council, *Miami Business Profile 1995-1996* (Miami: Beacon Council, 1996).

10. Beacon Council, *Miami's Multinational Business Community* (Miami: Beacon Council, 1994).

11. Jan Nijman, "Breaking the Rules: Miami in the Urban Hierarchy," *Urban Geography*, 17:5-22 (1996).

12. Rosabeth Moss Kantor, *World Class: Thriving Locally in the Global Economy* (New York: Simon & Schuster, 1995).

the machinations of its establishment. In their thesis on the "city as growth machine," Logan and Molotch point out that "the incessant lobbying, manipulating, and cajoling can deliver the critical resources from which great cities are made."[13]

The *New York Times* advertising supplements for Miami mentioned in the introduction of this article are illustrative of the particular character of Miami's aggressive and self-confident growth strategies. Most important of all, the growth machine has been a major force in the generation of a discourse that places Miami at the cutting edge of doing business internationally or even globally.

Tourism is still a major source of income, but it is increasingly aimed at international markets, especially Latin America and Europe. Besides tourism, international trade and real estate have become leading sectors of the Miami economy. All growth is welcomed, but the city is primarily promoted on the basis of its virtues as an international place. Miami's designation as the capital of Latin America, the Americas, and the Caribbean has been in vogue since the late 1970s and early 1980s.

The exceptional strength of Miami's growth machine derives from two factors. First, while other cities may have competing elites with different and conflicting growth strategies, in Miami there is an exceptionally strong consensus. This has to do with the city's celebrated location, which has proven an irresistible

13. John R. Logan and Harvey L. Molotch, *Urban Fortunes: The Political Economy of Place* (Berkeley: University of California Press, 1987), p. 293.

temptation to indulge in geographical determinism. Thus it is "obvious" to everyone that Miami should play a prominent role in the Americas because of its geographical position. The city is marketed and promoted as a natural winner in the era of global economic competition.

To the north, the city is promoted as a subtropical and exotic place with great access to Latin American markets: perfect for the location of companies with sales to and marketing oriented toward Latin America, as well as for real estate investments (a second home on what is called the American riviera). To the south, the city is sold as a haven of stability and opportunity, with one of the city's greatest assets being the combination of Latin culture with U.S. location. Southern investors have been particularly attracted to Miami's discrete and secure private banking opportunities and to its real estate. The city's growing trade business has proven attractive to northerners and southerners alike.

A second explanation for the strength of Miami's growth machine is the materialist culture that prevails in this city, something that catches the eye of many visitors. This materialist culture, in turn, is mainly the product of migration. The bulk of Miami's many immigrants came here in order to advance themselves economically. This is also true for the Cuban community, which was driven to prove Castro wrong by building their own economic success story. At the same time, many of the native whites in this city who chose to stay, did so predominantly for economic motives, and despite becoming a minority. In addition, to the extent that materialist culture replaces civic culture, it implies the absence of social constraints on the growth machine when it threatens to sacrifice public interests for private materialist gains. I shall return to this issue shortly.

The biggest local newspaper, the *Miami Herald*, neatly fulfills the role carved out for local news media in the urban growth machine:

The newspaper has no ax to grind except the one that holds the community elite together: growth. This disinterest in the specific form of growth, but avid commitment to development generally, enables the newspaper to achieve a statesman-like position in the community. . . . The publisher or editor is often the arbiter of internal growth machine bickering, restraining the short-term profiteers in the interest of more stable, long-term, and properly planned growth.[14]

In the early days of Miami's transformation, with stability gone and the future uncertain, the newspaper often took a critical stand against the massive influx of Hispanics. This changed with the unfolding of the city's promise as an international trading center and as the new urban growth machine got on track. Since the mid-1980s, the *Miami Herald*, complete with an independent Spanish edition, has been a strong advocate of multiculturalism and visibly the most important force in the forging of a stable community in this city, emphasizing the link between growth goals and better lives for Miami residents.

A good illustration of just how far the *Miami Herald* has come was a

headline on the front page on 14 June 1996 that exclaimed, "Vanishing Spanish." The article deplored the fact that only a small percentage of graduating high school students in metropolitan Miami are fully fluent in Spanish and that most second-generation Hispanic immigrants speak an imperfect sort of "home Spanish." This was described as an alarming trend since it erodes Miami's advantage as a bilingual community and diminishes its economic competitiveness.

The changed stand by the *Miami Herald* was ideological in its manifestations, but it was driven by the reconstitution of Miami's growth machine. In Miami, as Portes and Stepick put it, "bilingualism pays, monolingualism does not."[15]

THE RESTRUCTURING OF MIAMI'S ESTABLISHMENT

One common ingredient of the widely accepted narrative about Miami's transformation is the white flight from Dade County to the north, in response to the city's Latinization. White out-migration and Hispanic in-migration, in combination with the internationalization of the urban economy, had a notable impact on Miami's establishment and political economy. In Miami, more than in any city of comparable size, recent immigrants have been extremely upwardly mobile, and many have joined the city's ruling classes.

The Latinization of Miami makes a great story. Indeed, Miami's transformation into a foreign city has proven such an excitable and intrigu-

14. Ibid., p. 307.

15. Portes and Stepick, *City on the Edge*, p. 174.

ing theme that the continuing dominance of non-Hispanic whites has been pushed into the background. It is, however, one of the most interesting aspects of Miami's transformation, in that it exposes the flexible strength of the growth machine.

Considering the monumental changes in this city and the widely perceived threats to its social order, the native whites who stayed behind formed a rather selective crowd. Many of them were businesspeople, and many held key positions in the urban political economy. Even if the Latin so-called invasion was at first judged negatively, in due course many of the native whites acquired a sense of opportunity and a belief that Miami had great potential in terms of international growth. The growing power of Hispanics has only partially eroded the position of the older establishment of Miami. "Anglo hegemony" may have come to an end by 1980,[16] but non-Hispanic whites continued to be the major force in Miami's political and economic hierarchies.

Despite their growing importance on the political scene, Miami's Hispanics are still underrepresented in local government. Of 27 municipalities in Dade County, only 5 have a majority of Hispanics in their elected offices. Of the 6 largest municipalities (Miami, Hialeah, Miami Beach, North Miami, Coral Gables, and North Miami Beach), only Hialeah has a majority of elected Hispanics.[17] Altogether, there are more than twice

as many non-Hispanic whites as Hispanics in the elected offices of the county's local governments. Things look a bit better at the county level: of the 17 elected offices in the government of Dade County, 7 are held by Hispanics (all but 1 of whom are Cuban).

Interestingly, it is beyond the local government that Cubans are overrepresented: of all the Dade County representatives at the federal and state level, an overwhelming majority are Hispanic (14 of 25), all of them Cuban. This is a reflection of the concerns of Cuban Americans with issues regarding Cuba and Cuban refugees, which are mainly decided at the state and federal level. This suggests that the politicization of the Cuban American community applied especially to issues beyond the locale. The high visibility of Cuban American representation at the state and federal levels has probably contributed to perceptions of the rapidly growing political clout of Cuban Americans, but it is too easily assumed that this applies to the local level as well.

In economic terms, the continued dominance of non-Hispanic whites is unquestionable. From a listing of the 100 most powerful people in South Florida by a reputable local business journal in 1994, it can be learned that

---

16. Ibid., pp. 29-30.
17. Elected offices include the mayor, vice-mayor, commissioners or council members, clerk, manager, attorney, and chief of police.

Metropolitan Miami shows a striking pattern of political segregation in the sense that few local governments are ethnically mixed (the overarching metro government and the municipalities of Miami and South Miami are the best examples of ethnically mixed governments). Most municipalities have very large majorities of non-Hispanic whites, Hispanics, or blacks, respectively. These findings are based on data provided by the Dade County Department of Elections, 18 Apr. 1996.

21 of them were Hispanics and 4 were African Americans. The other 75 were non-Hispanic whites.[18] The same pattern applies to other indices, such as the 25 most highly paid executives, of whom only 2 were Hispanic. Of the top executives of the 50 largest employers in South Florida, 9 were Hispanic and they were predominantly with governmental, public, or semi-public institutions.[19]

While these figures are obviously high compared to other cities in the United States, they are low in view of the composition of Miami's population, in which Hispanics are the absolute majority and Cubans are the largest single ethnic group. It is especially revealing that these figures are surprisingly low to most local observers: they conflict with pervasive local discourses on Miami as a Latin city.

Another reason the role of native whites in Miami's establishment is underrated lies in the behind-the-scenes politics that form a standard ingredient of city growth machines.[20] An intriguing illustration in the case of Miami is the existence of the so-called Non-Group; the name of this group would have won the approval of political scientists Bachrach and Baratz, who coined the term "non-

decision-making."[21] Despite the fact that this group consists of the most influential businesspeople in Miami, not many locals have ever heard of it. The group, whose core is said to be made up of native whites, was formed by Alvah Chapman, Jr., the former chairman of Knight Ridder. In the local news media, Chapman has been referred to as "the linchpin in the Miami Business Machine."

Of course, native whites are not alone in their quest to promote this city. Power may not be distributed equally among Miami's ethnic groups, but the different elites share a preference for growth strategies that emphasize Miami as a growing international metropolis. To the Hispanic elites, one of the appealing aspects of the portrayal of Miami as a Latin city is that it highlights their own crucial role in Miami's rise to prominence. It is also essential to Miami's marketing image in South America, where the city is viewed with admiration and pride and as a testament to Latin ambition and creativity. However, even if the business elites favor Miami's internationalization, not all of the city's residents enjoy the benefits equally.

ECONOMIC INTERNATIONALIZATION AND SOCIAL POLARIZATION

A city's absolute economic growth does not necessarily benefit all its residents. Logan and Molotch point

18. "Who's Who: 100 People Who Make Things Happen in South Florida," supp., *South Florida Business Journal*, 29 Apr. 1994.

19. "The Book of Lists," supp., *South Florida Business Journal*, 22 Dec. 1995.

20. Over thirty years ago, Murray Edelman introduced the distinction between symbolic and real politics. The former is the politics that is played out on the front pages of the local newspapers. The latter is the kind that takes place in back rooms and on golf courses, less visible yet more important. See Murray Edelman, *The Symbolic Uses of Politics* (Urbana: University of Illinois Press, 1964).

21. The concept of non-decision-making reflects that the most important decisions are made outside of the formal political process. See Peter Bachrach and Morton Baratz, "Two Faces of Power," *American Political Science Review*, 56:947-52 (1962).

out that "just as new jobs may not change the aggregate rate of employment . . . they may also have little effect on unemployed individuals in a given place."[22] In Miami, the Latin success story overshadows the lot of many less fortunate Hispanics who face a daily struggle in this economically polarized city. More pertinently, in the case of Miami, the twining of growth and internationalization has resulted in social polarization with an important ethnic dimension. Miami's growth strategies tend to deprive Miami's blacks (natives and immigrants, such as Haitians) of equal opportunities in sharing the benefits of growth.

Miami's blacks have found themselves on the sidelines of the city's transformation and without an important role in Miami's growth machine. Growth has occurred mostly in the international sectors of the urban economy, and blacks are not well positioned to benefit from this. For example, black family incomes in 1990 were only 80 percent of Hispanic family incomes. In the same year, 27 percent of black families lived under the official poverty line, as compared to 16 percent of Hispanic families. The unemployment rate in 1990 for blacks was 13 percent, and it was 8 percent for Hispanics. Importantly, in contrast to Hispanics, blacks are also strongly underrepresented in terms of employment in the producer services sector, which has a strong international orientation and is one of Miami's fastest-growing sectors.[23]

The regression of blacks in Miami's development is rarely addressed explicitly in public debates, except by blacks themselves. To be sure, matters of poverty, crime, and homelessness are at the center of attention of the symbolic politics that cover the front pages of the local newspapers. But it is typical of the "underclass" discourse in many American cities in that it negates the role of race or ethnicity.[24] Part of the problem has to do with ideological predispositions of American society at large, but the negation of racial inequality, disharmony, and tension also flows from the logic of the growth machine. Apart from immediate destructive effects on the material environment, internal racial conflict has the potential to derail the growth machine as it damages the city's image and deters foreign investors. Thus structural conflict must be avoided, and, if it persists, it must be downplayed in rhetoric.[25]

Crime is a case in point. Miami's notoriously high crime rates can at least in part be attributed to social polarization, which tends to foster both opportunity (seen in the haves) and motive (on the part of have-nots).

22. Logan and Molotch, *Urban Fortunes*, p. 322.

23. Jan Nijman, "Class, Ethnicity, and the Economic Internationalization of Miami," in *Social Polarization in Post-Industrial Me-* tropolises, ed. J. O'Loughlin and J. Friedrichs (Chicago: Gruyter, 1996).

24. Norman Fainstein, "Race, Class, and Segregation: Discourses About African Americans," *International Journal of Urban and Regional Research*, 17 (1993), reprinted in *Readings in Urban Theory*, ed. S. Fainstein and S. Campbell (Cambridge, MA: Blackwell, 1996), pp. 216-45.

25. Miami has had its share of ethnic conflict. In 1980, Miami witnessed the worst race riots in the history of the United States since the Civil War (in terms of death and material damage), to be superseded only by the Los Angeles riots of 1992.

But while the local news media cover local violent crimes ad nauseum, these are never discussed in terms of race or ethnicity. This leads to remarkably contradictory situations. For example, when tourists are handed maps by car rental agencies showing areas that are unsafe and should be avoided, it will never be explicated that these are black areas. Acknowledgment of a structural race problem runs the risk of exposing structural deficiencies in the way our society is organized, and thus jeopardizes its legitimacy.

Local discourse seldom questions the material effects of Miami's growth strategies on the black population. Instead, it celebrates the virtues of multiculturalism and emphasizes civic pride in the city's international achievements. But to speak convincingly of a single civic community in Miami requires some imagination and not only because of the special position of blacks. One of the tasks of the elite in the urban growth machine that has proven particularly difficult in the case of Miami is to generate and sustain "the place patriotism of the masses."[26]

MIAMI AS A GLOBAL PLACE:
ETHNICITY AND THE
COLOR OF MONEY

In her description of Miami as a world-class trading center, Kantor acknowledged the city's problems in terms of the lack of social cohesiveness and the immaturity of its body politic. This is indeed an issue that threatens the long-term success of Miami's international growth machine, but it is reductionist to view social problems solely in terms of the threat they pose to continued economic growth.[27]

Miami's internationalization has an immediate effect on the social order and everyday lives of people in this city. This goes beyond the uneven distribution of the material benefits of international growth and resulting economic polarization. It is about social capital, rather than money, and about use values rather than exchange values.

Generally, the globalization of ethnic relations has a profound impact on local inter- and intragroup relations. With increased mobility, for many the nature of international migration has changed from a one-way and permanent settlement in a new destination to a much more flexible existence in two places simultaneously. Sociologist Alejandro Portes refers to these migrants as "global villagers," who give rise to "transnational communities."[28] Today's migrants are often capable of maintaining strong ties to the community of origin. While such communities continue to associate with their mother country, a large number of their members may be located in clusters around the world. Examples include San Francisco's Chinatown, Toronto's Greek community, and Miami's Little Haiti.

26. Logan and Molotch, *Urban Fortunes*, p. 299.

27. Another example of this reductionist approach to social problems in cities is Neal R. Peirce, *Citistates: How Urban America Can Prosper in a Competitive World* (Washington, DC: Seven Locks Press, 1993).

28. Alejandro Portes, "Global Villagers: The Rise of Transnational Communities," *American Prospect*, pp. 74-77 (Mar.-Apr. 1996).

But if communities are no longer necessarily place bound, what are the implications for urban areas with diverse population groups? According to Néstor Rodríguez, "Binational existence affects intergroup relations in immigrant settlement areas by reinforcing the immigrants' internal social and cultural infrastructure, reducing dependency on mainstream social resources."[29] Clearly, the implication is that immigrant groups, if they are sufficiently large, cohesive, and mobile, are less likely to assimilate into the existing urban mainstream.

The United States has a long and well-known history of immigration and population diversity. Hyphenated Americanism is a typical feature of that history: urban populations in the United States comprise Irish Americans, African Americans, Arab Americans, Chinese Americans, and so forth. As a rule, however, assimilation would occur, and, insofar as ethnic designations continued to be used, they were little more than folkloric window dressing.

In a city like Miami, however, positioned at the cutting edge of globalization, even hyphenated Americanism seems to be ruled out. Cuban Americans (most are naturalized) are known as Cubans, Nicaraguans are referred to as Nicaraguans, and so on. Presumably, there is little American about many people in this city. A good illustration of Rodríguez's point

about the lack of assimilation with regard to Miami's Cubans is a statement by Carlos Arboleya, one of the city's foremost Cuban businessmen: "Never in the history of the United States has there been such a number of immigrants concentrated in one specific area with an economic and social infrastructure that does not need the regular infrastructure of the place they live."[30]

Rodríguez pointed out that, "unless a common purpose binds them [the different ethnic groups in the same urban area] together, tribal hostilities will drive them apart."[31] As we have seen, Miami's different ethnic elites do indeed share a common purpose in terms of preferred economic growth strategies. But even if the elites share the same interests in the city's growth strategies, the large majorities of the respective ethnic groups remain largely segregated. This is true for blacks, as discussed earlier, but also for native whites and various Hispanic populations. Seen from this angle, Miami is at the forefront of the "disuniting of America."[32]

Money can function to bridge those gaps to some extent or to render one's ethnic identity partially irrelevant. But this solution applies only to the wealthy. Thus rich Hispanics and non-Hispanics live side by side in the affluent neighborhoods of Key Bis-

---

29. Néstor P. Rodríguez, "The Real 'New World Order': The Globalization of Racial and Ethnic Relations in the Late Twentieth Century," in The Bubbling Cauldron: Race, Ethnicity, and the Urban Crisis, ed. M. P. Smith and J. R. Feagin (Minneapolis: University of Minnesota Press, 1995), p. 215.

30. Pamela Varley, Language and the Melting Pot: Florida's 1988 "Official English" Referendum, Case #C-16-90-990 (Cambridge: MA: Harvard University, John F. Kennedy School of Government, 1990), p. 9.

31. Rodríguez, "The Real 'New World Order,'" p. 216.

32. Arthur M. Schlesinger, Jr., The Disuniting of America (New York: Norton, 1992).

cayne or Coral Gables, whereas many other Hispanics and blacks inhabit the more segregated areas of Hialeah (Hispanic) or Liberty City (black). Class overshadows ethnicity only in the upper echelons.

GLOBALIZATION AND CIVIC SOCIETY

The lack of community or unity in Miami affects the daily lives of many inhabitants of this city. It is striking how many people claim that they are here only temporarily, even if they have no firm future plans to relocate. Many live their lives within the confines of their own group—if they have one. Confronted with the city's transitory character, few seem intent on investing in their social environment. Newcomers to this city tend to experience Miami's social climate as cold and have difficulty in forging a social network that extends beyond their own ethnic group. At a different level, this lack of sociability and social control is reflected in the exceedingly large number of gated residential communities in Miami (reminiscent of some Latin American cities with their highly stratified social structure) and thriving security businesses.

The relative weakness of the social contract in this city, and the lack of a solid civic culture that spans all ethnic groups, may well play a part in the city's high crime rates.[33] Miami

acquired its notorious reputation for crime in the early 1980s. The *New York Times* of 23 December 1980 reported on its front page that crime had gone "berserk" in Miami, allegedly exceeding the crime rates in places like Los Angeles and New York.[34] In 1981, a *Time* magazine article depicted the city of Miami as a "paradise lost." In a ten-page cover story, it presented an extremely bleak and harsh picture of life in South Florida.[35] It suggested that the social costs of Miami's rapid growth and extraordinary development had been too high. Besides the direct problems caused by high immigration and ethnic tensions, the deteriorating image of Miami was closely linked to an impressive increase in crime.

The year 1980 was unusually violent, but in subsequent years Miami has not been able to rid itself of its image as a high-crime city. According to statistics of the Federal Bureau of Investigation, Miami ranked first in total crime among the nation's 79 large metropolitan areas in 1992 and 1993. It also ranked first in violent crime.[36] Miami acquired particular notoriety for the murders of tourists after a string of eight killings in a span of nine months ending in Sep-

33. The contrasting cases of Miami and Tokyo suggest a relationship between cultural diversity, civic culture, and crime. See Jan Nijman, "Wereldsteden in het proces van mondialisering," *Amsterdams sociologisch tijdschrift*, 22:206-24 (1995).

34. "Crime Termed 'Berserk' in Miami: Refugees and Drugs Blamed in Part," *New York Times*, 23 Dec. 1980.

35. "Trouble in Paradise: South Florida Is Hit by a Hurricane of Crime, Drugs and Refugees," *Time*, 23 Nov. 1981, pp. 22-32. Besides rising crime rates, the article was inspired by the Mariel boatlift, the race riots, and the influx of Haitian refugees, all of which converged in 1980.

36. Department of Justice, *Crime in the United States*, Uniform Crime Reports (Washington, DC: Department of Justice, 1994).

tember 1993.[37] It was at this juncture that the aforementioned maps were distributed by car rental agencies.

Materialism, as I indicated earlier, sometimes seems to function to compensate for Miami's social poverty. This penchant for materialism, in turn, implies that Miami lacks the social constraints on growth found in most other cities. Potentially corrective forces in defense of a collective civic culture and in opposition to the forces of growth are weak. The often-referred-to relationship between globalism and localism, in the sense of place-rooted reactionary movements against the perceived threats of globalization,[38] is virtually absent because so few of Miami's inhabitants are in fact rooted in this city. There are minimal constraints on the growth machine.

Ironically, the narratives generated by the growth machine emphasize the multicultural values of globalization, rather than the monetary rewards. The *Miami Herald*, again, can be seen to play a crucial role in the mobilization of these cultural motivations. The editorial columns show how the paper fits the role attributed to it by Logan and Molotch, constantly underscoring the reasons for civic pride in Miami's international achievements and holding Miami up as a shining example of multiculturalism to the rest of the nation.[39]

In a recent book, the Chinese American geographer Yi-Fu Tuan debates the importance to most human beings—even cosmopolites—of both the enlightenment of the "cosmos" and the comfort of the "hearth."[40] In its benign form, the hearth represents the trusted and familiar environment of the home, where there is a collective attachment to place and a sense of belonging. The cosmos, on the other hand, is the scale of worldliness, diversity, individual freedom, and rationality.

There is no question that, apart from economic gains, globalization brings a world of excitement, cultural enrichment, and broadening horizons. To the cosmopolites among us, Miami is an ultimately interesting city, a laboratory of urban change in the global era. But it is also the scene of the expansion of the cosmos and the fraying of the hearth. If cities are synonymous with civilization, Miami provides us with a glimpse of the fate of civilization in the global era.

What is at stake in Miami and other globalized cities is a social order and civility that do not come naturally, as in the environment of the traditional hearth. In a place like Miami, they have to be rationalized by enlightened cosmopolites. Tuan describes the ideal as follows: "Bonding based on propinquity and kinship is natural to us. By contrast, kindness to strangers who may not reciprocate and civility in impersonal transactions

37. "Tourist Is Killed in Florida Despite Taking Precautions," *New York Times*, 9 Sept. 1993.

38. See Zdravko Mlinar, ed., *Globalization and Territorial Identities* (Aldershot: Avebury, 1992).

39. Multiculturalism is a typical product of white Western culture, which reduces its vi-

ability in a setting where Western whites are a minority. In Miami, blacks and Hispanics rarely use the word.

40. Yi-Fu Tuan, *Cosmos and Hearth: A Cosmopolite's Viewpoint* (Minneapolis: University of Minnesota Press, 1996).

are a watermark achievement of civilization."[41] Herein lies a challenge of immense proportions to metropolitan Miami and other cities at the forefront of globalization: the making of the city into a cosmopolitan hearth.

41. Ibid., p. 40.

ANNALS, *AAPSS*, **551**, May 1997

Chicago's New Immigrants, Indigenous Poor, and Edge Cities

By RICHARD P. GREENE

ABSTRACT: The settlement pattern of new immigrants in the Chicago urban region diverges significantly from previous immigration periods, when employment was concentrated in the urban core. In recent decades, the rate of employment decentralization in the Chicago area has accelerated, giving rise to edge cities, which are acquiring an increasing share of the region's total employment. As a result, the new immigrants are in a far more favorable geographic position than the region's indigenous poor to compete in the local unskilled labor market. Meanwhile, with the absence of new immigrants settling the region's traditional port-of-entry neighborhoods, thus not replacing the exiting middle class, large sections of Chicago's urban core are being bypassed, further isolating the indigenous poor from the economic mainstream.

Richard P. Greene is currently associate professor of geography at Northern Illinois University. He has written on population redistribution, urban poverty, and the land conversion process at the urban-rural fringe.

THE assimilation of immigrants and other minority populations into American urban life has been a persistent theme in the urban policy and sociology literature. The focus of much of the current research on this topic concerns the degree of residential segregation among African Americans and the new immigrants, primarily composed of Hispanics and Asians, relative to their nonminority counterparts.[1] The existing research on the segregation of African Americans and new immigrants within metropolitan regions does not adequately address an important component of assimilation, namely, the degree to which immigrants and African Americans are spatially integrated within the metropolitan economy. Such an analysis requires an examination of the geographic distributions of African Americans, immigrants, and native-born whites relative not only to each other but also to the geographic distribution of jobs.

Many of the old models describing the entrance of immigrants into cities recognized that the new arrivals moved into neighborhoods that adjoined either the central business district or industrial districts close to the city center. In light of recent employment shifts out of central cities and the growth of employment in outlying "edge cities,"[2] there is a need to reexamine the residential patterns of the new immigrants relative to the changing employment geography of metropolitan areas.

In this article, the spatial distribution of jobs and the new immigrants are examined for Chicago and its neighboring suburbs. The importance of this study is that the global economy, characterized by flexible production and the growth of producer services,[3] is fueling the growth of Chicago's edge cities at the expense of its inner core; thus the new immigrants entering this transformed metropolis are encountering a different employment landscape from that encountered by the immigrants that came before them. An important side effect of the changing geography of immigrant enclaves within metropolitan regions is that the old neighborhood ports of entry, now occupied by the indigenous poor population of the region, are becoming increasingly obsolete. For Chicago, this zone includes many of the neighborhoods of the West Side and South Side of Chicago, whose indigenous poverty population is composed primarily of poor African Americans, recently referred to as the "underclass."[4]

The changing spatial pattern of jobs in metropolitan regions is being driven in large part by the increasing flexibility in the spatial organization of economic production.[5] The domi-

1. The phrase "new immigrants," appears in Alvar W. Carlson, "America's New Immigration: Characteristics, Destinations, and Impact, 1970-1989," *Social Science Journal*, 31(3):213-36 (1994).

2. Joel Garreau, *Edge City: Life on the New Frontier* (New York: Doubleday, 1988).

3. Peter Dicken, *Global Shift: The Internationalization of Economic Activity*, 2d ed. (New York: Guilford Press, 1992).

4. William J. Wilson, *The Truly Disadvantaged: The Inner City, the Underclass, and Public Policy* (Chicago: University of Chicago Press, 1987).

5. Paul Knox, "The Restless Urban Landscape: Economic and Sociocultural Change and the Transformation of Metropolitan Washington, DC," *Annals of the Association of American Geographers*, 81(2):181-209 (1991).

nant trend in the geographic redistribution of jobs in recent years has been the shift from the central city to the suburbs. Although the topic of suburban employment growth has received much attention, particularly since the publication of Joel Garreau's *Edge City*,[6] surprisingly few studies have considered its impact on the new immigrants' choice of residence within metropolitan areas. Yet the principal motivation for an immigrant's settlement choice is economic.[7] Thus an edge-city destination is likely to hold more economic promise for a new immigrant than an inner-city neighborhood that has experienced a decline in its industrial job base.

The modern-day edge-city landscape of Chicago stands in stark contrast to the nineteenth-century industrial landscape depicted in the Chicago school's classic model of immigrants in the city where employment was centered in an inner zone known as the central business district (CBD).[8] Immigrants, according to this classic model, initially inhabited a low-rent zone, referred to as the "zone in transition," which was adjacent to the CBD. Second-generation immigrants, those who had improved their economic standing, subsequently occupied the next outlying zone, "the zone of workingmen's homes." Because this model used social Darwinism and other tenets of plant ecology to explain the changing

spatial patterns of immigrants in the city, social scientists have long since dismissed many of the Chicago school's generalizations. Nonetheless, an understanding of the relationship between immigrants, jobs, and residential location is an important contribution of the Chicago school that has withstood the test of time. Warf, for example, has criticized modern urban studies of neighborhood change for abandoning these contributions of social ecology and constructing an "artificial chasm between 'social' and 'economic' geography, a division that assumes people either live or work in cities but do not do both."[9]

This article will demonstrate, through the analysis of the spatial distribution of jobs and the foreign-born population, that a significant number of the Chicago area's new immigrants are bypassing the traditional "zone in transition" for emerging job opportunities in the region's edge cities. While the new immigrants are bypassing the low-rent areas close to the city center, middle-class African Americans are abandoning these same areas at unprecedented rates. In the absence of sufficient demand, these bypassed neighborhoods have fallen into a cycle of landscape dereliction that is characterized by the decay of public infrastructure and large-scale abandonment of housing.[10]

6. Garreau, *Edge City*.

7. George J. Borjas, *Friends or Strangers: The Impact of Immigrants on the U.S. Economy* (New York: Basic Books, 1990).

8. Robert Park and Ernest Burgess, *The City* (Chicago: University of Chicago Press, 1925).

9. Barney Warf, "The Reconstruction of Social Ecology and Neighborhood Change in Brooklyn," *Environment and Planning D: Society and Space*, 8:76 (1990).

10. John A. Jakle and David Wilson, *Derelict Landscapes* (Savage, MD: Rowman & Littlefield, 1992).

DATA

This study is based on 1980 and 1990 census tract data on population characteristics including race, ethnicity, poverty, immigrant status, and year of entry into the United States. For employment information, the unit of analysis is the quarter-section, which has been adopted by the Chicago Area Transportation Study (CATS) for transportation planning purposes. Quarter-sections, normally 0.25 square miles in area, are part of the rectangular land-survey system of the region.

STUDY AREA

The official Chicago Consolidated Metropolitan Statistical Area (CMSA) now comprises 13 counties, of which 10 are in Illinois, 2 in Indiana, and 1 in Wisconsin, with a total of 6931 square miles and 8.2 million population in 1990. However, the CATS data files do not include the Indiana and Wisconsin counties and provide only limited coverage of four Illinois counties—Grundy, Kendall, DeKalb, and Kankakee—that were added to the CMSA in 1983 and 1992. CATS's emphasis is on the six-county area that formed the Illinois portion of the Chicago metropolitan area from 1959 to 1983.

Within the six-county area, three counties were chosen as the study area (see Figure 1). These are Cook County, at the core of the urban area; DuPage County, a rapidly developing suburban and outlying employment area south and west of Cook County; and Kane County, containing two satellite cities, Aurora and Elgin, which continued to be on the outer edge of heavy commuting and suburbanization into the 1990s. The remaining three counties—Lake, McHenry, and Will—were omitted because each has sizable areas for which place-of-work coding to areas as small as quarter-sections were not available. The study area includes 95.4 percent of the 1990 population of the six-county area and 88.2 percent of its jobs.

CHICAGO'S CHANGING EMPLOYMENT LANDSCAPE

The geographic distribution of jobs within the study area follows the historical progression of settlement within the greater Chicago region as demonstrated by the nodal and radial orientation of job density (see Figure 1). Job density is highest within the city center but sizable job corridors emanate from the center, with several satellite job centers strung out along the Fox River on the metropolitan fringe, including Elgin to the north and Aurora to the south. Smaller job concentrations correspond to suburban rail lines along the Lake Michigan shore, northwest, west (all three associated with suburban lines of the Chicago & Northwestern), and southwest (the Burlington). The interstate highway system has also reinforced the earlier railroad orientation of employment, particularly those clusters of employment along the East-West (I-88) and Northwest (I-90) tollways.

A procedure for delineating employment concentrations, based on a design from a previous study,[11] was

11. Richard Greene and Richard Forstall, "Spatial Patterns of Population and Job Distribution in the Chicago Urban Area, 1990 and 1980" (Paper delivered at the annual confer-

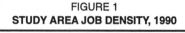

FIGURE 1
STUDY AREA JOB DENSITY, 1990

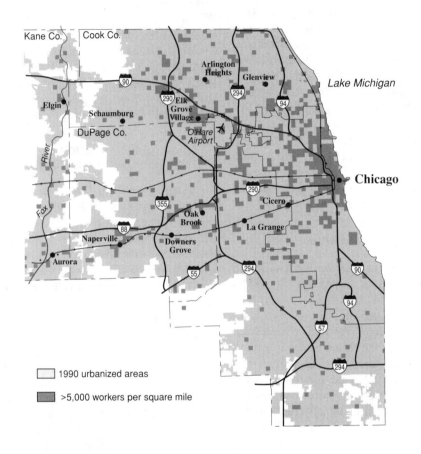

used for identifying job clusters in the three-county study area. In this procedure, each worker concentration includes at least one quarter-section with 1000 or more jobs per square mile and an employment/residence ratio of 1.25 or greater, or net in-commuting of at least 25 percent. Follow-

ence of the Association of American Geographers, Chicago, IL, 15 Mar. 1995).

ing this procedure, 209 concentrations of at least 500 jobs were defined, many of which were located outside the city of Chicago.

West and northwest of downtown Chicago, the suburban zone of the region is scattered with job concentrations, especially dense in parts of northern Cook County and in central DuPage County. The downtown Chicago cluster, which includes 586,000 jobs, represents the largest job concentration, with no other single cluster even approaching 100,000. The study area's second-largest concentration is found in the area comprising the community of Elk Grove Village and some adjacent locations, situated just beyond O'Hare Airport (see Figure 2). This area contains 90,000 jobs, with just over half in industry (manufacturing, mining, and wholesaling). In the 1960s, rapid development of industry occurred here, primarily in the form of planned industrial parks. O'Hare itself ranks eighth (42,000 jobs), and nearby Rosemont, dominated by hotels and other airport-related activities, is responsible for another 23,500 jobs. Des Plaines, with the tenth-largest concentration (34,000 jobs, 43 percent in manufacturing or wholesaling), adjoins both Rosemont and Elk Grove Village. Northwest of the O'Hare cluster lies the fifth-largest concentration, Schaumburg, with 45,000 jobs. Schaumburg is home to the region's largest shopping mall. Schaumburg, which was an entirely rural community in 1950, experienced rapid development after 1970.

On the east edge of DuPage County is Oak Brook, developed since the late 1950s and ranking ninth in the region, with 41,000 jobs, with retailing prominent. West of Oak Brook, along the Research and Development Corridor,[12] is Naperville, one of the more diversified concentra-

12. The East-West Tollway, also known as Route 88, has been designated the "Research and Development Corridor" because of the large volume of research and development being conducted by high-technology firms and government facilities along this stretch of highway.

tions within the Chicago CMSA. With 30,000 jobs, Naperville ranks twelfth in the region. Formerly a rural village and home to a small college, Naperville has undergone rapid suburban development, particularly since 1980.

Suburban
 employment growth

In order to display the geographic pattern of job growth in the region from 1980 to 1990, Figure 3 shows the 1980-90 percentage change in the number of jobs for incorporated places in the three-county study area with at least 5000 jobs in 1990. Chicago proper showed a job loss during the decade, while places outside of Chicago experienced an overall gain in jobs. At the county level, the fastest-growing areas were in DuPage County (50.1 percent), followed by Kane County and suburban Cook County. Nearly all increases of 50 percent or greater took place in DuPage or northwest Cook counties. The Fox Valley cities generally showed modest gains, such as 19 percent in Aurora, although Elgin suffered a slight loss.

Within the suburban area, the largest places tended to grow more rapidly than the smaller ones. Among the places with at least 25,000 jobs, Naperville in DuPage had by far the greatest job growth, 165.7 percent. This was followed by Arlington Heights, in northwest Cook County (87.2 percent), and Glenview, in north Cook County (83.9 percent). Growth also was substantial in Downers Grove, in DuPage (52.1 percent) and Schaumburg, in northwest

FIGURE 2
SELECTED SUBURBAN EMPLOYMENT CENTERS

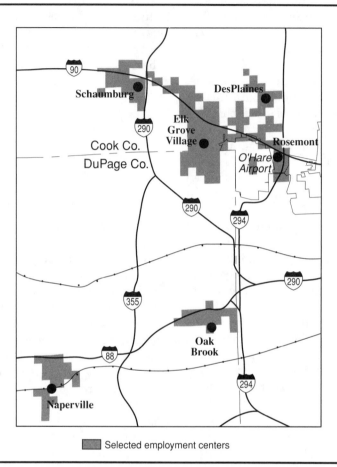

Selected employment centers

Cook (35.9 percent). On the other hand, Elk Grove Village grew only 10.9 percent, and Oak Brook had a job increase of only 7.9 percent.

Most newer suburbs had rapid job increases, but the pattern for older suburbs (those developed chiefly before 1940) was quite mixed. Immediately west, north, and south of Chicago in Cook County are old suburbs that have sustained job losses since 1980. Some of these losses were extreme, such as in Cicero (–44.8 percent, a loss of nearly 15,000 jobs), Northlake (–37.0 percent), and La Grange (–34.9 percent). In most, if not all, of these places, losses within the manufacturing sector accounted for the majority of lost jobs.

Although Chicago as a whole lost about 68,000 jobs (–4.7 percent), the downtown zone gained slightly (15,000 jobs, or 2.6 percent) during the same period. This gain was con-

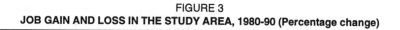

FIGURE 3
JOB GAIN AND LOSS IN THE STUDY AREA, 1980-90 (Percentage change)

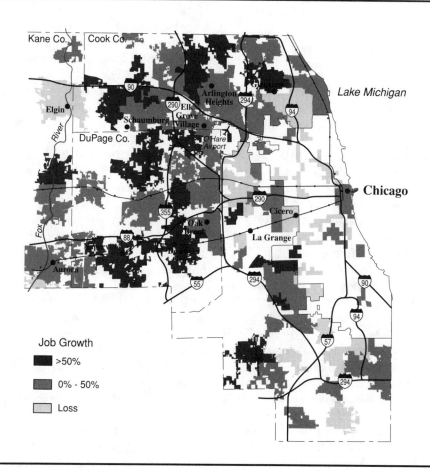

centrated on the western edge of the CBD, which is immediately west of the Chicago River. New office construction in the 1980s helped to expand the employment base from 48,000 to 81,000. Nearly all other areas within the city demonstrated declining employment bases during the decade, particularly the industrial areas along the belt railways. Exceptions that showed significant gains were the South Fork–Central Manufacturing area and the Burnside area north of Lake Calumet. A few large nonindustrial concentrations within the city fared much better; for example, employment opportunities in the vicinity of Midway Airport increased by 75 percent. Hyde Park, the neighborhood that is home to the University of Chicago, experienced a job increase of 19.7 percent. As a result of these spurious exceptions, job concentrations overall in the city of Chicago increased slightly, while the balance of the city, outside concentrations, lost at least 15 percent of its jobs.

CHICAGO'S NEW IMMIGRANTS

The term "new immigrants" refers to the changing number and composition of legal immigrants to the United States, which has gone from primarily European prior to the 1965 Immigration and Nationality Act amendments to primarily Latin American and Asian after 1965.[13] Borjas has shown that, with the exception of some European and Asian groups, the post-1965 immigrants tend to be less educated and less skilled, arrive with less money, and make less income than pre-1965 immigrants.[14] This would seem to discount the argument that the new immigrants would be more apt to suburbanize because of their higher skill levels. Indeed, it is the growth in suburban jobs, in all industrial sectors, that is luring immigrants to the suburbs.

Approximately 8 million legal immigrants entered the United States during the 1980s, and Illinois and five other states together received 75 percent of all newly arriving immigrants. Furthermore, outside of the Southwest, only Illinois has a sizable Mexican immigrant population. Chicago ranks behind only Los Angeles and Houston in Mexican population for metropolitan areas.[15] Frey has ob-

served a demographic "balkanization" as a result of the concentration of Asian and Hispanic immigrants in a small number of metropolitan statistical areas with especially high rates of out-migration of native-born populations.[16] The result of this balkanization is that selected metropolitan areas are disproportionately increasing their share of immigrants while others are disproportionately gaining in native-born populations. The Chicago metropolitan area has been designated a high-immigration metropolitan area, implying an increase in its minority population as a result of the arrival of new Hispanic and Asian immigrants and an out-migration that is largely white.[17] Frey's notion of a demographic balkanization can also be extrapolated inside metropolitan areas where the new immigrants compete with native-born populations for low-skilled jobs and affordable housing. This is especially important, as Borjas[18] notes that immigrants can displace less-skilled workers.

A number of studies have shown the relationship of migration flows to the push factors of poor economic conditions of the origin country,[19] while others have highlighted the importance of pull factors such as job opportunities and relatives in the United

13. Carlson, "America's New Immigration."
14. Borjas, *Friends or Strangers.*
15. Kevin E. McHugh, "Hispanic Migration and Population Redistribution in the United States," *Professional Geographer*, 41(4):429-39 (1989).

16. William H. Frey, "Immigration and Internal Migration 'Flight' from US Metropolitan Areas: Toward a New Demographic Balkanisation," *Urban Studies*, 32:733-57 (1995).
17. Ibid.
18. Borjas, *Friends or Strangers.*
19. Douglas Massey et al., *Return to Aztlan: The Social Process of International Migration from Western Mexico* (Berkeley: University of California Press, 1987).

States.[20] Early research suggested that, once in the United States, immigrants congregated in enclaves close to the CBD.[21] However, with the suburbanization of job centers, discussed earlier, the locational patterns of immigrant settlements have altered to reflect the changing location of employment. In addition, the immigrants entering the United States today are more likely to have relatives living in the suburbs than did previous generations of immigrants. By settling in suburban locations, new immigrants may discover job opportunities, through a variety of information channels, well before unemployed low-skilled workers living in the inner city learn of the opportunities.

Chicago's new immigrant zones

New immigrants are defined in the following analysis as the difference between a census tract's 1990 foreign-born population and its 1980 foreign-born population. A positive value implies that the tract has experienced an influx of immigrants during the 1980s, although some of these new immigrants could conceivably have been born abroad prior to 1980 if they had arrived at another port before entering the Chicago region, or a positive value could also imply redistribution from and to other tracts within the study area. Thus a mere increase in the foreign-born population of a tract between 1980

20. Borjas, *Friends or Strangers*.
21. David Ward, *Cities and Immigrants: A Geography of Change in Nineteenth Century America* (New York: Oxford University Press, 1971).

and 1990 does not necessarily imply an influx of recent immigrants. It is also not possible to cross-tabulate race and ethnicity with the foreign-born population at the scale of a census tract; as a result, the new immigrants, as defined here, may originate from places outside Latin America and Asia. To overcome these shortcomings, map overlays of race and ethnicity variables, as well as year-of-entry information, will be used to illustrate that, in many cases, the tracts with increases in foreign-born populations are the same areas with increases in Asians and Hispanics, herein referred to as the new immigrants.

As discussed earlier, Chicago's Loop remains the principal employment magnet for its urban region; however, the overall trend of the Chicago region's job growth in recent years has shifted west to northwest and away from the urban core. Similar to the spatial distribution of jobs, the foreign-born population of the Chicago region is also shifting west to northwest (Figure 4). Sustained immigrant clusters, defined as census tracts with 25 percent or more of the 1990 population born abroad, are all located within the city limits of Chicago. Similar to the pattern of job density, the highest-density immigrant neighborhoods are still located within the confines of the city of Chicago. However, it is worth noting the large number of census tracts with emerging immigrant clusters outside the city that experienced increases of 500 or more foreign-born persons since 1980. The substantial increase in the number of immigrants outside the city of Chicago has shifted the

FIGURE 4
IMMIGRANT AREA TYPES IN THE STUDY AREA

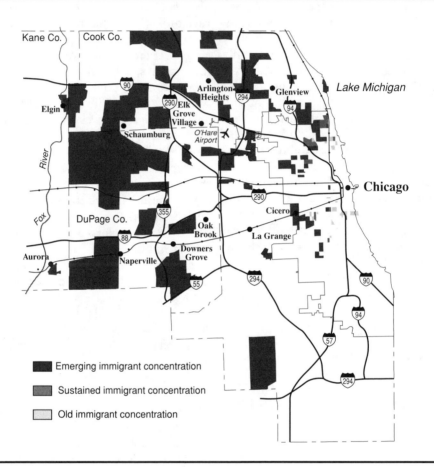

geographic center of the region's immigrant population in a northwest direction, which is an orientation that corresponds with the directional shift in the overall population and jobs for the Chicago region. Most of the sustained immigrant clusters gained in foreign-born population, while a handful closest to the city center experienced losses or only modest gains.

The relationship between Chicago's new immigrants and its indigenous poor

The most significant demographic trend for the Chicago region in recent decades has been population redistribution from the core of the region to its periphery. The most noticeable effect of this redistribution has been

FIGURE 5
JOB AND DEMOGRAPHIC MOVEMENTS IN THE STUDY AREA, 1980-90

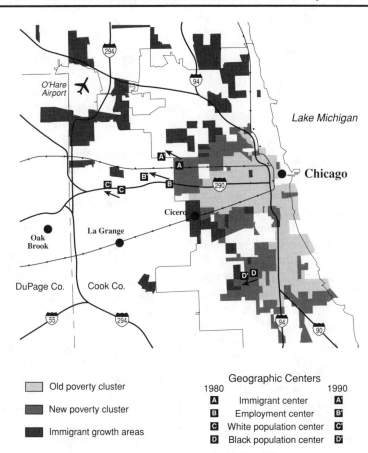

	Geographic Centers	
	1980	1990
Old poverty cluster	**A** Immigrant center	**A'**
New poverty cluster	**B** Employment center	**B'**
Immigrant growth areas	**C** White population center	**C'**
	D Black population center	**D'**

large-scale abandonment of housing in many of Chicago's inner-city neighborhoods, while the urban fringe, on the opposite side of the region, has been the recipient of large-scale reinvestment in its built environment. Although significant, the number of immigrants entering Chicago has not been able to offset the number of people leaving the region or relocating to its outlying suburbs. In the wake of the mass exodus of Chicago's middle class, the new immigrants find themselves with more housing choices than they would otherwise have if the immigrant flow were of a sufficient magnitude to offset the flow out of the city.

In order to illustrate where immigrants are locating relative to the declining areas of the core, Figure 5 shows that Chicago's largest contiguous poverty clusters, which are city areas experiencing the greatest population decline, do not correspond very well with immigrant growth areas. Most of the correspondence between the two area types, immigrant growth areas and poverty clusters, occurs on the outer edge of the poverty clusters. The population declines and subsequent territorial expansion of these poverty clusters have been well documented.[22] The area referred to in the figure as the old poverty cluster was built up prior to 1980 and has experienced high rates of population decline. The new poverty cluster emerged during the 1980s on the edge of the old poverty cluster as a result of a large exodus of middle-class African Americans. Meanwhile, many of the immigrants entering the region during this same period of poverty area expansion bypassed the inner poverty cluster and settled on the periphery of the outer poverty cluster or in areas entirely outside of the poverty clusters. As a consequence, between 1980 and 1990, the geographic center of the immigrant population moved northwest, in the same general direction and distance as the geographic centers of the white population and jobs. The outward migration of middle-class African Americans and the subsequent suburbanization oriented to the south are reflected in the southwest shift of the geographic center

of the African American population distribution.

CONCLUSION

The high employment growth rates exhibited by the outlying ring of municipalities surrounding the city of Chicago are an obvious magnet for new immigrants in search of job opportunities. The west-to-northwest suburban orientation in job and immigrant growth follows axial sectors established early on in the development of the Chicago region. The old port-of-entry neighborhoods and low-rent areas, close to the urban center, are not attracting new immigrants at a rate sufficient to offset the recent population declines incurred there by the outward migration of African Americans to the suburbs. As a result, these old bypassed neighborhoods are becoming the locus of the region's indigenous poor who are economically disadvantaged by location. The new immigrants, on the other hand, have been settling on the periphery of the region's traditional port-of-entry neighborhoods and are thus more strategically located with respect to the region's geographic distribution of jobs. Further employment and population decentralization in the Chicago region will continue to affect the residential decision process of new immigrants, while the indigenous poor, geographically isolated from the economic mainstream, will find it increasingly difficult to compete for the region's low-skilled jobs.

22. Richard P. Greene, "Poverty-Area Instability: The Case of Chicago," *Urban Geography*, 15(4):362-75 (1994).

ANNALS, *AAPSS*, **551**, May 1997

Globalization and the
Inner Periphery: A Mid-Bronx View

By RAY BROMLEY

ABSTRACT: The globalization literature on New York and other metropolises has focused mainly on control centers of the world system, typically located in central business districts, edge cities, transportation hubs, technology parks, and exclusive residential areas. The remainder of the metropolis is often depicted as just a source of labor power and consumers. Taking the case of CB-Six, a bureaucratically defined locality and low-income residential area in the Bronx, this article reviews the global dimensions of local history in the outer boroughs of New York City. Local and global issues are tightly interwoven through the changing numbers and origins of immigrants and through the impact of world wars, economic crises, and restructuring. The locality affects the world through its real and fictional roles in popular entertainment and through the missions of Fordham University, the Bronx Zoo, the Botanical Garden, and such bygone institutions as the Home for Incurables and the Starlight Amusement Park. Glory or notoriety could have resulted from silent movies, political assassination, soap opera, mass murder, or music and movie stars, but CB-Six never reached the Hall of Fame!

Ray Bromley is professor of geography and planning at the State University of New York at Albany. He has published extensively on urban, regional, and national planning and on casual labor and petty trading. His current research is on planning history, with case studies of the Bronx and Peru.

N EW York, often nicknamed "the Capital of the World," is in many senses the archetypal global city. The 1929 Wall Street crash triggered the worldwide Great Depression, New York City is the seat of the United Nations, and the Manhattan skyline is probably the world's best-known cityscape. Despite some recent losses to Washington and to Sunbelt cities, the New York metropolitan region (NYMR)[1] still boasts an impressive array of transnational corporations, foundations, and think tanks headquartered in Manhattan or in elite suburbs and edge cities like White Plains, Stamford, and Princeton. The NYMR is also one of the world's premier financial, news media, entertainment, and fashion centers, with some of the leading universities, museums, galleries, concert halls, and theaters.

During most of U.S. history, New York City has been the nation's principal gateway for foreign immigration, and immigrants have come from virtually every country on earth. New York has been variously dubbed "gateway," "global hub," "melting pot," "mosaic," and "stepping stone to the suburbs and the west," and it has fulfilled all these roles to some degree. The NYMR has generated numerous technological and cultural innovations, and it has developed many forms of cultural syncretism. New York has broadcast new forms of food, music, dance, dress, speech, journalism, radio, film, and television, and

these have been consumed, enjoyed, imitated, and reproduced in many countries.

Despite the depth and breadth of New York's global city status, and the ongoing globalization process in the world as a whole, New York is also a major center for local, parochial, and peculiar activities and sentiments. Most New Yorkers do not spend their lives constantly tuned into world affairs or playing a pivotal role in the world capitalist system. They play modest, globally trivial roles, just like most people in other parts of the world: parents, infants, homemakers, homeless, retirees, invalids, officials, cleaners, cops, construction workers, welfare recipients, and many more.

Most of the news watched, heard, and read in the NYMR focuses on such topics as weather, sports, crime, accidents, scandal, and celebrity gossip—standard media fare in most of the world. The news stories that catch the popular imagination are intensely personal and local. Just as Nero apocryphally fiddled while Rome burned, New Yorkers have used Amy, Joey, the Donald, Woody, Mia, Son of Sam, Iron Mike, and the never ending machinations of George Steinbrenner to keep themselves amused. New York's status as a global media center is not based on the breadth of its inhabitants' global vision. Instead, it is associated with the concentration of media corporations, the frequent use of the city as a setting for movies and television, and the constant projection of local gossip celebrities to a global audience.

The global image of New York, and the overwhelming majority of tourist

1. In this article, the NYMR is the Regional Plan Association's 31-county, tristate area. NYMR statistics are taken from Robert D. Yaro and Tony Hiss, *A Region at Risk* (Washington, DC: Island Press, 1996).

activity, is focused on Manhattan south of 125th Street. Many books about New York tourism, entertainment, and night life mention nowhere else or confine the remainder of the metropolitan region to brief sections at the end entitled "Airport Access," "Outer Boroughs," or "Suburbs and Beyond." Manhattan south of 125th Street *is* New York in so many ways. The major corporations, foundations, and organizations, the wealthy residents and highly skilled and creative workers, the entrepreneurs and the tourists who have moved beyond this area have usually chosen the outer suburbs of the NYMR or another region of the country. They have leapfrogged the inner city, the outer boroughs, and suburban cities like Yonkers, Hempstead, and Jersey City.

Nevertheless, of course, the four outer boroughs (the Bronx, Brooklyn, Queens, and Staten Island) and Manhattan north of 125th Street are important as places of residence and work for many ordinary New Yorkers. They account for 85 percent of the New York City population and 34 percent of the NYMR population and 90 percent of the New York City and 2.25 percent of the NYMR land area.

This article focuses on Bronx Community Board 6 (CB-Six), a 1.5-square-mile area at the geographical center of the borough. It is one of dozens of seemingly ordinary localities in the outer boroughs—never a transportation hub or a center for corporate headquarters, elite residence, or commerce. For over a century, CB-Six has been a cluster of ordinary, low- to lower-middle-income residential neighborhoods, one

of many in a city famous for big government, Manhattan centralism, and ethnic politics. It provides a case study of globalization at the local level in the outer boroughs, the "inner periphery" of what many would consider the twentieth century's premier global city.[2] The prime topics discussed will be immigration, metropolitan growth, popular entertainment, world wars, and political assassinations, five seemingly disconnected fields of study that interconnect in CB-Six and across the world.

CB-SIX: DEFINITION AND DEMOGRAPHY

New York City's Community Boards originated in the 1960s and were formally delimited in the 1975 City Charter revision, which divided the city into 59 board territories.[3] CB-Six is coterminous with Police Precinct 48 and includes most of Community School District 12 and parts of School Districts 9 and 10. In this article, the name "CB-Six" is projected backward to identify the territory of the current Community Board long before the boards were established. The use of the name "CB-Six" emphasizes that my focus is a spe-

2. Martin Shefter, ed., *Capital of the American Century* (New York: Russell Sage Foundation, 1993). For socioeconomic data on CB-Six, see New York City, Department of City Planning, *Socioeconomic Profiles* (New York: Department of City Planning, 1993); ibid., *Demographic Profiles*.

3. Peter Marcuse, "Neighborhood Policy and the Distribution of Power: New York City's Community Boards," *Policy Studies Journal*, 16(2):277-89 (Winter 1987); Robert F. Pecorella, *Community Power in a Postreform City* (Armonk, NY: M. E. Sharpe, 1994), pp. 97-190.

cific, bureaucratically defined territory, specified by boundaries that encompass a constantly changing population of individuals, households, communities, and neighborhoods.

CB-Six consists of several adjacent, overlapping, and very loosely defined neighborhoods—West Farms, Bronx Park South, East Tremont, Belmont, Fordham, Bathgate North, Fairmount, and Crotona Park North. Neighborhood names and approximate boundaries have varied over the last century, and many residents find it easier to define location by naming streets, intersections, buildings, or housing projects. CB-Six is bounded by Webster Avenue to the west, the Cross-Bronx Expressway and Crotona Park to the south, the Bronx River Parkway to the east, and Bronx Park to the northeast.

From early colonial times, there was some dispersed rural settlement in what is now CB-Six, and in the 1810s the village of West Farms emerged as a small manufacturing and commercial center by the Bronx River. It was not until the late nineteenth century, however, that large-scale subdivision and settlement affected most of CB-Six. The population of CB-Six rose from under 15,000 in 1890, to 102,000 in 1920, and to 136,000 in 1940—the all-time high. The 1920 census reported that 41.5 percent of the population was foreign-born, the principal immigrant origins being Italian and Russian (including Ukranian), followed by German, Austrian, Irish, Polish, British, Romanian, Swedish, French, and Canadian. Forty different national origins were specifically recorded, in-

cluding a few immigrants from Latin America, the Middle East, and Australia. While Americans of Irish, German, British, and Scandinavian extraction predominated in the nineteenth century, by the 1920s the southern part of CB-Six's population was mainly of East European Jewish extraction, while Belmont / Fordham, the northern neighborhood, was overwhelmingly Italian.[4]

By 1950 the population of CB-Six had fallen to 125,000, and by 1960, to 108,000. The total population held stable in the 1960s but fell dramatically in the 1970s to a low of 63,000 in 1980. From 1940 to 1980, CB-Six lost over half its total population, partly due to rising living standards, moves to better housing in New York City, suburbanization, and migration to other regions, and partly due to numerous public infrastructure and urban renewal projects, as well as widespread condemnation, abandonment, arson, and demolition of the aging housing stock. In addition to undergoing such a dramatic population loss, the locality underwent massive changes in population composition, with the out-migration of almost all the Jewish, Irish American, German American, Eastern European Catholic and Orthodox residents, and most of the Italian Americans, and a major influx of Puerto Ricans, African Americans, and some new immi-

4. Based on tract-level population data for the whole of CB-Six, compiled for each decennial census since 1920. See also Walter Laidlaw, ed., *Statistical Sources for Demographic Studies of Greater New York, 1920* (New York: Cities Census Committee, 1922): idem, *Population of the City of New York 1890-1930* (New York: Cities Census Committee, 1932).

grants from Latin America, the Caribbean, and the Balkans.[5]

Since 1980 the population of CB-Six has risen significantly because of new housing construction and rehabilitation and the continuing influx of Latin American and Caribbean immigrants, both documented and undocumented. CB-Six's current (1996) population is probably in the 70,000-80,000 range, accounting for about 1.0 percent of the New York City and 0.4 percent of the NYMR population. According to the 1990 census, the population was 42 percent Puerto Rican, 17 percent other Hispanic, 25 percent black non-Hispanic, 14 percent white non-Hispanic, and 2 percent Asian non-Hispanic and other. An analysis of the Immigration and Naturalization Service's Annual Immigrant and Naturalized Citizen Tape Files for 1983-89, covering the three zip codes that embrace CB-Six and adjacent areas, reveals that the largest number of legal immigrants came from the Dominican Republic, with 29 percent of the total, followed by Guyana and Jamaica, with 12 percent each. Over a hundred other countries of origin were represented, the most frequent being Honduras, Ecuador, Korea, India, Vietnam, China, Antigua-Barbuda, Guatemala, and Yugoslavia.[6]

5. The best summaries of the South Bronx odyssey are Jill Jonnes, *We're Still Here* (Boston: Atlantic Monthly Press, 1986); Nathan Glazer, "The South Bronx Story: An Extreme Case of Neighborhood Decline," *Policy Studies Journal*, 16(2):269-76 (Winter 1987).

6. New York City, Department of City Planning, *Demographic Profile*; idem, *The Newest New Yorkers: A Statistical Portrait* (New York: Department of City Planning, 1992).

The immigrant presence in CB-Six is particularly evident at the crowded Theodore Roosevelt High School on Fordham Road, where officials report that together, over fifty mother tongues are spoken in the homes of the 4000 students. Roosevelt hosts St. Rita's Center for Immigrants and Refugees, which assists students from 21 countries, most notably Vietnam, Cambodia, and Ghana. The group includes some Bosnians and Macedonians, and Euro- and Afro-Vietnamese children whose unknown fathers were in the U.S. military. A broader range of refugees, including many from the former Yugoslavia and Soviet Union, make extensive use of the Federation for European American Rights, an immigration counseling center in Belmont.

Like most other areas of New York City, CB-Six has an interesting range of ethnic businesses, institutions, and places of worship, linked to migration flows, past and present. Belmont's Italian heritage and the Irish roots of many of the Catholic institutions outside Belmont are well known. CB-Six also has many small businesses run by so-called ethnic entrepreneurs, some catering mainly to co-ethnics, others seeking a broader multiethnic clientele. The best-known and most widespread are Dominican, Italian, Albanian, Chinese, Korean, Puerto Rican, Jamaican, and Mexican, but numerous other ethnicities are present, notably Cuban, Cuban Chinese, East Indian Guyanese, and entrepreneurs from the smaller English-speaking Caribbean islands.

Three churches in dismal locations close to the Cross-Bronx Expressway were established to serve migrant concentrations of the 1945-65 period, but now they mainly serve middle-class commuter worshipers from the North and East Bronx, Westchester County, and further afield; aging upwardly mobile migrants who have moved away from CB-Six; and their friends and younger relatives who have never lived in CB-Six. The thriving Gethsemane Baptist Church is particularly associated with African American migrants from the Carolinas. Our Lady of Good Counsel Albanian Catholic Church is the only regular NYMR site for Masses in Albanian, though it will eventually be replaced by a new church and Albanian center in Hartsdale, Westchester County. The small congregation of St. Mary Protectress Ukranian Catholic Church is served by Ukranian-Brazilian priests who commute from a monastery on Long Island.

EDGES OF METROPOLIS AND LOCALITY

The northernmost part of CB-Six is the main campus of Fordham University, known as the Rose Hill Campus and initially established as St. John's College in 1841. The site was originally chosen by Irish American Catholic Bishop John Hughes because it offered cheap land adjacent to the Harlem Railroad, which was being extended from Manhattan to White Plains. It provided the perfect compromise: accessibility to the metropolis, a pastoral environment, and isolation from the temptations of the city. St. John's College was transferred to Jesuit administration in 1846, with an early predominance of French Jesuits and strong links to Francophone Canada. It was renamed Fordham University in 1907, and it currently has over 13,000 students, over half of whom study at the newer Manhattan and Westchester campuses. Fordham has strong Irish American connections, and it even established a school of Irish studies in 1928. Like most major U.S. universities, however, it has developed a broader international reputation through teaching, research, and almost 500 international students. Its philosophical and theological scholarship and its links to Catholic missionary activity and the global Jesuit diaspora are especially significant. In 1936 Fordham conferred an honorary degree on Eugenio Cardinal Pacelli, the Vatican's Secretary of State, who was elected Pope in 1939 and ruled as Pius XII until his death in 1958. Soon after, Mussolini protested to the Vatican that the university had no Italian department, and so Fordham established one in 1937. In the early 1960s, Fordham's Institute of Mission Studies helped to found CIDOC, the Intercultural Documentation Center in Cuernavaca, Mexico, a global focus for radical and libertarian Catholic scholarship inspired by the teaching of Ivan Illich.[7]

At the heart of CB-Six is St. Barnabas Hospital, originally established as the New York Home for Incurables in 1866. It was America's first chronic disease hospital and the

7. Fordham University, Office of Institutional Research, *Fact Book 1995-1996* (New York: Fordham University, 1995); Robert I. Gannon, *Up to the Present* (Garden City, NY: Doubleday, 1967), pp. 178, 208-13, 289. Ivan Illich's most famous book is probably *Deschooling Society* (New York: Harper & Row, 1971).

world's second.[8] Its location followed the same principles as St. John's College, accessible isolation: a rural location, with transport to Manhattan via the Harlem Railroad. It functioned as a chronic disease hospital for over a century and then converted to a general hospital with an emergency room in the 1970s. It is currently the largest employer in CB-Six. A few professionals and many auxiliary and support staff live in the locality, including significant numbers of immigrants from the English-speaking Caribbean, the Philippines, and South Asia.

The territory that now forms the borough of the Bronx was annexed by the expanding city of New York in two stages in 1874 and 1895, prior to the consolidation of Greater New York City with its present boundaries in 1898, adding the boroughs of Queens, Brooklyn, and Staten Island. The annexation of the Bronx was crucial to the city in two main ways—as new land for development, extending the mass transit axes running from south to north on Manhattan Island, and as access to the resources, especially freshwater, of the mainland. The Bronx Park to the northeast, Crotona Park to the south, and the dilapidated Crotona Parkway connecting the two are part of a grand vision developed and implemented in the 1880s for "lungs for the metropolis"—a system of six parks and connecting parkways for the northward expansion of the city.[9]

In the 1890s, Bronx Park was designated as the location for the New York Zoological Park, now known as "the Bronx Zoo," and the New York Botanical Garden. Zoo animals can be seen, heard, and smelled from some parts of CB-Six, and the Zoo and Botanical Garden have provided a century of construction, maintenance, and service employment opportunities. Animal and plant species native to every country on earth can be found within the bounds of the Zoo and Botanical Garden. These institutions are both microcosms of the world and important centers for scientific research, organizing expeditions to remote areas of the world and linking with laboratories, zoos, and gardens in many different countries.

The push to establish the Zoo and Botanical Garden was led by some of the nation's most eminent politicians, bankers, and industrialists. Theodore Roosevelt and Elihu Root, founders of the Boone and Crockett Big-Game Hunting Club, were prime movers in establishing the zoo, and J. Pierpont Morgan was a major early benefactor. Morgan was also one of the early managers and benefactors of the Botanical Garden, together with Andrew Carnegie, John D. Rockefeller, and Cornelius Vanderbilt II. Columbia University provided substantial institutional support, and the new institutions in the Bronx Park came to embody everything from America's "manifest destiny" to

---

8. St. Barnabas Hospital, *1991 Annual Report* (New York: St. Barnabas Hospital, 1992), pp. 4-7.

9. Bronx Museum of the Arts, *Building a Borough* (New York: Bronx Museum of the

Arts, 1986); Evelyn Diaz Gonzalez, *City Neighborhoods,* UMI 9318242 (Ann Arbor, MI: University Microfilms, 1993); New York State Commission to Select and Locate Land for Public Parks, *Report to the New York Legislature* (New York: Martin B. Brown, 1884).

popular entertainment. Exploration, hunting, geopolitics, military adventurism, and the corporate search for new raw materials and markets were interwoven with conservation, science, education, and recreation.

Opened in 1899, the Zoo attracted half a million visitors in its first year, and by 1914 it had 1290 species of mammals, birds, and reptiles. Its all-time peak attendance of over 3.3 million visitors was in 1941, with a daily high of 84,727 on 4 May just after inaugurating its African Plains exhibit. Though the Zoo's popularity has declined somewhat since the 1950s, it still received almost 2.1 million visitors in 1995.[10] By 1991, the Botanical Garden had accumulated 5.1 million specimens on file in its herbarium, and it had mounted over 900 expeditions on all seven continents. In 1995, it received about half a million visitors.[11]

ALMOST
A WORLD'S FAIR

In the early twentieth century, the section of CB-Six east of the Bronx River was a 135-acre estate owned by the Astor family, who also owned a substantial part of the Interborough Rapid Transit Company (IRT), which operated the two elevated railroads (Els) serving CB-Six, one up Third Avenue and the other along Boston Road.[12] These Els enabled Bronxites to commute to work in Manhattan, and they brought Manhattan and Brooklyn day-trippers to the Zoo and the Botanical Garden. With the backing of the IRT management and Bronx Congressman Benjamin Fairchild, the Astors established the West Farms Amusement Corporation in 1916 and then launched the idea of a Bronx International Exposition and a Starlight Amusement Park, which would be a world's fair and a permanent public entertainment complex.[13] Impressive grounds and pavilions were designed, but Congress did not approve the exposition because of the disruptions to international trade caused by World War I. Only one major pavilion was built and the remaining area was filled with outdoor amusements and flimsy structures.

The Starlight Amusement Park opened in 1918, and by the early 1920s IRT managers boasted that they could transport over 100,000 people per day to the park and the Zoo.[14] Starlight rivaled Coney Island in the 1920s; its attractions included a massive swimming pool, a stadium, two dance halls, a wide range of fairground activities, and such depictions of foreign lands as an under-

10. William Bridges, *Gathering of Animals* (New York: Harper & Row, 1974), pp. 362, 452; Wildlife Conservation Society, *Annual Report 1995* (New York: Wildlife Conservation Society, 1996), p. 80.

11. Ogden Tanner and Adele Auchincloss, *The New York Botanical Garden* (New York: Walker, 1991), pp. 121, 129.

12. George E. Horn, "New York's El Lines, 1867-1955," *Electric Railroads*, no. 25 (Dec. 1956); William F. Reeves, *The First Elevated Railroads in Manhattan and the Bronx of the City of New York* (New York: New York Historical Society, 1936).

13. Ronald O. Roth, "Starlight in the Bronx: From World's Fair to Amusement Park" (Manuscript, Bronx County Historical Society Library, 1990).

14. Ibid.; Clifton Hood, *722 Miles* (New York: Simon & Schuster, 1993), pp. 126-85.

ground Chinatown, the Hindu Palace, the Cairo Show, and the Canals of Venice. It was further enhanced in 1928 when the Convention Hall from the 1926 Philadelphia Sesquicentennial Exposition was dismantled and reassembled on the site as the New York Coliseum. Until it was requisitioned by the U.S. Army in 1942 and sold as a bus maintenance garage in 1946, the Coliseum was the city's largest covered arena, with a capacity double that of the old Madison Square Garden.[15] It accommodated the Ringling Brothers Barnum and Bailey Circus, numerous professional boxing bouts, and a wide range of indoor sports and expositions. Starlight was hard-hit by roller-coaster accidents, fires, the Great Depression, and the opening of free public swimming pools, playgrounds, and sports facilities resulting from New Deal public works programs, and it was closed by 1942.

MOVIES AND
BROADCASTING

In the early twentieth century, the Mid-Bronx was conveniently located to provide easy access, low rents, and moderate tranquility. It was chosen for the construction of two early movie studios, and it emerged as an area of residential upward mobility from lower-class to lower-middle-class status. It attracted German, Irish, Jewish, and Italian Americans from the crowded slums of the Lower East Side of Manhattan. CB-Six became a stage and a stepping-stone, and fact and fiction intermingled in

the production and setting of movies and broadcasting. In addition, of course, the people of CB-Six were avid consumers of movies and broadcasting, and around 1940, the locality had over a dozen movie theaters.[16]

Edison and Biograph

The silent movie industry was primarily located in New York, initially operating in makeshift Manhattan studios. Gradually, in the early 1900s, the expanding industry relocated to more spacious custom-built studios in the outer boroughs.[17] The Edison Studio was opened on Decatur Avenue in 1906, just one block outside CB-Six. D. W. Griffith made his movie debut there as an actor, and the studio later pioneered the development of cartoon films. Griffith began his directorial career and introduced the close-up into movies with the American Mutascope and Biograph Company in Manhattan. After Biograph opened its new studio on East 175th Street in CB-Six in 1912, he directed the indoor scenes of the first-ever full-length movie there, *Judith of Bethulia*. Griffith subsequently quarreled with the Biograph management, and most of the movie industry shifted to Hollywood in pursuit of easy all-year outdoor filming. Nevertheless, Mary Pick-

15. *Bronxboro*, 23(12):8 (Apr. 1946).

16. Michael Miller, *Marquee: Theaters of the Bronx* (Bronx, NY: Bronx County Historical Society, 1972).

17. John McNamara, *McNamara's Old Bronx* (New York: Bronx County Historical Society, 1989), pp. 127-28; Michael R. Cioffi, "The Origins of the Motion Picture Industry in Bronx County," *Bronx County Historical Society Journal*, 22(1):1-4 (Spring 1985).

ford, Douglas Fairbanks, and Fatty Arbuckle all acted at Biograph. The studios were refurbished in 1934 and again in 1956, and various talkie movies in English and Yiddish, numerous commercials, and some television series were filmed there.

Home for soap

From 1929 until 1958, with the successive sponsorship of the Pepsodent, Palmolive, Procter and Gamble, and General Foods corporations, Jewish American East Tremont was projected to national prominence as the home of the Goldbergs.[18] Most of the time, this fictional family lived in an apartment building on the corner of East Tremont and Vyse avenues. The anchor of the family was Molly Goldberg, played by Gertrude Stein, and the drama was played out on radio and later on television, in a movie, and in a Broadway play. *The Goldbergs* was the first great soap opera, with 10 million listeners per day during the 1930s following the affairs of the Goldberg family and hearing many soap and detergent commercials. Americans all over the nation were entertained, encouraged to wash more, and presented a vision of Jewish New Yorkers, the Bronx, and immigration. Gertrude Stein traveled the world as "Molly," one of America's most loved characters and godmother to a thousand soap operas in different countries.

Little Italy on record and screen

In the late 1950s, a group of Italian American teenagers from the Belmont neighborhood—Dion and the Belmonts—became an international pop music sensation with such records as *A Teenager in Love, Runaround Sue,* and *The Wanderer.* Dion explained his Bronx style: "You mix in R&B, street-corner doo-wop, some Hank Williams 'Honky Tonk Blues,' you filter it all through an Italian neighborhood full of wiseguys and all that, and it comes out with an attitude, like 'Yo.' "[19] Like so many groups in that period, the members of Dion and the Belmonts soon went their separate ways and moved away from the old neighborhood, but their example helped to inspire another Belmont boy, Chazz Palminteri, who has achieved movie stardom in the 1990s. Palminteri wrote a semi-autobiographical play, *A Bronx Tale,* set in Belmont, and he eventually co-starred with Robert De Niro in the movie of the same title, De Niro's directorial debut.[20] *A Bronx Tale* is a local story of loyalty, love, street life, organized crime, and interethnic turf wars that has been seen all over the world.

NEIGHBORHOOD ODYSSEYS

Until the 1950s, Belmont was overwhelmingly Italian American

18. Jack Long, "Her Family Is Her Fortune," *American Magazine,* no. 154, pp. 108-13 (Dec. 1952); Morris Freedman, "The Real Molly Goldberg: Baalebosteh of the Air Waves," *Commentary,* 21(1):359-64 (Jan. 1956); Gertrude Berg, *Molly and Me* (New York: McGraw-Hill, 1961).

19. *Dion, Bronx Blues: The Columbia Recordings (1962-1965),* Sony, 1991, jacket; *A Teenager in Love: The Best of Dion and the Belmonts,* CEMA Special Markets, 1992.

20. *A Bronx Tale,* Savoy Pictures, HBO Video, 1993; John Parker, *De Niro* (London: Victor Gollancz, 1995), pp. 221-45.

and covered a sixty-block area south of Fordham University and between the Third Avenue El and the Zoo. Since then, most of the Italian Americans have migrated to more prosperous neighborhoods and suburbs, and the remaining housing stock has been occupied by Puerto Ricans, African Americans, and recent immigrants. Nevertheless, a tenacious Italian American merchant community has maintained and enhanced a Little Italy within Belmont, extending two or three blocks outward from the intersection of Arthur Avenue and East 187th Street. The Italian character of this small area is greatly strengthened by the Mount Carmel Catholic Church, which has ministered to the Italian American community and offered Mass in Italian since 1906; by the Arthur Avenue Market, a thriving indoor market established by Mayor Fiorello La Guardia in 1943; by the Enrico Fermi Italian Cultural Center, established in 1981; and by the Italian American Playhouse, established in 1991. The area also has several Italian bakers, butchers, and food wholesalers; various Italian restaurants, pastry shops, and groceries; and a store specializing in old Italian gramophone records. In short, it is a classic Little Italy, more authentic in many ways than its Manhattan equivalent.[21]

Belmont is renowned as a neighborhood success and a minor tourist attraction, but East Tremont, to the south, has acquired notoriety as the neighborhood destroyed by Robert Moses and the Cross-Bronx Expressway. Robert Caro's famous biography of Moses, *The Power Broker*, devotes two chapters to East Tremont, using the neighborhood to illustrate the human tragedies associated with expressway construction and Moses' ruthless determination to overcome community opposition and push his projects through.[22]

THE BIGGEST
MASS MURDER

On 25 March 1990, Julio Gonzalez, a Cuban immigrant who had come to the United States ten years earlier on the Mariel boatlift, lit a fire in the entrance of the Happy Land Social Club on Southern Boulevard. The club had no windows or back door, and 87 of the 93 people inside were killed, primarily by smoke inhalation. Gonzalez was eventually convicted of murder, and though the Oklahoma City bomb blast may soon displace it, for the moment the *Guinness Book of Records* lists Happy Land as the biggest mass murder in U.S. history.

The club was owned by Elias Colón, a Puerto Rican former merchant seaman who had remodeled the building after taking a seven-year sublease. Colón's landlord was

21. Belmont Arthur Avenue Local Development Corporation, *Belmont: Alive and Flourishing*, Diamond Pictures, 1993; Rocky D'Erasmo, *Memories of Fordham* (San Diego, CA: Private, 1987); Anthony L. LaRuffa, *Monte Carmelo* (New York: Gordon & Breach, 1988); Our Lady of Mount Carmel Parish, *Golden Jubilee 1906-1956* (Bronx, NY: Our Lady of Mount Carmel Parish, 1956).

22. Robert A. Caro, *The Power Broker* (New York: Alfred A. Knopf, 1974), pp. 850-94; Marshall Berman, *All That Is Solid Melts into Air* (New York; Simon & Schuster, 1982), pp. 287-312.

Queens Apple Realty, the agents for One Peach Associates, a company presided over by Jay Weiss, husband to actress Kathleen Turner. One Peach, in turn, had a 30-year lease on the building from Clarendon Place Corporation, owned by Alexander DiLorenzo III, a leading New York property speculator frequently pilloried in the *Village Voice* as one of the city's "Landlords from Hell."

Happy Land was totally inadequate to function as a place of public assembly, yet various official inspections over the previous two years had failed to close it down for more than a few weeks at a time. The club had a large sign outside, operated three nights a week, and was just two blocks from a firehouse. It was a multicultural social center where young people could meet, listen to music, drink, and dance, and new immigrants could make contacts to find jobs and housing.

Of the 87 dead, 59 were of Honduran origin, 12 were Puerto Rican, and the remainder were American, Dominican, Salvadoran, Guatemalan, Ecuadoran, and British. The two successive managers who ran the club for Colón, the two disc jockeys, and about a quarter of those who died in the fire, were Garifuna from the northern coast of Honduras. Happy Land was one of two Garifuna-run clubs in the Bronx, known for punta, an Afro-Honduran dance rhythm, but also offering salsa, merengue, lambada, rock, disco, and reggae.

The Garifuna are an Afro-Carib people with their own language. They were deported by the British from St. Vincent to the island of Roatan off Honduras in 1797, accused of hoarding land, conspiring with the French, and supporting slave revolts. The deportees soon defected to the Spanish-ruled mainland, assumed Spanish names, and engaged in fishing and small farming. In the twentieth century, many Garifuna men became merchant seamen, working on the banana boats and taking general cargo jobs during World War II, when the British and U.S. merchant fleets were desperately short of crew. Some formally immigrated to the United States, while others did not rejoin their ships after visiting U.S. ports. Thus, legally and illegally, often legalizing later through amnesties, marriage, and family reunification, substantial numbers of Garifuna have settled in New York and New Orleans. Their remittances help to sustain the impoverished Garifuna communities on the Caribbean coast and the continuing migration of Garifuna to the United States.[23]

Through the Mariel boatlift, municipal negligence, Weiss, Turner, and DiLorenzo, Happy Land connects to the pinnacles of government, diplomacy, wealth, and prestige. Nevertheless, its handling by the city of New York and the mass media was primarily as a poor people's tragedy, rather than a set of outrageous crimes. News coverage concentrated

23. Peter Matthews, ed., *The Guinness Book of Records 1994* (New York: Facts on File, 1993), p. 184; Ray Bromley, *The Happy Land Tragedy* (New York: Department of Mental Health, Mental Retardation and Alcoholism Services, 1991); Juan Gonzalez, *Roll Down Your Window* (London: Verso, 1995), pp. 101-13; Nancie L. Gonzalez, *Soujourners of the Caribbean* (Urbana: University of Illinois Press, 1988); Andy Logan, "Happy Land," *New Yorker*, 23 Apr. 1990, pp. 102-9.

on the frustrated dreams of the victims and the grief and poverty of their relatives. Only Julio Gonzalez went to jail. Weiss, DiLorenzo, and their insurers paid some modest fines and compensation to the victims' families and their attorneys, and the city of New York avoided any liability for negligence. CB-Six now has a monument and "Boulevard of the 87" signs outside the club site.

KOSOVO: NEW NATION
OR NEXT BOSNIA?

As well as providing a home for first-generation Italian immigrants, over the last fifty years Belmont has attracted substantial numbers of immigrants who came to the United States via Italy. Most notable are the ethnic Albanians, some from Albania, others from the predominantly Albanian Kosovo province of Yugoslavia, from the Albanian-speaking areas of Macedonia, or from the Albanian minorities in Serbia and Montenegro. Little Italy in the Bronx has at least 1500 residents of Albanian descent; it has the editorial offices of *Illyria*, the world's premier international Albanian newspaper; and it has some Albanian American clubs, restaurants, and real estate firms.[24]

In March 1996, the *New York Times* published a quarter-page advertisement, an open letter to President Clinton from "The Coalition of Albanian-American Communities

supporting the Republic of Kosova," based at 605 Crescent Avenue in Belmont. The letter noted that

the Albanian community is very happy to see the successive U.S. warnings to dictator Milosevic of Serbia not to provoke any conflicts in Kosova, which has, until now, escaped brutal "ethnic cleansing." This farsighted policy not only has saved thousands of lives, but it has avoided a conflict that would have drawn in the neighboring countries of Albania, Macedonia, Greece, Bulgaria, and possibly Turkey. A conflict in Kosova would have diplomatically pitted the United States against Russia, which supports control of Kosova. And it would have inevitably spilled into neighboring Macedonia, a country with some 40 percent Albanian population.

The letter pleaded for U.S. recognition of the independence of Kosovo, declared on 7 September 1990, and for U.S. support to achieve Kosovo's admission to the United Nations. It called on the president to avoid a repeat of the genocide in Bosnia-Herzegovina by protecting the rights and sovereignty of the over 2 million ethnic Albanians in Kosovo and to protect them from "Serbian military occupation, police terror, political oppression, economic strangulation, cultural neglect and social discrimination bordering on apartheid."[25]

In the election year of 1996, the U.S. government apparently decided to ignore Kosovo, repeating its policies toward Bosnia-Herzegovina of the early 1990s—a sort of benign neglect. Meanwhile, in Belmont and adjacent areas of the Bronx, the inflow of Bosnian, Albanian, and other Balkan refugees continues, and there is considerable anxiety in the Albanian

24. Mark Goret, "The Bronx Albanians," *Bronx County Historical Society Journal*, 21:25-29 (1984); Tim Golden, "Changes in Albania Rekindle Pride in Immigrants," *New York Times*, 18 Mar. 1991.

25. *New York Times*, 27 Mar. 1996.

community about relatives back home and scattered around the world.

WHAT MIGHT HAVE BEEN

On Saturday, 21 October 1944, a raw, windy, and rainy day, President Franklin Delano Roosevelt made a fifty-mile trip in an open car through Brooklyn, Queens, the Bronx, and Manhattan, accompanied by his wife, Eleanor, and Mayor La Guardia. As the presidential motorcade was proceeding northward through CB-Six, a young man with a gun was surprised by two local women on the rooftop of the CB-Six building where he lived, 465 East Tremont Avenue. The rooftop had an excellent view of the oncoming motorcade. The young man shot and wounded the two women and then fled the site with the police in hot pursuit. He killed himself with the gun so as to avoid arrest, and the news of the attack and its potential consequences was suppressed for over a decade "for reasons of security."[26]

If FDR had been assassinated in CB-Six on that fateful Saturday, the history of the United States and the world might have been dramatically changed. It was just two weeks before the presidential elections, in which FDR faced New York's Governor Thomas Dewey, a Republican with more isolationist and pro-business views. Roosevelt was running for a fourth term, even though he had serious health problems and the accepted maximum was two terms.

U.S. forces had just begun the recapture of the Philippines from Japan, and Allied forces had recently invaded Germany from the west and east. While U.S., British, and Canadian forces were advancing slowly, Soviet forces were moving much more rapidly, acquiring control of most of Eastern Europe. Marshal Tito's National Liberation Movement had just captured Belgrade, and Churchill and Stalin had just met in Moscow to discuss the future of Poland and the Baltic and Balkan states. The Allied advance up the Italian peninsula was stalled, and Mussolini still ruled northern Italy as a German puppet.

The rain-soaked open-car trip through New York City was classic Roosevelt electioneering, designed to show his courage, to celebrate war victories, and to convince the electorate that he was in good health. Roosevelt defeated Dewey by the narrowest margin of his four presidential victories, and when he delivered his Inaugural Address on 20 January 1945, he was visibly trembling. Soon after, he traveled to meet Stalin and Churchill at Yalta, and on 12 April 1945 he died in Warm Springs, Georgia.[27]

CONCLUSION: GLOBAL AND LOCAL INTERTWINED

Traditional social history has given us a vision of ordinary people as producers and consumers, as participants in a labor process and a social system, as subject to the vagaries of restructuring, and as victims

---

26. See *New York Times*, 22 Oct. 1944; Walter Propper, "Footnote to Bronx History," *Bronxboro*, p. 9 (Winter 1959).

27. Harold F. Gosnell, *Champion Campaigner* (New York: Macmillan, 1952), pp. 198-218.

of wars and crises of world capitalism. Consideration of the global-local interface goes further, however, showing how strategic locations change through time and how ordinary places can be the scene for extraordinary events. Major events reverberate around the world, interconnecting with one another in thousands of localities and in many curious ways.

The twentieth century has been marked by four great traumas that have affected every nation on earth: World War I, the Great Depression, World War II, and the Cold War. The trigger for World War I was the assassination of the archduke of Austria by a Bosnian Serb in the city of Sarajevo, Bosnia-Herzegovina. As the century closes, Sarajevo, Cold War hangovers, and interethnic tensions in the Balkans continue in the news. Just as New York can be viewed as the archetypal global city of the twentieth century, Sarajevo might be viewed as the ultimate world city! Superficially, its intense conflicts are mere local vendettas based on age-old enmities, but they echo historic struggles between major polities and religions for dominance of the known world. Sarajevo's timing in world history is synchronized to a geopolitical clock. Events in peripheral localities often respond to global forces, and they may trigger profound changes in the global cores.

The neighborhood concerns of CB-Six focus mainly on such mundane issues as noise, garbage, crime, vandalism, graffiti, traffic and parking problems, the poor quality of the public schools, community school board

corruption, and police brutality.[28] Ethnicity is frequently discussed and used as a badge of identity, and public works and the changing ethnic composition of the population are popular explanations for neighborhood change. These problems and explanations are shared by most cities and many suburbs in the United States and by many major cities around the world.

Local history is often viewed as the last refuge of esoteric, empirical, and trivial research. Yes, George Washington slept in CB-Six, on what is now the Fordham campus! Yes, Tremont was named by Hiram Tarbox, the first postmaster of Upper Morrisania, considering it as the area between three small hills—Mount Hope, Mount Eden, and Fairmount! Such facts are noteworthy for jeopardy games and local tours, but they have little broader significance.

The local historical facts, and the fictitious images and media events described in this article, are of a different type. They illustrate the many complex ways in which a locality affects the world and the world affects a locality.

28. A broad overview of neighborhood concerns can be gleaned from local interest articles in the *Bronx Press Review*, other Bronx newspapers, and major New York City newspapers and from attendance at the monthly public CB-Six and Police Precinct 48 meetings. Other key sources are Harry Keifetz, *A Decade of Service* (Bronx, NY: Community Board Six, 1974); Lydia G. Segal et al., *Power, Politics and Patronage* (New York: Special Commissioner of Investigation for the New York City School District, 1993); Robert M. Brenner et al., *From Chaos to Corruption* (New York: Special Commissioner of Investigation for the New York City School District, 1993).

Some local events and images are intimately tied to New York's global city status. It was no accident that parks, a chronic disease hospital, a botanical garden, and a zoo were established on the fringe of the expanding metropolis, or that the early movie industry developed in New York and established new studios on the edge of the city. Even in fiction, reputation, plausibility, and notoriety are crucial. Thus it is hardly surprising that the soap opera Goldbergs lived in New York and moved from the Lower East Side to the Mid-Bronx, or that numerous slum-gang action movies have been set in a fictional Bronx, most recently Jackie Chan's *Rumble in the Bronx*, filmed in Vancouver![29] Smaller places do not have the concentration of market, capital, and talent, or the global media coverage and reputation that New York offers. The Bronx has worldwide recognition because of its substantial population, its vital stepping-stone role for immigrant Americans, its distinctive name, and the 1970s South Bronx crisis of abandonment and arson. Its name reverberates because of the Bronx Zoo and the Bronx Bombers (the New York Yankees).

Occasionally, local connections may be pure coincidence! In 1968, for example, Dion DiMucci recorded a new worldwide hit, *Abraham, Martin and John*, a folksy song about America's most famous victims of assassination. Five years had lapsed since Dion's last hit record; he had moved

to Florida; he no longer had the Belmonts as a backing group; and his old home on East 183rd Street had been demolished for the Twin Parks East urban renewal.[30] There was no obvious connection to the possible but frustrated assassination of FDR on East Tremont Avenue.

Local events can have repercussions in far-off places. Abraham was assassinated in Washington, D.C., Martin in Memphis, and John in Dallas. The United States has lost four presidents to assassins' bullets: Lincoln, Garfield, McKinley, and Kennedy. The only obvious parallel to the attempt on FDR is the presidential motorcade. FDR's 50-mile procession in New York in October 1944 set an eerie precedent for JFK's similar procession through Dallas. If the 1944 incident on East Tremont Avenue had been publicized, JFK might never have risked an open-car motorcade through Dallas. If FDR had been assassinated in the Bronx, JFK might never have become president!

In the ultimate global city, fact and fiction, both local and global, become intertwined. Just as the fictional Sherman McCoy, "Master of the Universe," came to grief in the Bronx's *Bonfire of the Vanities*,[31] the real Franklin Delano Roosevelt might have fallen prey to an assassin's bullet in CB-Six. Sherman's demise resulted from the city's byzantine ethnic politics. In contrast, President Roosevelt's potential demise opened so many ethnic, national, and political enmities at such a difficult time

29. *Rumble in the Bronx*, directed by Stanley Tong, New Line Cinema, 1996. See also *Escape from the Bronx*, directed by Enzo G. Castellari, Media Home Entertainment, 1985.

30. *Dion*, Right Stuff, 1994, jacket.
31. Tom Wolfe, *The Bonfire of the Vanities* (New York: Farrar, Straus & Giroux, 1987).

that it was kept secret. Depending on the national origin, links, and assumed motives of the potential assassin, even a failed assassination attempt might have had a major impact on world history.

ANNALS, *AAPSS*, **551**, May 1997

The Rise and Fall and Rise of Cleveland

By BARNEY WARF and BRIAN HOLLY

ABSTRACT: Cleveland, Ohio, long the quintessential blue-collar, working-class American city, has been fashioned through a series of periodic transformations tightly linked to the changing rhythms of the national and global economies. After a brief review of the city's historical development, this article explores Cleveland's descent in the face of massive and traumatic deindustrialization. In the 1990s, as the midwestern economy has become thoroughly restructured around the prerequisites of post-Fordism, Cleveland has enjoyed an unexpected renaissance, including an incipient high-technology sector, producer services, and as a center of cultural consumption. A consistent theme throughout is that the details of Cleveland's experience can be understood only in reference to the city's changing competitive position; in this light, it offers a lens through which national and global tendencies conjoin in unique local contexts.

Barney Warf is professor and chair of the Department of Geography at Florida State University, Tallahassee. His interests lie within the broad domain of urban and regional development, straddling contemporary political economy on the one hand and traditional quantitative, empirical approaches on the other. His work currently focuses primarily on defense spending, services, and telecommunications.

Brian Holly is associate professor of geography, Department of Geography, Kent State University. His research centers upon urban and economic geography, including industrial systems, business services, technological change, and regional economic development. His work includes studies of commercial banking, high-technology firms in Ohio, and the geography of wine production.

ON the shores of Lake Erie at the mouth of the Cuyahoga River, Cleveland, Ohio, offers a fascinating example of the intersection of global forces and local context, of the manifold ways in which the periodic long-wave restructuring brought on by the changing global economy has played out within the unique context of northeastern Ohio. Long the quintessential blue-collar city, Cleveland in the 1970s and 1980s embodied the worst aspects of the Rustbelt: deindustrialization, population loss, rising poverty, ugly landscapes, and a notoriously poor reputation. In the 1990s, however, Cleveland has enjoyed an unanticipated renaissance and has swiftly moved from backwater to the forefront of contemporary urban change. In surfing the business cycle, Cleveland serves as a mirror of how larger forces have periodically reshaped the fabric of urban America.

This article attempts to capture the complexity of Cleveland's changing circumstances in the twentieth century. It opens with a review of the city's historical context, stressing its competitive advantage throughout the late nineteenth and early and mid-twentieth centuries. Next, it ponders its slide from jewel of the Manufacturing Belt to the "mistake on the lake" during the 1970s and 1980s, detailing the city's abandonment by capital. Third, it examines the city's recovery in the 1990s, including the emergence of post-Fordist production systems, producer services, and cultural consumption. Throughout, it links Cleveland's temporal and spatial changes to the rhythms of national and global capitalism.

CLEVELAND'S
HISTORICAL CONTEXT:
AN ABBREVIATED
SYNOPSIS

In 1776, a surveyor for the Connecticut Land Company, Moses Cleaveland, surveyed the state's western reserve; his employers were interested in land speculation in what promised to be a lucrative new market. Cleaveland stayed only three months, but his namesake (whose spelling now excluded the first "a") lives on. In the post–Civil War boom that fashioned the Manufacturing Belt along the southern shores of the Great Lakes, Cleveland emerged as the premier center of industrialism between Buffalo and Chicago. The city's ascendancy was guaranteed when it became the northern terminus of the Ohio River–Lake Erie Canal, while the Erie Canal farther east guaranteed access to powerful eastern markets.[1] With a locational advantage augmented by ready access to the resources of Appalachia, cheap water transportation on Lake Erie, and a well-developed matrix of rail lines, the city evolved from the 1860s to the 1920s into a diversified node of durable goods production.[2]

Early industries included dairying, agricultural processing and im-

1. Harry Margulis, "Cleveland: Making the Transition from a Corporate to an Advanced Industrial City," in The Changing Heartland: A Geography of Ohio, ed. L. Peacefull (Needham Heights, MA: Ginn Press, 1990).

2. C. Miller and R. Wheeler, "Cleveland: The Making and Remaking of an American City, 1796-1993," in Cleveland: A Metropolitan Reader, ed. W. Keating, N. Krumholz, and D. Perry (Kent, OH: Kent State University Press, 1995).

plements, and coal mining. Riding a boom in petroleum processing, Clevelander John D. Rockefeller made his city the headquarters of Standard Oil Corporation in 1870, although this industry would soon move to the richer wells of Texas and Oklahoma. The city's steel industry blossomed in the 1870s and 1880s, driven by the newly invented Bessemer open hearth furnace and rising demand propelled by rapid industrialization and a thriving national urban middle class, as part of the world's largest steel-producing district. Westinghouse was founded in Cleveland in 1886. Tire making flourished in nearby Akron during the bicycling craze of the 1880s.

By 1900, the region had become covered with a dense mesh of firms, including iron and steel foundries, electrical motors, machine tools, meatpacking, clothing, paint, and varnish. As argued by Scott, such conglomerations typically saw small, labor-intensive, vertically disintegrated firms cluster near the city center while larger, more capital-intensive, vertically integrated companies located on the urban periphery, typically along transport lines.[3] Cleveland surpassed Cincinnati as Ohio's largest city, reaching 560,000 people at the turn of the century. Detroit's emergence as the epicenter of global automobile production further accelerated Cleveland's growth, particularly given the numerous backward linkages from that industry, many of which stretched into northeastern Ohio, including the production of tires,

steel, paints, and electrical equipment. In the 1920s, when Cleveland was the nation's fifth-largest city, Shaker Heights, a wealthy suburb, exhibited the highest per capita income of any city in the United States. During World War II, the demand for tanks, trucks, and artillery further strengthened the city's manufacturing base.

These capital investments were accompanied by rapid population growth. From 1870 to 1930, despite its severe lakeside climate, Cleveland saw an average decadal growth rate of 47 percent. Until World War I, much of the labor supply was generated by a steady influx of immigrant labor, particularly from Italy and Eastern Europe. By the 1880s, three-quarters of the city's population was foreign-born or first-generation immigrants.[4] Immigrants soon segregated themselves into a potpourri of ethnic neighborhoods.[5] A stream of Appalachian whites and black migrants from the South from the 1940s through the 1960s fueled the city's growth anew; blacks eventually composed roughly 40 percent of the populace. In short, Cleveland was born and matured during the classic period of Fordism, the epoch of production characterized largely by mass markets, mass production, homogeneous goods, vertically integrated firms, oligopolistic market structure, and semiskilled labor.[6]

4. Miller and Wheeler, "Cleveland."

5. E. Miggins and M. Morgenthaler, "The Ethnic Mosaic: The Settlement of Cleveland by the New Immigrants and Migrants," in *The Birth of Modern Cleveland, 1865-1930* (Cleveland: Western Reserve Historical Society, 1988).

6. Ash Amin, ed., *Post-Fordism* (Cambridge, MA: Basil Blackwell, 1994).

3. Allen Scott, "Production System Dynamics and Metropolitan Development," *Annals of the Association of American Geographers*, 72:185-200 (1982).

Northeastern Ohio prospered greatly during the post–World War II boom, an era characterized by unprecedented U.S. hegemony in the world system. In the 1950s, the completion of the St. Lawrence Seaway allowed large commercial ships to reach the Great Lakes, contributing to a steady growth in Cleveland's status as an international port. The flourishing steel industry saw numerous ships carrying iron ore from northern Michigan and Minnesota. In the 1960s, the economy of metropolitan Cleveland roared in conjunction with that of the nation. Manufacturing generated high-paying jobs in a variety of industries, notably iron and steel, automobile assembly, machinery, and fabricated metals. Total manufacturing employment in the Cleveland standard metropolitan statistical area was maximized in 1967 at 306,700. Labor unions operating under national contracts (primarily AFL-CIO) protected workers' wages, jobs, and benefits.

DEGENERATING INTO THE "MISTAKE ON THE LAKE"

In the 1970s, the world and national economies changed in such profound ways that the economy of this grittiest of Rustbelt cities was permanently disemboweled. As American manufacturing found itself rocked by "petro shocks" and increasingly besieged by foreign competition, employment began to drop, often precipitously. Deindustrialization, numerous plant closures, and rising unemployment led to enormous socioeconomic dislocations, including the metamorphosis of the

Manufacturing Belt into the Rustbelt.[7] Many large multi-establishment firms in mature industries, increasingly mobile in a competitive world economy and hampered by the high-cost, unionized labor of the Midwest, evacuated the decaying cities of the Great Lakes and northeastern United States to find greener pastures—and higher profits—in the Sunbelt or overseas.[8]

In the Cleveland metro region, this process initiated a dramatic restructuring in the late 1970s and early 1980s. Total private employment plummeted from a high of 780,000 in 1979 to 675,000 in 1993, a 13 percent drop, although when public sector employment is included, there was little change; manufacturing jobs, the core of the regional economy, fell from 280,000 in 1979 to less than 190,000 in 1994, a drop of 40 percent. The largest losses during the period of 1979-94 were in nonelectrical machinery, which lost 19,700 jobs, fabricated metals (15,200), and transportation equipment (13,300). For example, U.S. Steel Corporation closed its Cleveland plant, LTV Steel shut its Youngstown facilities and reduced employment drastically in nearby plants, and USX closed its plant and sold its Lorain mill to Japan's Kobe Steel. White Motors' truck assembly plant and General Motors' Coit Road factory—both located in Cleveland—closed abruptly. Westinghouse closed its lighting products

7. Barry Bluestone and Bennett Harrison, *The Deindustrialization of America* (New York: Basic Books, 1982).

8. Michael Storper and Richard Walker, *The Capitalist Imperative: Territory, Technology, and Industrial Growth* (Cambridge, MA: Basil Blackwell, 1989).

factory in 1979, General Electric shut down six factories, and the Harris Corporation moved its headquarters to Florida.[9] Other producers such as Eaton, which made automobile parts, diversified into more recession-resistant sectors. In the rubber industry, tire production moved to Georgia and Tennessee, although Akron remained the headquarters of the Big Four firms in this industry such as Firestone and Goodyear. As a result, Clevelanders' real median family income, which had risen 22 percent throughout the 1960s, slid by 11 percent in the 1970s. To add insult to injury, in 1969 the Cuyahoga River, coated with a thick layer of oil and toxic waste, caught fire, adding ridicule to an already tarnished reputation.

The dramatic downturn in jobs was accompanied by demographic losses. Between 1970 and 1980, the metro area lost 8 percent of its population, or 165,000 people, while the city of Cleveland lost 24 percent, or 177,000 people, one of the steepest declines in U.S. urban history (Table 1). Rapid out-migration was selective; those who could leave did, with the poor, elderly, and structurally unemployed or marginally unemployable remaining behind. Housing values went into a precipitous decline, especially in the inner city, often losing one-half to two-thirds of their 1967 value, and did not recover until a decade later.[10] Abandoned houses and commercial

buildings began to blight the landscape in large numbers. Blue-collar neighborhoods were hit the hardest, particularly black communities on the city's eastern side. The poverty rate, correspondingly, rose from 27 percent in 1980 to 40 percent in 1987. Like many U.S. cities, Cleveland became a depository for the poor, infirm, and those dependent upon public services.[11] By 1975, Cleveland stood in the nation's highest quintile among cities in terms of poverty, unemployment, poor housing, violent crime, and municipal debt.[12]

The transformation of labor and housing markets had important repercussions for the public sector. Always a low-tax state, Ohio left its communities largely to fund themselves through local property, sales, and income taxes. Declining population, incomes, and real estate values, however, reduced the earnings base of many cities, even as the demand for public services by the elderly and impoverished climbed steadily. To make matters worse, aid from the federal government tapered off in the 1970s and, in the 1980s, fell substantially, making the costs of public transit and housing even more difficult to sustain.[13] With falling tax revenues and a burgeoning service-dependent population, municipal debt began to rise rapidly.[14]

9. Edward Hill, "The Cleveland Economy: A Case Study of Economic Restructuring," in Cleveland, ed. Keating, Krumholz, and Perry.

10. Edward Hill and Thomas Bier, "Economic Restructuring: Earnings, Occupations, and Housing Values in Cleveland," Economic Development Quarterly, 3:123-44 (1989).

11. Ibid.

12. K. Bradbury, A. Downs, and K. Small, Urban Decline and the Future of American Cities (Washington, DC: Brookings Institution, 1982).

13. David McKee and Richard Bennett, eds., Structural Change in an Urban Industrial Region (New York: Praeger, 1987).

14. Bradbury, Downs, and Small, Urban Decline.

TABLE 1

**POPULATION OF THE CLEVELAND
METROPOLITAN REGION,
1940-90 (Thousands)**

Year	Cleveland	Standard Metropolitan Statistical Area
1940	878	1,320
1950	915	1,533
1960	876	1,909
1970	751	2,064
1980	574	1,899
1990	503	1,880

SOURCE: *Statistical Abstract of the United States* (Washington, DC: Government Printing Office, 1993).

The growing crisis reached its apex under Cleveland Mayor Dennis Kucinich (1977-79), who promoted an urban populism antithetical to the corporate establishment, opposing tax abatements and subsidies for firms and only reluctantly increasing the local income tax. Simultaneously, Cleveland emerged as a laboratory for urban planning; under the leadership of Planning Director Norman Krumholz, the city's planners invented "advocacy planning," which explicitly challenged conventional planning guidelines as essentially do-nothing strategies that protected a highly uneven status quo.[15] Advocacy planning, in contrast, actively sought to plan on behalf of the poor and powerless, emphasizing social equity over efficiency by stressing, for example, public housing and public transportation.

15. Norman Krumholz, Janice Cogger, and John Linner, "Make No Big Plans . . . Planning in Cleveland in the 1970s," in *Planning Theory in the 1980s*, ed. R. Burchell and G. Sternlieb (New Brunswick, NJ: Rutgers Center for Urban Policy Research, 1978).

Kucinich's populism alarmed the business community, who denounced his anticorporatism and brought the full wrath of the local "growth machine" elite to bear. In December 1978, matters came to a head: bankers, who held the city's debt, led by Cleveland Trust, demanded the sale of Municipal Light to a privately owned utility in order to roll over the city's notes; Kucinich refused, charging blackmail.[16] Cleveland became the first U.S. city to default on its bonds since the Great Depression. Kucinich was ousted in 1979 after one two-year term, and Republican George Voinivich, now governor of Ohio, was elected (1979-89). Urban politics subsequently returned to "normal," with extensive tax abatements to firms that later helped set the stage for the downtown's recovery. Kucinich's brief reign illustrates that politicians who contradict the powerful vested interests of corporate capital enjoy short careers.[17]

FROM JOKE
TO JEWEL

The 1980s saw a widespread restructuring of the U.S. economy, including massive technological change and a tsunami of corporate layoffs as firms downsized to meet the prerequisites of bone-crushing global competition. This transition, which was acutely painful for mil-

16. Todd Swanstrom, "Urban Populism, Fiscal Crisis, and the New Political Economy," in *Cleveland*, ed. Keating, Krumholz, and Perry.

17. John Logan and Harvey Molotch, *Urban Fortunes: The Political Economy of Place* (Berkeley: University of California Press, 1987).

lions of households, also laid the grounds for a sustained recovery in productivity, wages, and, to a lesser extent, employment. U.S. manufacturing is now among the most productive in the world. As the East and West coasts suffered from office overbuilding, the collapse of financial firms, and reductions in military spending, the Midwest has witnessed renewed prosperity. In the face of intense international competition, the region has recovered from the traumatic restructuring of the 1980s to become a highly productive center.

In the 1990s, Cleveland has enjoyed an abrupt reversal in status and fortunes that few could have foreseen during the bleak previous decade.[18] Several factors contributed to this change, including a surprising reindustrialization. The absence of large military contractors isolated the region from the post–Cold War defense cutbacks. Devastated by two decades of deindustrialization, the cost of doing business in northeastern Ohio had reached parity with the rest of the nation; meanwhile, the region also offered a well-developed infrastructure and skilled blue-collar workforce. One important force has been a reinvigorated automobile industry. The demand for automobiles, fueled by cheap petroleum, has assisted northeastern Ohio's parts producers and assemblers. Throughout much of Ohio, Japanese "greenfield" transplants in the automobile indus-

try have created numerous jobs.[19] Ford has reinvested in its Brook Park plant, and Ford and Nissan set up a new minivan plant near Lorain.

Other forms of industry are also flourishing, if with fewer workers. American Steel and Wire reopened the old U.S. Steel plant in 1986. The instruments industry has seen new producers of circuit boards (such as Techmar) and calibration equipment. British Petroleum's absorption of Sohio included a movement of its world headquarters from New York to Cleveland. In chemicals, paints, and industrial coatings, Sherwin Williams and Glidden are headquartered in Cleveland's Public Square, the city's historic and commercial center, while the Ferro Corporation, with 800 employees, is headquartered nearby.[20] LTV Steel Corporation, whose Cleveland plant is the nation's largest flat-rolled facility, has entered into a joint venture with Sumitomo Metals.[21] Farther south, in Hudson, Ohio, Little Tykes, a division of Rubbermaid, has innovated plastic molded toys (a booming market given the birth of the baby boomlet).

The globalization of the U.S. economy also played a role in Cleveland's renaissance. Ohio is the nation's seventh-largest exporter of merchandise. The Center for Regional Eco-

18. Dennis Keating, "Cleveland: The 'Comeback' City. The Politics of Redevelopment and Sports Stadiums Amidst Urban Decline," in *Reconstructing Urban Regime Theory: Regulating Urban Politics in an Urban Economy*, ed. Mickey Lauria (Thousand Oaks, CA: Sage, 1997).

19. Andrew Mair, Richard Florida, and Martin Kenney, "The New Geography of Automobile Production: Japanese Transplants in North America," *Economic Geography*, 64:352-73 (1988).

20. Edward Hill, "Cleveland, Ohio: Manufacturing Matters, Services Strengthened, But Earnings Erode," in *Economic Restructuring of the American Midwest*, ed. Richard Bingham and Randall Ebberts (Boston: Kluwer, 1990).

21. Hill, "Cleveland Economy."

nomic Issues estimates that the Cleveland metro area exported $3.8 billion worth of commodities in 1993, employing 72,000 of the region's labor force. The top export industries included chemicals ($969 million), industrial machinery ($616 million), electronic equipment ($493 million), instruments ($312 million), transportation equipment (that is, automobiles, $310 million), and fabricated metal products ($294 million). The region's largest trading partners include, in order, Canada, Mexico, Great Britain, Germany, Japan, Taiwan, and France.[22] Cleveland also benefited from the implementation of the U.S.-Canada Free Trade Agreement in 1989;[23] because many of the region's exports were hampered in the Canadian market by tariffs and nontariff barriers, and because they exhibit relatively high price elasticities of demand, this trade agreement may generate an increase in Ohio exports between 4.5 and 5.9 percent.

As northeastern Ohio has been catapulted into the age of post-Fordism, characterized by niche markets, vertical disintegration and increased subcontracting, flexible production systems, just-in-time inventories, and enhanced skill levels,[24] a network of high-technology

firms has flourished in industries such as industrial machinery, chemicals, electronic equipment, and instruments production.[25] The NASA-Lewis Research Center tests equipment for space flight and trains astronauts. The region has become a leading center for research into polymers and liquid crystals. The Edison Biotechnology Center and the Great Lakes Manufacturing Technology Center, in Cleveland, and the Edison Polymer Innovation Corporation, in Brecksville, have provided assistance as well. The growth of such companies has been aided by the Cleveland Advanced Manufacturing Program, which assists manufacturers with technical assistance, quality control, worker training, marketing, and adherence to international standards.[26]

Simultaneously, services have grown steadily in northeastern Ohio. Many of the region's hospitals, banks, and law and accounting firms arose as providers for the mammoth industrial firms in the late nineteenth century. Services have increased in their absolute and relative shares of the local labor market. In 1993, 592,000 people in the Cleveland metropolitan area worked in services, compared to

22. Case Western Reserve University, Weatherhead School of Management, Center for Regional Economic Issues, "REI's Profile of the Northeast Ohio Economy," 1995, World Wide Web http://weatherhead.cwru.edu/dept/rei/neo_prof.html.

23. Barney Warf and James Randall, "The U.S.-Canada Free Trade Agreement: Impacts on U.S. States and Canadian Provinces," *International Regional Science Review*, 17:99-119 (1994).

24. Erica Schoenberger, "From Fordism to Flexible Accumulation: Technology, Competitive Strategies and International Location," *Environment and Planning D: Society and Space*, 6:245-62 (1988); Amin, *Post-Fordism.*

25. Audrey Clarke, "Spatial Linkages and Subcontracting Relationships Among High-Technology Industries in the Northeastern Ohio Region," *Environment and Planning A*, 26:1579-1603 (1994); Audrey Clarke and Brian Holly, "The Organization of Production in High Technology Industries: An Empirical Assessment," *Professional Geographer*, 48:127-39 (1996).

26. Center for Regional Economic Issues, "REI's Profile."

TABLE 2
FORTUNE 500 COMPANIES HEADQUARTERED IN CLEVELAND, 1995

Company	Industry	*Fortune* 500 Rank
TRW	diversified, auto	68
Eaton	diversified, auto	115
LTV	basic metals	123
Sherwin-Williams	paint, coatings	163
Parker-Hannifin	industrial equipment	187
Reliance Electric	electronics	253
American Greetings	greeting cards	255
MA Hanna	rubber, plastics	268
Nacco Industries	industrial equipment	272
Lubrizol	chemicals	276
Ferro	chemicals	355
Geon	chemicals	369
Lincoln Electric	industrial equipment	396
Figgie International	industrial equipment	418
Standard Products	rubber, plastics	420
Sealy	furniture	461
RPM	chemicals	491

SOURCE: Center for Regional Economic Issues, 1995.

185,000 in manufacturing. Surprisingly, the region has witnessed a rapid growth in health services, which employed 99,600 people, a reflection of the area's aging population and the rising share of gross national product spent on medical care. For example, the Cleveland Clinic rivals Minnesota's Mayo Clinic as a world-renowned center of specialized medical care and generates $300 million in extra-local revenues.[27] Other large services include retailing (SIC 53-59, employing a total of 85,000), wholesale trade (63,000), eating or drinking establishments (52,000), and business services (55,900).

Cleveland's services include a disproportionate number of headquarters (which perform functions such as administration and research).

Largely a legacy of its industrial past, 21 headquarters of the *Fortune* 500 are located in the Cleveland metro region (Table 2), including TRW, Eaton, LTV, Reliance Electric, and Parker-Hannifin. While the Cleveland metropolitan area is nineteenth largest in the nation, it ranks fourth in headquarters, following New York, Chicago, and Houston.

Many of the region's services are exported extra-locally. Goe found that even in a traditionally manufacturing-dependent economy such as that of northeastern Ohio, producer services (financial and producer services sold primarily to firms, not households) are exported elsewhere.[28] Cleveland producer service firms derived, on average, 36.3 per-

27. M. Magnet, "How Business Bosses Saved a Sick City," *Fortune*, 27 Mar. 1989.

28. Richard Goe, "Producer Services, Trade and the Social Division of Labour," *Regional Studies*, 24:327-42 (1990).

cent of their gross revenues from clients in other cities, including 19.5 percent from outside of Ohio and 3.6 percent outside of the United States. Cleveland is the headquarters to 14 of the nation's 500 largest legal services firms.[29] Such firms reflect the growing demand for specialized expertise that producer services provide, as well as the increases in subcontracting that typify the emerging post-Fordist global, national, and regional economies.[30]

Unfortunately, services tend to pay lower salaries than manufacturing jobs: the average service worker in northeastern Ohio receives only 56 percent of the income of the average manufacturing employee.[31] Cleveland, like much of the nation, has seen the substitution of relatively well-paying blue-collar jobs by lower-paying pink-collar and white-collar jobs. The distribution of income today in the region has grown more unequal over time.[32] Today, Cleveland's employment profile closely mirrors that of the United States as a whole: for the northeastern Ohio region, manufacturing accounts for 20.5 percent of total employment, compared to 15.7 percent nationally. In losing much of its regional economic uniqueness, the region has also become less sensitive to cyclical fluctuations.[33]

Cleveland's success is also attributable to the aggressive efforts of its

public authorities. In 1988, the city's Planning Commission released its Civic Vision 2000, which outlined plans for a rejuvenated downtown retailing and entertainment district, including multi-use public spaces along the lakefront and river, streetscape beautification, and strengthening the Dual Hub Corridor linking Tower City Center with the businesses, institutions, and neighborhoods along eastbound Euclid Avenue.[34] Northeastern Ohio has the largest chamber of commerce in the nation, the Greater Cleveland Growth Association. A privately funded development strategy group of fifty local chief executive officers, Cleveland Tomorrow, created a Technology Leadership Council in 1974 to facilitate research and university–private sector interaction. The Cleveland Industrial Retention Initiative, a combined project of the Cleveland Advanced Manufacturing Program, the Growth Association, the City of Cleveland, and the Cleveland Neighborhood Development Corporation, works to minimize plant closings, provide regulatory relief, and clean up brownfield sites of contaminated land. At the federal level, Cleveland in 1994 was designated as one of eight national Empowerment Zones under the federal Empowerment Zone Act of 1993, which generated $87 million in Economic Development Initiative grants and $3 million in Title XX grants, as well as $1 million in incentive financing from the Ohio Department of Development.[35]

29. Barney Warf and Chand Wije, "The Spatial Structure of Large U.S. Law Firms," *Growth and Change*, 22:157-74 (1992).

30. Schoenberger, "From Fordism to Flexible Accumulation"; Amin, *Post-Fordism.*

31. McKee and Bennett, eds., *Structural Change*, p. 174.

32. Hill, "Cleveland, Ohio: Manufacturing Matters."

33. Ibid.

34. Cleveland City Planning Commission, *Cleveland Civic Vision 2000* (Cleveland: Cleveland City Planning Commission, 1988).

35. Center for Regional Economic Issues, "REI's Profile."

Cleveland City, Cuyahoga County, the Cleveland Port Authority, and the Chamber of Commerce formed the Greater Cleveland International Trade Alliance to encourage international trade through northeastern Ohio and to provide export assistance.

In many respects, Cleveland has come to rival Baltimore as a poster child of urban redevelopment. Rouse, the real estate developer widely responsible for gentrified inner-city projects in Baltimore, Boston, and elsewhere, will lead a waterfront redevelopment project on the Lake Erie shore. The Flats, an ensemble of dining and musical entertainment places in restored nineteenth-century industrial buildings, has infused new energy into the city's night life. A collection of aging movie houses has been transformed into Playhouse Square, while Tower Center has arisen around the old Baltimore & Ohio Terminal Tower. Several new real estate projects have given the central business district a badly needed facelift (see Table 3). In 1995, Clevelanders celebrated the opening of the $300 million Gateway Center, an urban baseball park with attendant restaurants, retail, and parking facilities (although the Cleveland Browns promptly abandoned the city for Baltimore). The Cleveland Indians enjoy a new home at Jacobs Field, while the $92 million Rock-and-Roll Hall of Fame and Museum is designed to "lift Cleveland beyond the old age of steel and into the age of Steely Dan."[36] Four miles east of Public Square, the University Circle dis-

trict serves as Cleveland's Mecca of high culture, including the Cleveland Philharmonic; the Natural History, Art, and Children's museums; and Case Western Reserve University. Cedar Point, in Sandusky, and Sea World, in Hudson, offer further attractions. In Akron, the newly built Inventor's Hall of Fame and, in Canton, the Football Hall of Fame hold promise for a long-sought tourist alley stretching through northeast Ohio. Contrary to the old gag about spending a year in Cleveland one weekend, the region now attempts to make itself "the pre-eminent visitors' destination between New York and Chicago."[37] Indeed, Cleveland—long a city with a notorious reputation as an uncultured, working-class city void of sophistication—has emerged as an important center of cultural consumption, with a reputation as the "Comeback City" carefully crafted by the local growth machine.

This effort should be viewed as part of Cleveland's attempts to position itself vis-à-vis neighboring cities. As Hill notes, "Cleveland is engaged in a competitive struggle with Pittsburgh, Columbus, and Detroit to become the economic capital of the eastern end of the Great Lakes region."[38] Pittsburgh's well-known success in remaking itself from a steel-producing city to an economy centered around business and medical services has become a role model for many Rustbelt communities. One adage holds that "Cleveland seeks to

36. Iver Peterson, "The 'Mistake' Wakes Up, Roaring," *New York Times*, 10 Sept. 1995.

37. A. Schorr, ed., *Cleveland Development: A Dissenting View* (Cleveland: Case Western University, Mandel School of Applied Science, 1991).

38. Hill, "Cleveland, Ohio: Manufacturing Matters," p. 135.

TABLE 3
MAJOR REAL ESTATE PROJECTS IN CLEVELAND IN THE 1980S AND 1990S

Firm	Type of Activity
Ohio Bell	new headquarters
Eaton Corporation	new headquarters
British Petroleum	new headquarters
Galleria	shopping mall
Society Center	mixed land use center
Cleveland Union Terminal	mixed land use center, transit
Playhouse Square	revived entertainment district
North Coast Harbor	waterfront promenade
Gateway	sports complex
Rock and Roll Hall of Fame	museum
Hyatt Regency	hotel
Marriott	hotel

SOURCE: Compiled by authors from various sources, esp. Edward Hill, "The Cleveland Economy: A Case Study of Economic Restructuring," in *Cleveland: A Metropolitan Reader*, ed. W. Keating, N. Krumholz, and D. Perry (Kent, OH: Kent State University Press, 1995).

be like Pittsburgh, and Detroit seeks to be like Cleveland." In the current climate of increasingly mobile, internationalized capital flows, Cleveland's attempts to create a good business climate reflect the reconstructed relations between capital and space that characterize the late twentieth century.

Despite its successes, Cleveland still struggles with the legacy of decades of economic decline. The rapid growth of the suburbs, which constitute three-quarters of the metro area's population, has intensified the exodus of middle-class whites (a phenomenon subsidized by the federal government through the interstate highway system). In addition to older communities such as Shaker Heights, a pros-

perous collection of communities is found in cities such as Beachwood, Mayfield Heights, and Randall Park, all of which exemplify the growth of low-density, sprawling communities on the urban fringe.[39] Within Cleveland proper, especially east of downtown, large areas consist of dilapidated warehouses and abandoned storefronts and houses. Forty percent of Clevelanders, half of whom are black, remain below the poverty level. Indeed, a map of Cuyahoga County's median family income in 1990 (see Figure 1) reveals the familiar archipelago of wealth surrounding an impoverished central city. Despite the growth of high-end retail malls downtown and on the urban periphery, central-city housing abandonment has accelerated, and thousands remain homeless.[40] Many inner-city blacks are denied access to the labor market by a lack of skills, a crime- and drug-ridden environment, racism, and a poor educational system.[41] Half of Cleveland's high school students fail to graduate. Trapped by poverty, lack of education, inadequate transportation, and little access to burgeoning suburban housing and labor markets, Cleveland's black population suffered much of the brunt of deindustrialization and few benefits of the recent renaissance in growth. In the 1980s, reductions in federal aid to cities and welfare pro-

39. Joel Garreau, *Edge City: Life on the New Frontier* (New York: Anchor Books, 1988).
40. Hill and Bier, "Economic Restructuring."
41. William J. Wilson, *The Truly Disadvantaged: The Inner City, the Underclass, and Public Policy* (Chicago: University of Chicago Press, 1987).

FIGURE 1
MEDIAN FAMILY INCOME, CUYAHOGA COUNTY, 1990

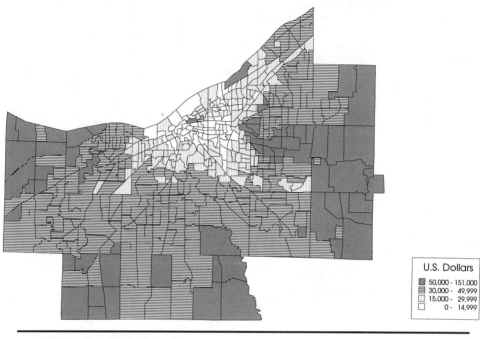

U.S. Dollars
▨ 50,000 - 151,000
▤ 30,000 - 49,999
▥ 15,000 - 29,999
☐   0 - 14,999

SOURCE: Compiled by the authors.

grams augmented the suffering of the city's poor and powerless.

CONCLUSION

Like many urban places, Cleveland has surfed through numerous restructurings, riding successive waves of capital investment and disinvestment over different historical epochs. Rapid growth in the late nineteenth and early twentieth centuries created an economy centered around durable goods, particularly steel and automobiles. To a steel- or autoworker living in the region during the 1920s, the notion that Cleveland's prosperity would not last indefinitely would have been inconceivable. The 1970s and 1980s,

however, saw devastating deindustrialization as Cleveland proved to be vulnerable to the new global economy; correspondingly, the region suffered massive capital disinvestment, population losses, rising unemployment and poverty, and real estate abandonment.

In the 1990s, a new wave of growth has washed over the city. The revival of manufacturing reflects the conjunction of the post-Fordist production systems that have re-energized the Rustbelt and the city's retention of its centralized location at the heart of North America. The Cleveland metro area has become centered around services and is less vulnerable to the oscillations of the business cycle. Through serendipity and aggressive promotional efforts, the city has enjoyed a remarkable transformation from cultural backwater to avant-garde avatar of chic. Although the metro area is now predominantly white-collar in nature and heavily suburbanized, the problems of the ghettoized inner city have persisted.

These periodic episodes have been driven largely by Cleveland's changing competitive position within the national and, increasingly, global division of labor. Each of these bouts left an indelible imprint on the local landscape, creating a unique mixture of peoples and places that defines northeastern Ohio. In many ways, Cleveland serves as a mirror to reflect the ways in which Kondratieff waves are given expression in the urban landscape, including capital investment and disinvestment, industrialization and deindustrialization, suburbanization and ghettoization, white flight and a black underclass, the growth of services, and a dual economy. Given the instability of capitalism, in which the only constant is change, the only certainty is that the current renaissance will not last indefinitely.

The Philadelphia Experience

By CAROLYN T. ADAMS

ABSTRACT: While Philadelphia has developed many links to the global economy, this city region does not qualify as a world city on a par with New York or Los Angeles. Ironically, in an era of increasing globalization, Philadelphia's regional economy is arguably more locally oriented than during the heyday of manufacturing because services are not as exportable as manufactured goods. This article identifies some of the advantages and problems associated with Philadelphia's status as a regional city rather than a world city. It examines the prospects for city-suburban cooperation to enhance the region's competitive economic position. The politics of regional cooperation are illustrated by three examples of physical infrastructure: the Pennsylvania Convention Center, the ports of Philadelphia and Camden, and the Naval Shipyard. The author concludes that even to promote infrastructure that supports business, the political and business leaders have difficulty cooperating.

Carolyn T. Adams is dean of the College of Arts and Sciences at Temple University, where she teaches courses in urban development, urban politics, and public policy. Her publications focusing on Philadelphia include a coauthored study of the transformation of that city's economy and politics since World War II, entitled Philadelphia: Neighborhoods, Division, and Conflict in a Postindustrial City.

THE evidence of Philadelphia's multiplying links with the global economy is abundant. Global trends have affected this east coast metropolis in many of the same ways they have affected other cities discussed in this volume. Foreign capital has become increasingly influential in the region's economy, most visibly in its real estate market. During the 1980s, Japanese banks and insurance firms held prominent interests in downtown office buildings, hotels, and retail complexes. French lenders helped finance major office construction projects and the massive renovation of the city's main passenger rail station at 30th Street, while Japanese lenders helped refinance what has become the largest suburban shopping center in the region, in King of Prussia.

Foreign investors bought some of the region's best-established corporations. One noteworthy example was the purchase of SmithKline Beckman Corporation by Britain's Beecham Group in 1989, which shifted to foreign owners one of the leading pharmaceutical firms. In another important example, France's Elf Aquitaine acquired Pennwalt, a prominent chemical firm. Although pharmaceuticals and petrochemicals are two of the region's leading sectors,[1] they are increasingly vulnerable to corporate decisions made half a world away. The local impact was immediate when in 1996 the merger of a Swiss drug firm, Ciba-Geigy, with a Swiss chemical company, Sandoz, threatened employees at a suburban Philadelphia plant that had been acquired only two years earlier by Ciba-Geigy.[2]

More and more Philadelphia firms, both large and small, are aligning themselves with overseas partners: a large specialty chemical company, Rohm & Haas, has formed a joint venture with German partners to develop and sell petroleum additives; a small suburban instrument manufacturer has a joint venture with Saigon Tourist Cable Television to install scrambling systems for the Vietnamese cable company; a suburban mutual fund is teaming with an Irish fund-processing firm to provide off-shore services for U.S.-based investment managers. Similar examples appear daily in local business media.

Philadelphia is attracting international labor as well as investment. The importance of international immigration is obvious when we consider that without Asian and Latino newcomers, the region would have registered no net population gain between 1980 and 1990. If we define "immigrants" as those with a different national and linguistic identity, then Puerto Ricans (who are U.S. citizens) compose the largest group of newcomers. Their spatial concentration in North Philadelphia neighborhoods contributes to their visibility in local politics and culture. Since 1980, Korea has sent the next largest group, followed by India, Vietnam, Jamaica, the Philippines, Cambodia, and China. Another smaller but still important group is East European,

1. At present, the Philadelphia region has five times the national average of pharmaceutical jobs and twice the national average of jobs in synthetics, plastics, and high-end chemical manufacturing.

2. Steve Sakson, "A Swiss Merger Could Mean Cuts in the Area's Jobs," *Philadelphia Inquirer*, 8 Mar. 1996.

mainly Soviet Jews and Poles. Although Philadelphia attracts far fewer immigrants than New York or Los Angeles, their presence is highly visible. Rather than seeking to assimilate, many retain strong national identities and ties to their homeland by frequent travel and telephone contact.[3]

Like other regions embedded in the global economy, Philadelphia has experienced an increase in its informal economy that is significant though hard to document accurately. Reflecting the rising importance of subcontracting as a strategy for manufacturers, small plants have emerged as suppliers to larger firms in the apparel trade, woodworking, and metalworking. These small enterprises tend to employ nonunion immigrant workers to whom they pay piecework wages and few benefits. When the U.S. Labor Department cites garment sweatshops that have violated wage and hour laws, Philadelphia subcontractors often make the list.[4] They can be found in both the city and suburbs of the region.

In addition to international economic relations, the changing military situation has had profound consequences for the region. Philadelphia suffered serious job losses in the demobilization of federal defense installations during the 1990s. The base closings included the Philadelphia Naval Shipyard, Naval Hospital, and Defense Clothing Factory, which together employed over 4000 civilian workers, plus a Naval Air Warfare Center in suburban Bucks County that generated employment for almost 4000 more. Neither the city nor Bucks County has yet developed a conversion plan.

Yet, for all these signs testifying to the increasing ties with events and people in distant parts of the globe, Philadelphia does not qualify as a world city—one of what Castells called "concentrated decision-making units in a few commanding heights of the international economy."[5] While Philadelphia possesses two of the three defining characteristics of world cities,[6] it is missing the third, most critical component:

1. Like world cities, Philadelphia exhibits an extremely high concentration of producer services, services to businesses that are easier for them to buy from outside than to provide with the company's own employees. This is the single fastest-growing segment of the region's economy, encompassing insurance, financial services, design, legal services, accounting, software, and many other supports to business.

2. Philadelphia possesses a rich physical and social infrastructure. Its physical assets include a distinctive historical center; an attractive pedestrian-oriented downtown busi-

3. Judith Goode and JoAnne Schneider, *Reshaping Ethnic and Racial Relations in Philadelphia* (Philadelphia: Temple University Press, 1994), p. 96.

4. Susan Warner, "Garment Sweatshops? Contractors Unclothed," *Philadelphia Inquirer*, 4 May 1996.

5. Manuel Castells, ed., *High Technology, Space and Society* (Beverly Hills, CA: Sage, 1985), p. 30.

6. The three determining characteristics are cited in Arie Sachar, "World Cities in the Making: The European Context," in *North American Cities and the Global Economy*, ed. P. K. Kresl and G. Gappert (Thousand Oaks, CA: Sage, 1995), p. 154.

ness district; a well-developed mass transit system serving large parts of the region with commuter rail lines; and convenient rail connections to New York, Washington, and other east coast cities. The region's sociocultural infrastructure includes a larger number of higher education institutions than can be found in any U.S. metropolis except Boston, and a sophisticated cultural community that includes a major symphony orchestra and an abundance of museums, libraries, theaters, multicultural and community centers, and historic landmarks.

3. What Philadelphia lacks, however, is a management and financial center of global reach. It is no longer a banking center. In 1980 Philadelphia boasted eight large hometown commercial banks. Now CoreStates is the only major bank headquartered in the region. All the others have been merged or taken over. For example, Girard Bank and Philadelphia Savings Fund Society—both well-established Philadelphia institutions—were bought by Mellon Bank and are controlled from Pittsburgh. The region has also lost major corporate headquarters, many of them to international acquisitions. One indication that this is no longer a headquarters town is the composition of Greater Philadelphia First Corporation (GPFC), established in 1983 as a coalition of chief executive officers from the largest corporations in the region who banded together to promote economic development. By 1996, about half of the 32 seats on its board of directors were not filled by chief executive officers but by regional managers, local partners, or heads of subsidiaries.

A REGIONALLY ORIENTED ECONOMY

Ironically, in this era of increasing globalization, the prevailing economic trends render the Philadelphia economy more locally oriented than ever. This region's experience supports the ideas set forth in an intriguing article by Persky and Wiewel.[7] They argue that the economies of many large metropolitan areas in the United States are now more locally oriented than ever because of the decline of manufacturing and the rise of local consumer services. More highly educated workforces demand more extensive and sophisticated local services, whose importance in metropolitan economies outweighs that of globally oriented jobs. To test their hypothesis, Persky and Wiewel assembled data for 45 metropolitan regions showing for every industrial category the share of local demand that was met by local supply. Comparing estimates from 1969, 1979, and 1989, they found that the local-oriented share of economic activity in these regions rose significantly over the two decades because the rise in internationally oriented activities was more than offset by the combined results of dwindling manufacturing exports and rising local services.

The Philadelphia region mirrors those national trends. Table 1 shows the dramatic loss of manufacturing employment in the city over recent decades, but it also portrays an entire region whose manufacturing base diminished substantially between 1970

7. Joseph Persky and Wim Wiewel, "The Growing Localness of the Global City," *Economic Geography*, 70(2):129-43 (Apr. 1994).

TABLE 1

NONAGRICULTURAL EMPLOYMENT BY INDUSTRY CLUSTER,
1970 AND 1990 (In thousands of jobs)

	City			Metropolitan Region		
Employment Category	1970	1990	Percentage change	1970	1990	Percentage change
Manufacturing	235.7	82.2	−65%	549.0	348.4	−37%
Services	180.8	266.6	+47%	325.2	695.7	+114%
Finance, insurance, and real estate	71.4	65.0	−9%	102.1	162.1	+59%
Transport and utilities	67.1	40.3	−40%	104.9	100.5	−4%
Wholesale	63.1	40.8	−35%	104.6	136.5	+30%
Retail	115.4	95.8	−17%	265.3	371.9	+40%
Construction	32.9	15.8	−52%	82.5	100.7	+22%
Government						
Federal and military	67.1	56.9	−15%	88.4	80.1	−9%
State and local	86.9	86.1	−1%	176.2	227.7	+29%

SOURCE: Janice Madden and William Stull, *Work, Wages and Poverty: Income Distribution in Post-Industrial Philadelphia* (Philadelphia: University of Pennsylvania Press, 1991), pp. 193-96.

and 1990. In contrast, the categories of greatest growth for the region were in the service sector: services; finance, insurance, and real estate; wholesale trade; and retail trade.

Whether the shift to services necessarily creates a more locally oriented economy depends upon whether the region can export a large share of the services it produces. There is considerable debate about this question. Obviously, personal services like retail, social services, janitorial, security, and so on are consumed locally. But what about services to businesses? Can they be exported? Clearly, some can, in the way New York exports advertising and banking services, or Boston exports computer software services. But the competitive advantage of most service firms is eroded by the increasing dispersion of business services across metropolitan areas. Stull and Madden document the limitations on exporting services to businesses. They

conclude that business services provided by firms located outside the metropolitan area are less competitive than those provided locally: "Producer service jobs are increasingly tied to the area where their output is utilized."[8]

GPFC, the pro-development business coalition mentioned earlier, appears more optimistic. GPFC has designed an economic development strategy for the region based primarily on boosting the export of services, particularly health care services, finance, insurance, marketing, printing and publishing, law, engineering services, higher education, and hospitality services (through tourism and conventions).[9] Many of these are

8. William Stull and Janice Madden, *Post-Industrial Philadelphia: Structural Changes in the Metropolitan Economy* (Philadelphia: University of Pennsylvania Press, 1990), p. 51.

9. Greater Philadelphia First, *Gaining the Lead in the Global Economy: An Economic Development Strategy for the Greater Philadel-*

the kinds of business services that Stull and Madden argue will be difficult to export as more and more communities develop their own local suppliers.

It is worth noting that one positive feature of the shift to a service economy is that it increases the stability of the local economy. Manufacturing is footloose and disruptive of the local economy, but many services have a stake in the city. Further, employment in services is less vulnerable to the fluctuations of the business cycle than employment in manufacturing is.[10]

SHOULD PHILADELPHIA ASPIRE TO WORLD CITY STATUS?

Should Philadelphians lament the fact that they do not inhabit a world city? Perhaps not. The advantages of living in one of the world's command-and-control centers are lessened by some important drawbacks. One is the sharp rise in the price of commercial rents, industrial services, and other business services characteristic of world cities. The consequence of bidding up these prices is to make it increasingly precarious for moderately profitable firms to survive. Many less profitable firms are forced to operate informally or may go out of business altogether.[11]

There is little evidence that Philadelphia corporations are bidding up

commercial rents in this fashion. The boom in downtown office development during the 1980s, fueled by federal tax incentives, created gleaming new towers of quality space and emptied many older buildings of their tenants. Rather than inflating rents, the boom produced an increase in the vacancy rate for office space, which climbed from 8 percent in 1985 to almost 20 percent in 1993. Many suburban office districts were similarly overbuilt, for example, parts of Burlington and Camden counties in South Jersey and the Pennsylvania suburbs of Fort Washington and Willow Grove. The glut of office space has kept rents reasonable for entrepreneurs with plans for start-ups or expansions.[12]

Nor is it clear that losing corporate headquarters brings financial ruin. The choice of headquarters appears less and less to be the determinant of where a company creates jobs. Corporate operations may be widely dispersed, going wherever makes the most business sense. Thus maintaining a world headquarters is no guarantee of securing a substantial number of jobs. For example, one of the worldwide firms headquartered in Philadelphia is Aramark, a food service firm. A decade ago, its headquarters staff of 230 managed a worldwide employee force of 110,000. By 1995 its widely dispersed workforce had expanded to 148,000 but the company still employed the same number in its headquarters.[13]

---

phia Region (Philadelphia: Greater Philadelphia First, 1995).

10. Stull and Madden, *Post-Industrial Philadelphia*, p. 51. See also *Business Review* (Federal Reserve Bank of Philadelphia) (Dec. 1975). This is a special issue on "Jobs in Philadelphia: Experience and Prospects."

11. Saskia Sassen, "Cities and Communities in the Global Economy," *American Behavioral Scientist*, 39(5):633-34 (Mar.-Apr. 1996).

12. David Turner, "City Office Vacancies at Record High," *Philadelphia Inquirer*, 23 July 1993.

13. Andrew Cassel, "Is It a Big Deal that Scott Paper Is Leaving?" *Philadelphia Inquirer*, 19 Mar. 1995.

Another drawback to the world city status is its tendency to aggravate the income polarization already inherent in the postindustrial city. Admittedly, this point can be debated. Sassen argues that world cities exhibit the sharpest income polarization because their leading sectors are structured to offer either very high-wage or very low-wage jobs. Furthermore, the highly paid classes demand increasing levels of consumer services, which creates even more low-wage jobs in the economy.[14] Other analysts caution that there may be many other, equally important determinants of income inequality in U.S. cities. Burtless, a Brookings economist, shows income inequality rising at comparable rates in both the internationally linked sectors and the local sectors. He emphasizes other factors accounting for inequality: changing technology that reduces the demand for low-skilled workers, the growth of single-parent households, and the cuts in government assistance to the poor all depress the incomes of some households while the high employment rates among middle- and upper-class women generate affluence for other households.[15]

In a recent study of Philadelphia,[16] my colleagues and I found that the flight of manufacturing and the ad-

vent of the service economy had contributed to divergent incomes, stratifying residential neighborhoods, and even stratifying the political process. We found a large number of the city's neighborhoods had simply become disconnected from the region's structures of opportunity. These widening disparities are reflected particularly strongly in the operation of the housing market, which produces scenes of gentrified splendor next to dilapidated public housing. They also strain the region's political infrastructure, which seems unable to mediate between groups with increasingly divergent stakes in the city. Even as a regional city, then, Philadelphia displays polarization. The likelihood is that this picture would be considerably worsened by ascending to world city status.

UNABATED SUBURBANIZATION

Perhaps even more than world cities, regional cities are subject to powerful forces of decentralization. According to Sassen:

Firms in more routine lines of work and with predominantly regional or national markets increasingly appear to be free to establish their headquarters outside cities or to relocate there. Firms in highly competitive and innovative fields or with a strong world market orientation (or both) appear to benefit from locations at the center of major international business centers, no matter how high the costs.[17]

14. Saskia Sassen, *Global City: New York, London and Tokyo* (Princeton, NJ: Princeton University Press, 1991).

15. Gary Burtless, "Worsening American Income Inequality: Is World Trade to Blame?" *Brookings Review*, 14(2):26-31 (Spring 1996).

16. Carolyn Adams et al., *Philadelphia: Neighborhoods, Division, and Conflict in a Postindustrial City* (Philadelphia: Temple University Press, 1991).

17. Saskia Sassen, "Urban Impacts of Economic Globalization" (Occasional Paper Series in Comparative Urban Studies, no. 5, Woodrow Wilson International Center for Scholars, 1993), p. 10.

In short, transnational corporations, whose operations are dispersed over many locations—some of them in nations with different legal, commercial, and cultural systems—require complex and specialized business services that concentrate in downtown locations. By contrast, companies that lack high levels of overseas activity and require less specialized services need not locate downtown.

The locally oriented firms that now predominate in Philadelphia's economy are tied to the region but not to a specific location within the region. They can locate anywhere in the metro region.[18] This fact engenders sometimes-fierce competition between neighboring jurisdictions, such as the 1996 rivalry between Philadelphia and Camden for a back-office operation of PNC Bank Corporation that guaranteed 1200 jobs. To outbid its neighbor across the Delaware River, Philadelphia offered almost $11 million in grants and loans supplemented by an additional $6.5 million from the state government, plus a promise that the company could count part of its property taxes toward repayment of the city loans.

Under these conditions, the forces favoring dispersion to suburban office parks and malls are likely to remain more powerful for a regional city than they would be for a world city, where the premium location is unquestionably at the center. The major public planning agency at the regional level, the Delaware Valley Regional Planning Commission (DVRPC) has created a model to estimate the land consumption likely to be associated with economic and

population growth to the year 2020. The region's modest population growth of around 11 percent and employment growth of 20 percent between 1990 and 2020 will consume another 11 percent of the total land area.[19] The greatest growth, it forecasts, will occur at the ex-urban fringe where low-density, single-family detached housing developments and office parks will locate on fields or farmland along highway corridors.

The prospect of losing more open space to continuing sprawl alarms many in the region. To minimize the impact of economic and population growth, the DVRPC recommends concentrating new development in a hierarchy of existing and emerging regional centers rather than dispersing it to new areas. But coordinated planning is extremely difficult because Pennsylvania grants to each of 239 municipalities in the region almost total control over land use within its borders. The regional planning commission has the power only to exhort municipalities to fashion zoning ordinances to encourage higher-density development and preserve open spaces. It cannot impose any plan.

PROSPECTS FOR
REGIONAL COOPERATION

Both Neal Peirce[20] and David Rusk[21] have asserted that global com-

18. Persky and Wiewel, "Growing Localness," p. 139.

19. Delaware Valley Regional Planning Commission, *Guiding Regional Growth* (Philadelphia: Delaware Valley Regional Planning Commission, 1995), p. 17.

20. Neal Peirce, *Citistates: How Urban America Can Prosper in a Competitive World* (Washington, DC: Seven Locks Press, 1993).

21. David Rusk, *Cities Without Suburbs* (Washington, DC: Woodrow Wilson Center Press, 1993).

petition in exporting goods and services absolutely requires cities and suburbs to cooperate within regional frameworks. As he did for a dozen other cities in the United States, Peirce acted as a consultant to Philadelphia and produced a broad-ranging report with a multitude of policy recommendations exhorting the region's leaders to seek greater regional cooperation: "Why think regionally? . . . Because only cohesive, efficient urban regions are going to make it in the new world economy."[22]

What are the region's prospects for implementing Peirce's brave vision of the Philadelphia citistate? We can approach this question by focusing on three of the region's strategic physical assets. Physical development projects are often the linchpin of local economic development efforts.

No city offers more proof of the power of concrete images for promoting development. Back in 1947, the Better Philadelphia Exhibition mounted at Gimbel's Department Store featured a motorized scale model, 14 feet by 30 feet in size, of the central business district. The model's component sections flipped over to reveal the gleaming new structures and streets that were proposed to replace those of the worn-out city center. This exhibit, designed by city planners to sell their idea, is credited with launching a downtown development campaign that lasted three decades.

Because they afford concrete images, physical development projects are often easier to sell to various constituencies than are intangible pri-

22. Neal Peirce and Curtis Johnson, "Reinventing the Region: The Peirce Report," special insert, *Philadelphia Inquirer*, 26 Mar. 1995.

orities like education, training, or social welfare. Yet, for all their concrete character, the following three cases illustrate the difficulty of achieving broad-based cooperation to develop the region's physical infrastructure.

*Pennsylvania
Convention Center*

In the early 1980s, the Reading Company proposed to build a 1-million-square-foot convention complex centered on its former train shed on five city blocks in the heart of downtown. The project was embraced by civic leaders as the largest single development project in the city's history, at a cost of a half billion dollars. Planning for the giant facility plodded forward for a dozen years, through three different mayoral administrations. The jobs and contracts it represented became the focus of conflict between the populist forces in City Council and the project's backers in the mayor's office and business community.

When the bill authorizing the state's contribution came before the state legislature in 1986, several dozen state legislators representing Philadelphia suburbs tried to block it. As Republicans, the suburban legislators were not swayed by their Republican governor's support for the investment. Their opposition was a tactic to protest the wage tax that Philadelphia levies on suburbanites employed within the city limits. To suburbanites, this tax has represented taxation without representation. That long-standing feud spilled over into legislative debate on the Convention Center project. Suburban politicians, however, were not the only opponents threatening to block the project. Legislators representing the city's minority neighborhoods lobbied for minority hiring provisions. To the embarrassment of the city's mayor and business leaders, who were pressing for state support of the project, 9 of 22 members of the Philadelphia delegation voted against the state's appropriation to support the facility because the bill contained no assurances of jobs for minorities and women. The legislation passed only after an assurance came from the builders trade unions that they would abide by minority hiring guidelines even in the absence of legislative requirements.

The Convention Center finally opened in June 1993 in a public relations flurry. One recent analysis of its prospects estimated that, by 2004, it will have created 1708 new jobs and generated $17.8 million in city and state taxes.[23] Notwithstanding this optimistic forecast, the Convention Center nevertheless will continue to require taxpayer subsidies from Philadelphia city government for another decade. (That subsidy is estimated at $21 million for 1996.)

*Ports of Philadelphia
and Camden*

Maritime trade along the Delaware River is one of the region's primary links to the global economy. Historically, the cities of Camden and Philadelphia, sitting directly across the river from one another, have operated independently, sometimes

competing for shipping trade. In 1952, Pennsylvania and New Jersey created a bistate compact to cooperate on promoting maritime commerce along the river. They established the Delaware River Port Authority (DRPA), with a board of eight commissioners to represent each state. In addition to promoting river commerce, the DRPA was charged to maintain several strategic links between southeastern Pennsylvania and South Jersey: four toll bridges across the river plus one high-speed rail line from Philadelphia to the commuter suburbs of New Jersey.

However, rather than pursuing a unified regional agenda for port development, the DRPA turned into a vast patronage machine oiled by the cash from bridge tolls, which now amounts to over $100 million a year. For the past decade, its main focus has been on how to use the substantial surpluses generated every year, splitting the money between the two states.

Periodic skirmishes have occurred that reinforce the principle of equal shares for the two states. For example, in the early 1990s, rising subsidies to New Jersey's high-speed commuter rail line appeared to give New Jersey more than its fair share of the agency's resources. In 1993, at a strategic moment during the New Jersey gubernatorial campaign, Pennsylvania commissioners threatened to cut off the $12 million annual subsidy to the rail line and thereby inconvenience thousands of New Jersey commuters, unless Pennsylvania received more equal treatment. To avoid public embarrassment, New Jersey Governor Florio instructed his

23. Pennsylvania Economy League, *The Economic Impact of the Pennsylvania Convention Center, FY 1995–FY 2004* (Philadelphia: Pennsylvania Economy League, 1995).

commissioners on the DRPA, who quickly agreed to exchange the continuing subsidies to New Jersey trains for payments totaling $15 million to Philadelphia projects. Rather than tolerate an unequal split of the agency's bounty, the Pennsylvania commissioners were willing to paralyze a major commuting artery that transports thousands of daily commuters between Philadelphia and New Jersey. The leading negotiator from Philadelphia who forced the compromise explained unabashedly, "I had nothing to lose and everything to gain. . . . I could care less if they shut PATCO [the rail line] down . . . because none of my constituents rides it."[24]

Complicating relations between the states in this compact are the tensions between Philadelphia's interests and those of the Republican Pennsylvania governor. Since his election in 1994, Governor Ridge has struggled to wrest control over the Pennsylvania delegation from the Philadelphia Democrats who had been appointed by the previous governor, a Democrat. He has been only partially successful; the Democratic incumbents have vigorously resisted his efforts to oust them from a position that confers such obvious patronage benefits. Meanwhile, as the contest for political control was being fought in the early 1990s, the port was losing its share of some shipping trade, especially winter fruit from Chile, which had been a major con-

24. Pennsylvania State Senator Vincent Fumo, quoted in Marc Duvoisin and Nancy Phillips, "Fumo Reigns as Gatekeeper of Port Authority," *Philadelphia Inquirer*, 13 Nov. 1995.

tributor to the port's economy during the 1980s. This threat was among the factors highlighting a need for the states and cities to cooperate not just at the policy level but at the level of everyday operations. In 1994 DRPA formed a new subsidiary, the Ports of Philadelphia and Camden, to combine the workforces and docks on the two sides of the river into a unified operation. As of this writing, the unification, which was to have been completed in late 1995, still has not been completed, because of last-minute objections from several New Jersey commissioners.

Philadelphia
Naval Shipyard

In 1991, as part of the federal downsizing of its defense installations, the U.S. Navy announced it would end its 200-year ownership of the 1000-acre shipyard in South Philadelphia, which had at one time provided 10,000 jobs. After several years of considering and discarding conversion ideas that ranged from a Disney theme park to a gambling-based resort, the city's economic planners were heartened to learn that a German shipbuilding firm named Meyer Werft proposed to locate a world-class shipbuilding facility at the site, creating over 6000 jobs.

The German proposal called for the governments of Pennsylvania, New Jersey, and Philadelphia to contribute $167 million, with another $179 million furnished in federal loan guarantees. By the summer of 1995, the proposal had secured the endorsement of all parties except Pennsylvania's governor, who told the German company to put up more of its own capital and depend less on public investments. Meyer Werft responded by modifying the proposal, but not enough for Governor Ridge, who then issued a blistering public commentary about the German firm's unreasonable demands.

Philadelphia politicians, alarmed that the deal might fall through, used their political clout to persuade the DRPA to contribute $110 million to subsidize the package. Although this hastily crafted package was similar to his initial proposal, the owner of the German firm refused to consider it. He was unwilling to risk the soundness of his enterprise, and perhaps the welfare of the workers in his company's headquarters in Papenburg, Germany, for a deal brokered by Philadelphia politicians. Meyer was quoted as remarking that, "if you base your company's future on politicians, you have real problems when the politics changes."[25] The site remains available, with no successor project yet in sight.

CAN LOCAL POLITICIANS FORGE REGIONAL SOLUTIONS?

These cases illustrate two important points about regional cooperation. First, they show that regional cooperation led by politicians has inherent limitations. For political actors, relying on support from their local base, it is irrational to undertake cooperation that costs their con-

25. Bernard Meyer, quoted in Henry Holcomb, "Painful Lessons Can Be Learned from Meyer Deal," *Philadelphia Inquirer*, 9 Oct. 1995.

stituents more than it delivers. Hence, in Philadelphia as in other metropolises, private sector actors are central to the movement toward regionalism. The cooperative projects that businesspeople are most likely to support involve building and maintaining infrastructure that is directly supportive of private enterprise.

Even in such cases, however, the business community does not always play an active role. Of the three examples described earlier, only the Convention Center enjoyed consistent support from the business community. Neither the port unification nor the Navy yard stirred much interest among the region's business leaders. How much less likely are business leaders to champion projects like education, human services, or open-space planning that improve the quality of life for the region's citizens. They see that as a responsibility of the political establishment.

A renewed case for regional cooperation led by the political sector has recently been brought to town by a Minnesota state legislator, Myron Orfield, who was commissioned by the Pennsylvania Environmental Council to analyze the prospects of forging a political alliance between Philadelphia and the subset of older, distressed suburban communities. Orfield's experience in Minnesota has been that because they share many of the city's problems—housing deterioration, stagnating tax bases, childhood poverty, drugs, crime, eroding educational systems—the older suburbs can be drawn into a city-suburban coalition to address these problems cooperatively. Such a coalition operated within the Minnesota state legislature to pass one initiative on property tax sharing and another on sharing affordable housing across metropolitan regions. In his Philadelphia report, Orfield concluded that fully 69 percent of the region's population lives in communities for whom a city–inner suburban political alliance would make sense.[26] It remains to be seen whether Orfield's ideas can attract a serious following among the region's political leadership.

The second important point illustrated by our three cases is one that is underemphasized by Neal Peirce in *Citistates*. It is the importance of

26. Myron Orfield, "Philadelphia Metropolitics: A Regional Agenda for Community and Stability" (Draft report, Pennsylvania Environmental Council, Dec. 1995).

state government and the handicap suffered by a region that spans two different states that often find themselves bidding against one another for regional assets like corporate offices or sports teams. More than just metro-level cooperation is required to achieve development. In each of the examples cited, the relation of city and suburban leaders to state politics was crucial—in securing state dollars for the massive Convention Center, in developing the combined ports of Camden and Philadelphia, and in successfully converting abandoned defense facilities. The vertical linkages needed for regional cooperation have not received the attention they deserve as our major metropolitan regions are transformed by the global economy.

ANNALS, *AAPSS*, **551**, May 1997

State and Local Revitalization Efforts in East St. Louis, Illinois

By KENNETH M. REARDON

ABSTRACT: This article explains how the processes of suburbanization, deindustrialization, disinvestment, and globalization combined to destroy the economic security of East St. Louis, Illinois, a once-thriving industrial and transportation center. The article discusses the impact that the city's 1991 economic collapse had on its ability to maintain basic services. It describes how state and federal officials worked together during a six-year period to support the community-stabilization efforts of local officials. The article shows how specific state and federal initiatives reinforced the actions of municipal authorities to strengthen the city's fiscal well-being, enhance its municipal services, improve its housing stock, expand local business and employment opportunities, and lessen the city's most serious environmental problems. The case illustrates the powerful role that enlightened state and federal policies can play in mitigating the most serious consequences of contemporary economic restructuring on local populations.

Kenneth M. Reardon is an assistant professor of urban and regional planning at the University of Illinois at Urbana-Champaign, where he engages in research and teaching activities focused on the empowerment efforts of low-income urban communities and serves as a faculty coordinator for the university's East St. Louis Action Research Project.

E AST St. Louis is a small central city located directly across the Mississippi River from downtown St. Louis, Missouri, in southwestern Illinois. Originally called Illinoistown, East St. Louis was established in 1826 to serve the fresh-food needs of St. Louis's growing urban population.[1] The settlement was soon transformed into a major transshipment point for midwestern agricultural products being moved down the Mississippi River by barge to the cities of the eastern seaboard. The discovery of extensive coal deposits in nearby Cahokia led to East St. Louis's further development as a major railroad center in the mid-1850s. East St. Louis's central location, ample water supply, excellent river- and rail-based transportation facilities, rich coal deposits, and disciplined labor force helped transform the city into a thriving manufacturing community in the late 1800s. The city's intense demand for labor during its so-called Golden Era caused its population to increase from 15,000 to 75,000 between 1890 and 1920.

While industrialization produced thousands of jobs, it did little to create a tax base to meet the city's infrastructure and municipal service requirements. A significant number of area firms chose to build factories outside of East St. Louis, where they found cheaper land, lower taxes, weaker unions, and more pro-business municipal governments. Assisted by the Illinois state legislature, several firms created company towns beyond the East St. Louis city limits where they could exert maximum political control over their workers and minimize their tax liabilities. Efforts by East St. Louis officials to annex these rapidly growing industrial enclaves were thwarted by state legislators who feared losing these firms to neighboring Missouri. East St. Louis began to experience serious fiscal problems in the 1920s when such outmigration by business caused tax revenues to fall short of infrastructure and services expenses. The city's growing economic problems were first documented in Harland Bartholomew's *Comprehensive City Plan for East St. Louis, Illinois,* which was published in 1920. According to this report, "Of 131 cities in the United States having a population of 50,000 or over, East St. Louis has next to the lowest assets and value of public property and is very nearly the lowest in revenue receipts from taxes and in expenditures for governmental purposes."[2]

A dramatic increase in the demand for East St. Louis's industrial products and transportation services during World War II provided a temporary solution to the community's financial problems. However, a powerful set of social, economic, and political factors combined in the post–World War II period to undermine the city's economy. Coal's fading popularity as an energy source left thousands of East St. Louis residents, miners, and railroad workers without jobs. The nation's shift from rail to auto-

1. Carl Baldwin, "East St. Louis History," in *East St. Louis Revitalization Project,* vol. 2, *Student Architecture Design Studios,* ed. Carolyn L. Dry (Champaign, IL: University of Illinois, School of Architecture, 1989), pp. 6-11.

2. Harland Bartholomew, *A Comprehensive City Plan for East St. Louis, Illinois* (East St. Louis, IL: War Civics Committee, 1920), pp. 1-4.

mobile-based transportation caused additional unemployment in the city's rail yards and warehouses. The development of refrigerated railroad cars and trucks made it more economical to slaughter livestock on the range, thereby reducing the need for regional meatpacking centers like East St. Louis. These technological changes caused the number of East St. Louis businesses to fall from 1527 to 383 and the supply of local jobs to drop from 12,423 to 2699 between 1967 and 1991.[3]

East St. Louis's business and employment losses eroded the strength of the city's retail sector, which provided the lion's share of East St. Louis's tax revenues, and left the community ill prepared to compete in an increasingly global marketplace. Between 1960 and 1992, the city's property tax base declined from $562 million to $162 million, forcing local officials to raise real estate taxes to nearly 23 percent of assessed values to maintain basic municipal services.[4] When these tax increases failed to produce balanced budgets during the 1970s and 1980s, the city eliminated most municipal services, including local trash collection from 1987 until 1992. In spite of these cutbacks, the city's municipal debt grew to nearly $100 million in the early 1990s, forcing it to spend nearly half of its operating budget on debt service payments.

Skyrocketing unemployment, increasing taxes, declining municipal services, growing deficits, bank redlining, and blockbusting prompted many to abandon the city between 1960 and 1990.[5] The city's residential population fell from 88,000 to 43,000 during this period, making abandonment of housing a major issue. The departure of a significant portion of the city's Caucasian and African American working-class and middle-income families dramatically altered the community's demographic profile. Between 1960 and 1990, the African American portion of the population increased from 45 percent to 98 percent, the unemployment rate rose from 10.5 percent to 24.6 percent, the percentage of female-headed households rose from 21 percent to 62 percent, and the percentage of families living in poverty jumped from 11.0 percent to 39.2 percent.[6] In the mid-1980s, these changes prompted the U.S. Department of Housing and Urban Development (HUD) to identify East St. Louis as "the most distressed small city in America."[7]

Efforts by city officials to use the Housing Act of 1949 throughout the 1950s and 1960s to stem the tide of disinvestment, deindustrialization, and depopulation that were destabilizing the community produced dis-

3. U.S., Department of Commerce, Bureau of the Census, *County and City Data Book: 1994* (Washington, DC: Government Printing Office, 1994).

4. John Tegley, *Report on Essential Services in East St. Louis, Illinois* (East St. Louis, IL: East St. Louis Financial Advisory Authority, 1992).

5. *Census of Population* (Washington, DC: Department of Commerce, Bureau of the Census, 1960); ibid. (1990).

6. U.S., Department of Commerce, Bureau of the Census, *County and City Data Book: 1962* (Washington, DC: Government Printing Office, 1962); idem, *County and City Data Book: 1994* (1994).

7. Jonathan Kozol, *Savage Inequalities: Children in America's Schools* (New York: Harper Perennial, 1991), pp. 7-39.

appointing results.[8] Like many American cities, East St. Louis used urban renewal funds to demolish blocks of deteriorating commercial buildings within its central business district and make major infrastructure investments to stimulate new private investment. The only significant investments in the city's various renewal areas, however, were made by state and federal agencies.

Efforts to improve the quality of the city's housing stock using the federal government's various public housing programs also ran into difficulties. Large numbers of low-income families were moved into high-density public housing complexes that were poorly designed, managed, and maintained. When a significant part of the city's public housing units became uninhabitable in the mid-1980s, HUD took the unusual step of placing the East St. Louis Housing Authority under federal receivership. The private agency selected by HUD to manage the local housing authority received permission in the early 1990s to demolish more than 640 existing housing units at two high-density complexes. Efforts to replace these eight-story apartment buildings with low-density townhouse apartment complexes have encountered widespread community opposition from neighborhood organizations whose leaders question the continued concentration of the poor and the property management record of the housing authority and receivers.

HITTING BOTTOM IN THE EARLY 1990s

The city's economic condition declined throughout the early 1990s as businesses and families left the community in search of greater economic opportunity and improved quality of life in the suburbs. Its financial problems reached a climax on 28 September 1990 when it defaulted on a court-mandated payment compensating an individual who had been seriously injured in the municipal jail.[9] When the city informed the court that it lacked the resources to meet its $3.4 million legal obligation to the injured party, the judge asked for an inventory of its assets. The judge then attempted to compensate this individual by awarding the East St. Louis City Hall, along with 220 acres of city-owned riverfront property, to his estate. The city's impending loss of its municipal building became an important national newspaper and television news story.

This story put considerable pressure on local and state officials to create an effective partnership to address the city's major problems. The leaders of St. Louis's business community—who were involved in efforts to construct a regional light rail system connecting both sides of the river, build a new hockey arena, develop a new indoor football stadium to attract a National Football League team, and build legislative support for legal gambling—feared the impact that continued coverage of East St. Louis's decline might have on these new ventures. Public officials representing the suburban areas sur-

8. Robert Mendelson and Dennis Judd, *The Politics of Urban Planning: The East St. Louis Experience* (Urbana: University of Illinois Press, 1973), pp. 1-40.

9. Isabel Wilkerson, "A City Floundering at Rock Bottom," *New York Times*, 4 Apr. 1991.

rounding East St. Louis were concerned about the possible spread of East St. Louis's economic and social problems to their communities. The area's most important corporate leaders, while attending a regional economic development conference, identified East St. Louis's decline as the most important factor affecting the area's future. The city's state legislators were subjected to harsh community and media criticism for their perceived lack of leadership on this issue. Governor Jim Edgar was encouraged by his political advisers to strengthen his electoral base in southern Illinois by committing state resources to the stabilization and revitalization of East St. Louis.

STATE ACTION
FOR COMMUNITY
STABILIZATION

The Illinois state legislature passed the Illinois Financially Distressed Cities Act of 1990 to save the city of East St. Louis from bankruptcy. The bill provided East St. Louis with $34 million in state credit, which enabled the city to restructure its burgeoning municipal debt. These resources were funded through low-interest, general obligation bonds issued by the state of Illinois. The bill also established a state-appointed financial oversight commission, comprising seven individuals jointly appointed by the governor and the legislature, with the power to approve all city budgets, employment contracts, and service agreements. The East St. Louis Financial Advisory Authority (ESLFAA) is responsible for working with the East St. Louis mayor, City Council, and city

manager to enhance the effectiveness of the city's financial planning and management systems. With the ESLFAA's assistance, the city was able to negotiate its outstanding debt from $88 to $34 million and refinance it using low-interest state funds. This dramatically reduced the portion of the city's budget devoted to debt service, enabling East St. Louis to increase spending on basic municipal services. The ESLFAA will remain in existence, according to the Illinois Financially Distressed Cities Act, until the city produces 10 consecutive balanced budgets.

In 1991, the state legislature surprised many political observers by granting East St. Louis one of four highly coveted riverboat gambling licenses. The town of Sauget had been viewed as the community in southwestern Illinois most likely to be selected for this honor. But Gordon Bush, the newly elected mayor of East St. Louis, worked with a group of St. Louis investors to develop a competitive proposal. He then lobbied county and state officials to secure the license for East St. Louis by pointing out the desperate economic problems of his city. The St. Louis investors built a $43 million gambling boat and administrative complex on a riverfront site provided by the city of East St. Louis.[10] The Casino Queen Riverboat has been one of the most profitable gambling facilities in the state of Illinois. It has generated more than 1200 permanent jobs, 25 percent of which are

10. April Hattori, "East St. Louis Hopes Its Luck Will Change with Help from Mammoth Riverboat Casino," *Bond Buyer*, 12 July 1993, pp. 1, 28.

held by East St. Louis residents. The $10 million to $12 million in annual gross receipts taxes produced by the boat has enabled East St. Louis to expand and improve its municipal services while reducing its combined property tax levy from 23 percent to 16 percent of assessed values. The boat's success recently led its investors to acquire an additional 55 acres of nearby waterfront property on which they plan to build a hotel, entertainment complex, and recreational-vehicle park at an estimated cost of $30-50 million.[11] The large number of people brought to the city by gambling since 1992 has resulted in a dramatic expansion of the city's retail sector.

In 1990, more than sixty homicides took place in East St. Louis, three-quarters of which were alcohol- or drug-related. A thirty-person task force, comprising neighborhood leaders, school officials, police representatives, treatment specialists, and public health professionals, was established by the governor to develop innovative approaches to alcohol and drug abuse prevention, intervention, and treatment.

The task force was instrumental in founding the Metropolitan Enforcement Group of Southern Illinois, which is credited with establishing a regional database on alcohol- and drug-related crimes that can be used to direct local enforcement efforts. The task force has also helped local neighborhood organizations establish crime watches to provide information on illegal activities to law en-

forcement agencies and has recruited staff from local, county, state, and federal agencies to participate in anti-drug patrols and raids in East St. Louis. When a review of local substance abuse programs revealed the need for additional treatment beds, it worked with officials from St. Mary's Hospital to secure the funds to establish an in-patient facility for twenty adults. The task force also assisted local, regional, and state agencies to develop new programs for at-risk children to prevent them from becoming involved with alcohol or drugs. Several after-school and summer educational, recreational, and cultural programs are now operating in local schools, social service agencies, and public housing complexes as a result of the task force's efforts.

In 1995, the Illinois State Board of Education appointed a three-person committee to oversee the management of School District 189 in East St. Louis. This action was prompted by community protest against the deterioration of school facilities and the declining quality of education, widespread irregularities in local hiring and contracting, and a mid-season walkout of the city's highly regarded high school football coach. The state board appointed Richard Marks, the chief executive officer of East St. Louis's St. Mary's Hospital, as its chairperson. Marks has instituted widespread reforms within the district that have produced cleaner schools, better access to school supplies and instructional resources, and more classroom teachers. He is currently working with parents, teachers, and principals to overhaul the school district's antiquated cur-

11. Telephone interview with Joseph Quinn, Comptroller's Office, Casino Queen, 15 Oct. 1996.

riculum and to secure state-of-the-art multimedia instructional materials.

At the request of State Representative Wyvetter H. Younge, the University of Illinois at Urbana-Champaign, the state's land-grant university, has become deeply involved in community stabilization efforts in East St. Louis.[12] Since 1987, the university has spent more than $100,000 a year to fund student and faculty research and technical assistance addressing East St. Louis's community development problems. Since 1990, the university has concentrated its efforts on building the organizational capacity of community-based organizations through its East St. Louis Action Research Project (ESLARP). Participating students have worked with residents of the city's five poorest residential neighborhoods to complete comprehensive stabilization plans. Teams of students have also worked with neighborhood leaders to develop proposals, create designs, secure funding, and mobilize volunteers to complete the improvement projects featured in these plans. During the past six years, more than 800 students have completed over 100 planning and design projects for eight community-based organizations. Three neighborhood playgrounds and a municipal farmers' market housing eight minority businesses have been constructed, and more than thirty homes have been renovated.[13] The Winstanley/Industry

Park Neighborhood Organization, the community-based organization that the university has worked with the longest, has developed into a highly effective community development corporation with a professional staff of three and an operating budget of more than $300,000.

In 1995, the university assisted eight East St. Louis neighborhood organizations in securing funding from the U.S. Environmental Protection Agency to establish a citywide coalition to work on common problems. In the fall of 1996, the university opened its Neighborhood Technical Assistance Center (NTAC), where a professional architect, urban planner, and nonprofit management specialist are available to assist local residents, businesses, community associations, and municipal agencies to implement new community development projects. The NTAC is being jointly funded, on a pilot basis, by the city of East St. Louis and HUD.

FEDERAL ACTION
FOR COMMUNITY
STABILIZATION

The federal government's involvement in East St. Louis community development projects increased dramatically following Bill Clinton's election as president in 1992. The federal government has become an important participant in local efforts to improve police protection, housing conditions, economic opportunities, transportation services, and the quality of the urban environment. The federal government's contribu-

12. Kenneth M. Reardon, "Action Research in East St. Louis," *Planning and Public Policy*, 6(1):1 (Fall 1991).

13. Kenneth M. Reardon, "Creating a Community/University Partnership That Works: The Case of the East St. Louis Action

Research Project," *Metropolitan Universities: An International Forum*, 6(2):47-59 (Spring 1995).

tions to these local improvement efforts will be briefly described here.

W. Charles Grace, the U.S. Attorney for the Southern District of Illinois, launched a major new anti-crime effort in East St. Louis in early 1993. Grace recruited representatives from 13 local, county, state, and federal law agencies to work with neighborhood organizations and municipal agencies on crime prevention efforts. Bruce Reppert, first assistant U.S. Attorney, was assigned to assist participating organizations and agencies in devising a comprehensive approach to crime prevention in East St. Louis.

Reppert worked with local law enforcement officials to develop a uniform reporting form that residents could use to notify law enforcement agencies of suspicious or illegal activities taking place in their neighborhoods. The U.S. Attorney's Office launched a highly visible series of raids, which resulted in hundreds of drug-related arrests in response to thousands of citizen-generated crime report forms. The U.S. Attorney has also assisted the East St. Louis Police Department in securing funds to implement a community policing program. In the past three years, the city has successfully operated this program, which has transformed the role of the patrol officers assigned to these areas from that of reactive crisis intervention manager to pro-active facilitator of community problem solving. The assistant U.S. Attorney has also collaborated with local police officials in organizing two crime prevention classes, called the East St. Louis Police Academy, which more

than fifty community activists have completed.

The federal government has also become involved in several activities aimed at preserving and expanding the city's stock of decent affordable housing. The East St. Louis Housing Authority has received federal funds to rehabilitate more than 500 units of existing public housing in need of major renovation. This agency has also received a federal grant to replace two high-density apartment towers containing 640 apartments with low-density townhouse complexes.

The federal government has also been involved in housing improvement via HUD. HUD's Community Development Block Grant Program has provided funds to make emergency repairs to single-family homes that are at risk for abandonment. HUD's new HOME Program has been used to assist local community organizations involved in the renovation of single-family, homeowner-occupied housing. HOME funds have also been used to assist first-time buyers in purchasing units in two new East St. Louis subdivisions that have been successfully developed by local builders through a combination of conventional financing and municipal subsidy.

Another source of federal involvement in housing has been the executive branch. The Clinton administration's more vigorous enforcement of the Community Reinvestment and Home Mortgage Disclosure acts has led local lenders whose institutions had redlined the city to make significant new investments in its residential and commercial sectors.

The federal government has also attempted to support the city's various local economic development initiatives. HUD provided the city with a small planning grant to help it prepare an application for federal designation as an Enterprise Community. The city was subsequently designated 1 of 24 Enterprise Communities; this designation will provide it with an additional $3 million in economic development funds. The city has also received a $900,000 Youth Build contract from HUD to be used in training young unemployed workers in basic construction trades on sites where new affordable housing is being created. The federal government's decision to expand the Jefferson Memorial National Park along the East St. Louis riverfront has served to reinforce interest in the city's ongoing waterfront development initiatives.

One of the most critical federal government contributions to East St. Louis's economic recovery has been in the field of mass transportation. Federal support has enabled the Bi-State Coordinating Council to complete the first phase of a $464 million regional light rail system. The completed portion of the system connects St. Louis's Lambert International Airport to downtown East St. Louis via the St. Louis central business district. The MetroLink System, as it is called, is the nation's most successful new light rail system, and plans are currently being made to extend the line to the St. Clair County Airport. Seven and a half million passengers rode the MetroLink in 1994, and 12.4 million passengers used the system in 1996, representing nearly a 65 per-

cent increase over the previous year's totals.[14]

The MetroLink has dramatically increased the access of East St. Louis residents to the region's major new employment center, located close to the St. Louis airport. Hundreds of formerly unemployed East St. Louisans who do not own automobiles are now able to get to and from relatively well-paying jobs in the factories and warehouses near the airport. Plans to extend the light rail line from downtown East St. Louis to the St. Clair County Airport were recently modified to include passenger stations in two of the city's most distressed neighborhoods. Local community activists hope these stations will spur new commercial and residential investment in their communities.

The federal government has also attempted to work with East St. Louis officials to improve the quality of the urban environment in East St. Louis. A successful suit developed by an assistant U.S. Attorney during his off-hours against a Wall Street bond house resulted in a $7 million out-of-court settlement that funded a successful cleanup of illegally dumped trash within the city. The Federal Emergency Management Agency has acquired nearly 100 East St. Louis homes affected by recurring flooding caused by development in the suburban communities on the bluffs surrounding the city. The U.S. Environmental Protection Agency has cooperated with local officials throughout the Metro East region to create a new storm water management and flood control plan for the

14. Bi-State Development Agency, World Wide Web home page, www.bi-state.org.

watershed. The Environmental Protection Agency has used a portion of its remaining Superfund resources to mitigate serious industrial contamination at two former manufacturing sites in East St. Louis. The agency has also supported a wide range of environmental assessment, educational, and advocacy activities that were carried out by four different citizen organizations within the region. Finally, this agency has created an informal coalition of citizen organizations, private businesses, municipal governments, and federal agencies, called the Mississippi River Gateway Initiative, to promote community-based environmental planning to protect and enhance the environment of the Mississippi River watershed.[15] The U.S. Department of Agriculture has initiated a new $900,000 per year program, called the Urban Resources Partnership, which provides small grants that enable community-based organizations to implement local projects to improve urban environment. The Corporation for National and Community Service, a recently established federal initiative, has funded twenty internship positions through its AmeriCorps Program, offering East St. Louis residents the opportunity to become involved in local environmental enhancement and neighborhood beautification projects.

THE STATE AND FEDERAL
GOVERNMENTS' ROLE IN
STABILIZING EAST ST. LOUIS

On 26 April 1991, Gordon D. Bush was elected mayor of East St. Louis

15. Karen Lumino, *The Mississippi River Gateway Initiative* (Chicago: Environmental Protection Agency, 1995), pp. 1-5.

on a good-government and municipal reform platform. The broad base of support he enjoyed from the city, county, and region's economic and political leaders created a willingness on the part of many state and federal officials to assist his administration.

This increased level of state and federal government support saved East St. Louis from certain bankruptcy in 1991 and has enabled the city to restore many of its basic municipal services. These changes have, in turn, contributed to a dramatic improvement in the quality of life enjoyed by East St. Louis residents. Some of the city's most important achievements in each of these areas, which are described in this section, would not have been possible without the additional state and federal aid previously discussed.

The financial health of the city of East St. Louis has improved dramatically since 1991, when it was at risk for bankruptcy. The Illinois Distressed Cities Act of 1991 gave East St. Louis access to skilled public administration and municipal finance consultants, who assisted the city in reorganizing the municipality's human resources and municipal finance policies and procedures. The act also provided $34 million in supplemental state credit services, which enabled East St. Louis to retire a portion of its debt, allowing the city to expand its municipal services. The $12 million in receipts tax revenues generated by the Casino Queen Riverboat has helped the city to further expand its municipal services while reducing its combined property tax rate from 23 percent to 16 percent during the past four years. State action to restore the fiscal integrity of East St. Louis has been reinforced by an increase of approximately $5 million a year in discretionary grants from the federal government through its AmeriCorps, Enterprise Zone, HOPE, HOME, and Youth Build programs. The city, as a result of these changes, has posted three consecutive balanced budgets while reducing its combined real estate taxes, which enabled it to successfully reenter the municipal bond market in 1995.

These improvements in East St. Louis's financial condition have permitted the city to hire additional employees and purchase new equipment in order to improve the quality of its municipal services. Recent surveys conducted in several of the city's largest residential neighborhoods by the University of Illinois at Urbana-Champaign reveal a dramatic increase in resident satisfaction with the basic services offered by the city. Residents report more visible police patrols, shorter police and fire response times, better-maintained streets and sidewalks, cleaner playgrounds and parks, and restored municipal trash collection.

The city's physical appearance has also shown a dramatic improvement in recent years due to the combined efforts of state and federal officials. The U.S. Attorney's documentation of the malfeasance of a Wall Street bond house that failed to market city paper resulted in a settlement that produced $7 million to capitalize the East St. Louis Community Fund, a new foundation. These resources were leveraged by the fund's officers to cover the costs of removing tons of illegally dumped trash from vacant city lots and streets. Repaving and reinstallation of traffic lights along several of East St. Louis's main arteries by the Illinois Department of Transportation has further enhanced the city's appearance. The development of the Casino Queen waterfront district, the lower State Street area, the Lake Ana Estates subdivision, and the South End Homes subdivision—with funds provided, in part, by HUD—gave several of the city's busiest districts a much-needed facelift. Local beautification projects completed by the federally funded AmeriCorps and Urban Resources Partnership programs have supported ongoing neighborhood stabilization and revitalization efforts in several of the city's older residential areas.

Public safety is one of the areas in which the combined efforts of the state and federal governments have had the greatest impact. The coordinated approach to crime prevention launched by the Governor's Task Force on Alcohol and Drugs and developed by the U.S. Attorney's Violent Crime Initiative has improved crime reporting systems, provided police personnel with new equipment and technology, intensified police patrols, and coordinated local, state, and federal prosecutorial efforts. Systematic efforts have also been made through the federally funded Community Policing Program and the Citizens' Police Academy to enlist East St. Louis's neighborhood organizations in various crime-prevention activities. As a result of these and other activities, the annual number of homicides in East St. Louis has dropped from 62 to 35 between 1990 and 1995.

Investment in the city's residential housing has significantly increased in the past few years as a result of state and federal government regulatory and subsidy activities. Local lenders have responded to the federal government's tougher enforcement of the Community Reinvestment Act and Home Mortgage Disclosure Act by forming the Metro East Lenders Group to promote reinvestment in the community. In 1993, this consortium provided a $25,000 grant to the Winstanley/Industry Park Neighborhood Organization to provide credit counseling to residents seeking to enter the housing market. The success of this private sector initiative in helping East St. Louis residents secure conventional mortgages and home improvement loans led HUD to award the same neighborhood organization a $70,000 grant to extend its credit counseling services. As a result of these activities, as well as a $1 million direct-deposit program established by the state of Illinois and nearly $1.9 million in annual subsidies made available under HUD's Community Development Block Grant and HOME programs, the number of home rehabilitation projects being undertaken by local residents has increased dramatically. The number of public housing units being rehabilitated has also increased as a result of HUD's various rehabilitation programs. New single-family homes are now being built in East St. Louis with state and federal government assistance following 25 years when few such homes were erected. In 1994, ten new homes priced between $69,000 and $89,000 were sold in the newly developed

Lake Ana Estates subdivision in East St. Louis. These new homes were made affordable to working-class and middle-class East St. Louis residents by subsidies provided through the state of Illinois's Tax Incremental Financing Program and the federal government's Community Development Block Grant Program. In 1995, eight single-family homes were successfully developed in the city's South End by Community Planners and Designers, a private real estate development corporation, through a similar mix of state and federal subsidies.

The city's economic health has also benefited from state and federal government planning and subsidy programs:

1. The state's decision to award a riverboat casino license to East St. Louis has been the single most important factor in the city's economic recovery. Casino gambling has created more than 1000 new jobs, brought tens of thousands of visitors to the city, generated millions of dollars in new tax revenues, and led to the development of dozens of new retail businesses.

2. The second most important state and federal stimulus to the East St. Louis economy has been the establishment of the MetroLink light rail system, which enables city residents to access the growing number of new jobs created by firms located near the St. Louis International Airport.

3. Federal plans to expand the Jefferson Memorial National Park on the East St. Louis side of the river have generated considerable developer interest in the city's waterfront district. The developers of the city's

successful casino boat, who recently acquired an additional 55 acres of waterfront property where they plan to build a hotel, entertainment complex, and recreational-vehicle park, cited the federal government's park expansion project as a major factor in their decision to make additional investments in East St. Louis.

4. The federal government's selection of East St. Louis as an Enterprise Community will provide the city with an additional $3 million in economic development funds and will give the community's other federal funding requests immediate priority.

These public sector investments have led to several important new private sector investments, including the expansion of St. Mary's Hospital and the construction of the Gibson Health Services building.

CONCLUSION

The city of East St. Louis has been stabilized and is currently enjoying a period of modest economic growth. The quality of life enjoyed by most of its residents has improved dramatically, and many families are begin-ning to feel guardedly optimistic regarding the future. While the election of a highly effective mayor committed to good government and municipal reform set the stage for the city's recovery, a significant commitment of state and federal resources was necessary to save this aging industrial city. These public investments enabled the city to avoid bankruptcy, restore basic municipal services, and improve conditions within its major residential areas.

The East St. Louis case highlights the critical contribution state and federal government can make toward stabilizing smaller industrial cities, which have been devastated by suburbanization, deindustrialization, and globalization in the postwar period.[16] In a period when hundreds of smaller industrial cities are experiencing dramatic disinvestment due to global competition, the successful stabilization of East St. Louis offers important lessons for individuals seeking to assist these communities.

16. Robert A. Catlin, *Racial Politics and Urban Planning: Gary, Indiana 1980-1989* (Lexington: University Press of Kentucky, 1993), pp. 1-16.

Book Department

INTERNATIONAL RELATIONS AND POLITICS

STEINBERG, BLEMA S. *Shame and Humiliation: Presidential Decision Making on Vietnam.* Pp. ix, 397. Pittsburgh, PA: University of Pittsburgh Press, 1996. $40.00. Paperbound, $17.95.

In commendable depth, Blema Steinberg has researched the lives of Presidents Dwight Eisenhower, Lyndon Johnson, and Richard Nixon and contends that their early-life child-parent relationships shaped their personalities then and later, with far-reaching implications. Eisenhower, psychologically secure, was able to reject the urging of advisers in 1954 that he intervene in Vietnam. Johnson, a "humiliated narcissist," could not bring himself to reject prestigiously pedigreed advisers (brought into government by John F. Kennedy, subsequently martyred) who told LBJ that American intervention was necessary in 1965. (I entertained this thesis, which I no longer find especially compelling, in part of a 1988 *Political Science Quarterly* article, from which Steinberg plausibly draws.) Nixon, an "angry narcissist" whose life was a string of "repeated humiliations," responded to painful attacks on his administration by displacing his anger with the 1970 invasion of Cambodia.

To Steinberg's credit, she approaches old stereotypes of LBJ critically. I often found the portrait of Nixon's private life sensationalized, however. Goodness knows, he and Johnson were complex figures with insecurities; Eisenhower was indeed comparatively secure.

Early on, Steinberg writes that her psychological analysis is a complement to, not a substitute for, accounts of those presidents' decision making on Vietnam that emphasize environmental constraints and opportunities, including ideology, public opinion, foreign policy precedents, and partisan politics. Subsequently, however, she treats the political environment in ways that are not quite credible. For example, in comparing Eisenhower's decision not to intervene in Vietnam in 1954 with Johnson's 1963-65 deliberations, she portrays the environments of the two periods as similarly malleable: the fluid "domestic political environment was not a significant determinant of policy," she writes. Alert readers will anticipate such a conclusion when, drawing on George Reedy, she asserts earlier that it would not have been "especially difficult" in the early days of his presidency (November 1963, mind you) for LBJ to withdraw U.S. forces from

Vietnam. Though not unprecedented in the literature on the war, it is a remarkable claim about the American political environment in the immediate aftermath of JFK's assassination. My countersuggestion: the momentum of Vietnam policies across the Truman, Eisenhower, and Kennedy administrations would have made it distinctly hard (though not impossible, given a president's power) to choose such a policy in the 1963-65 period. Fewer Vietnam precedents burdened Eisenhower.

In the aftermath of Steinberg's and other scholars' analyses of Eisenhower and Vietnam in 1954, I urge future scholars also (or instead) to address, in depth, Ike's subsequent Vietnam policymaking that entrenched the U.S. in Vietnam. David Anderson's *Trapped by Success: The Eisenhower Administration and Vietnam, 1953-1961* (New York: Columbia University Press, 1991) made a good start at this.

Overall, I do not find the causal connections drawn in *Shame and Humiliation* between childhood, presidential psychology, and U.S.-Vietnam policies particularly persuasive. Still, those wishing to explore the possibilities of such causation ought to examine Steinberg's account.

DAVID M. BARRETT

Villanova University
Pennsylvania

AFRICA, ASIA, AND LATIN AMERICA

GREEN, MICHAEL J. *Arming Japan: Defense Production, Alliance Politics, and the Postwar Search for Autonomy*. Pp. xii, 206. New York: Columbia University Press, 1995. $40.00.

In the name of defense, nations rise to all manner of challenges, real and imaginary. Ronald Reagan convinced the U.S.

Congress to double his defense budget without a war in sight, and Dwight Eisenhower convinced the nation to fund highways and education—all in the name of national security. Today's citizens have finally realized that security means more than foreign marauders at their doorstep; it means jobs, profits, and superpower status, all of which emanate from hosting the world's most massive defense industry.

With the intense concentration on U.S. defense policy, few are aware of the raging battle that occupied Japanese politicians and bureaucrats during the postwar period. Michael Green has filled that need with the fullest exploration to date of *kokusanka*, the attempt to indigenize Japan's armaments production. Led by civilian officials from the defense agency who were abetted by members of the military establishment, the argument focused on the nation's security needs, namely, the resistance to increasing dependence on the United States, coupled with the ongoing dread of aggression from the Soviet Union. Interestingly, those in the hawks' camp had never been tested on the battlefield, since Japan had enjoyed relative peace and extraordinary commercial growth during this time period.

Advocates of *kokusanka* met fierce resistance from political forces. Doves cited Article IX of the Japanese Constitution, which prohibits excessive expenditures on defense for fear of the resurgence of the strain of militarism omnipresent in Japanese culture that led to World War II. Budget-minded voters and their allies in the government's budget bureau opposed copying the notorious U.S. example of bankrupting the treasury by simultaneously cutting taxes and raising defense expenditures. Japan also attracted opposition to *kokusanka* from American opponents, who suspected their trading partners of trying to cash in on their defense business.

Green's book is especially strong in detailing the interagency wars that crested in Japan in the 1980s and early 1990s, and providing a historical context for the mysteries of modern Japanese politics. It also offers profound insights into the effects of international economic shocks, such as the "floating dollar" of the Nixon period. The analysis reflects Green's expertise in Japanese politics, an understanding of the bureaucratic culture, and great skill at unraveling the nuances of the difficult and subtle Japanese language. He interviewed scores of respondents, pored over relevant documents, and won access to the highest levels of policymaking. *Arming Japan* represents a real contribution to the literature on U.S.-Japan relations, Japanese politics and government, and international security policy.

SUSAN J. TOLCHIN

George Washington University
Washington, D.C.

UNITED STATES

GREENAWALT, KENT. *Fighting Words: Individuals, Communities, and Liberties of Speech.* Pp. xi, 189. Princeton, NJ: Princeton University Press, 1995. $24.95.

At his lapidary best, Kent Greenawalt is the Canaletto of First Amendment scholarship, master alike of the big picture and exquisite detail. But modern constitutional law does not always provide structures worthy of this technique. *Fighting Words* compares recent United States and Canadian Supreme Court decisions about the proper scope of free expression in constitutional democracies only to discover that in law, as in architecture, sometimes more is less.

Greenawalt analyzes several controversial and sometimes contradictory rulings on flag burning, hate speech on and off the college campus, workplace sexual harassment, and obscenity and pornography. Although he criticizes the U.S. Supreme Court's "categorical boxes and blindness to nuance," he approves its general requirement that government demonstrate both a compelling interest and a genuine necessity to justify the regulation of expression because of its content or viewpoint. The Canadian Supreme Court, despite its "flexible and intelligent" balance of free expression against reasonable democratic limits under the 1982 Canadian Charter of Rights and Freedoms, restricts expression that the First Amendment would protect.

Unlike many liberal theorists, Greenawalt takes seriously—though he mostly rejects—the contention of various judges, feminists, communitarians, and other critical scholars that freedom of speech has gone too far. He weighs the familiar values of robust political debate and self-expression against arguments that some speech can inflict irreparable harm—on individuals by diminishing their dignity and autonomy, on sexually or racially identified groups and their members by denying them political, economic, and social equality, or on national or local communities by damaging their identity and cohesion.

Though he prefers practical reason to unwavering principle, he considers expressive flag-burning an easy case. Even if it undermines the flag's inspirational power and impedes national unity, political dissent is still the primary democratic virtue: flag worship is no "substitute for critical thought about government policy." The harder cases occur when speakers wield words or images—especially sexual, racial, or religious epithets, or pornography that degrades women—as weapons that "reinforce feelings of prejudice and inferiority and contribute to social patterns of domination."

Greenawalt searches for precise boundaries that will free serious proponents of ideas to express deeply offensive opinions without impairing other people's rights. Narrow government regulation may be permissible, he suggests, if the speaker deliberately humiliates specific persons in face-to-face encounters by hurling insults or epithets that communicate no idea except racial, sexual, or religious hatred or bigotry. He would protect nearly all other demeaning speech in public places. On the job and at the university, he would ban only direct harassment of workers or students who first ask the speaker to desist. He nevertheless challenges liberal individualists to acknowledge more fully the importance of "the threads of community in human life," of group identity and diversity in democratic society, and of equal rights and equal respect for listeners as well as speakers in constitutional law.

MARY ELLEN GALE

Whittier Law School
Los Angeles
California

SOCIOLOGY

KITTRIE, NICHOLAS N. *The War Against Authority: From the Crisis of Legitimacy to a New Social Contract.* Pp. xx, 304. Baltimore, MD: Johns Hopkins University Press, 1995. No price.

Throughout history, social theorists have written about rebellions against authority and crises of legitimacy. Authority also has been one of the basic unit-ideas of modern social science, which has produced a deep body of theory about the intimate relationship of authority, legitimacy, politics, and rebellion. It would thus take an extraordinary book to say something new and exciting about these subjects, but *The War Against Authority* does not take us be-

yond what we already know about legitimacy and rebellion.

The War Against Authority reports on who rebels against authority, when, where, why, and how. The range of principal actors here, however—from members of the Black Panther Party, leaders of Students for a Democratic Society, and airplane skyjackers to Russian revolutionaries, American civil rights leaders, and founding fathers, just to name a few—is too broad, and the coverage of them too shallow for effective analysis.

Attempts at analysis are further hampered by a seemingly haphazard use of theoretical material. Thus Kittrie emphasizes minor theories, such as Mosca's "political formulae," but gives little space to Weber's monumentally important theories of legitimacy.

Other theoretical weaknesses are also notable, including unsupported assertions. For example, Acton's famous aphorism, "Power corrupts and absolute power corrupts absolutely," is said to be a paraphrase of something Bakunin said. I know of no evidence that Acton was either influenced by Bakunin or that he paraphrased him in his now famous 1887 correspondence with Creighton. (The supposedly earlier statement by Bakunin did not appear until 1905, and only in Italian, in his book *Socialism and Mazzini.*) In the same vein, some sources are misquoted, such as Hannah Arendt, who wrote that "Negroes and Indians . . . had never been included in the original *consensus universalis* of the American republic." The word "original" is left out of the quoted version, leaving a very different impression from what Arendt meant to convey.

Democracy often makes it difficult to separate mere politics from rebellion and dissent. After all, democracy makes politics possible, and politics, not democracy per se, is the real basis of freedom, including the freedom to dissent, if not rebel.

The War Against Authority makes little effort to explore the meaning of authority and rebellion against authority in democracies as opposed to other forms of government. Clichés about changing the American ideal of the melting pot to one of a "people's potpourri," or about new social contracts, are no substitute for hard-nosed analyses of why democratic legitimacy has come under fire.

In the end, *The War Against Authority* promises more than it delivers. The book is selectively derivative, recapitulating as it does some parts of the massive literature on this subject but never getting beyond it. It may serve, at best, as a primer on this topic for those approaching it for the first time.

HOWARD G. SCHNEIDERMAN

Lafayette College
Easton
Pennsylvania

ECONOMICS

KAUFMAN, ALLEN, LAWRENCE ZACHARIAS, and MARVIN KARSOHN. *Managers versus Owners: The Struggle for Corporate Control in American Democracy.* Pp. xiv, 271. New York: Oxford University Press, 1995. $39.95. Paperbound, $19.95.

The authors of *Managers versus Owners* established an ambitious agenda for this small book. Kaufman, Zacharias, and Karsohn argue that managers developed a "professional ideology" of management to protect their large firms from political and financial controls. Furthermore, this group identity had a significant impact on the long-running American debate about the role of large firms and their managements in a society that traditionally viewed a decentralized economy as the best means of preserving liberty.

The authors seek to bring business history, specifically Martin Sklar's *Corporate Reconstruction of American Capitalism* (1988) and what they characterize as the "firm-specific" work of Alfred D. Chandler, into current management analytical frameworks through collective-action theory and interest group analysis. This works best in their treatment of the origins and development of the New Deal regulatory state. Drawing on Berle and Means's characterization of alternative approaches to corporate regulation as "trust" and "contract," Kaufman and his coauthors see debates about the proper role of the large corporation in political life as crucial to an understanding of the period. Relations with specific corporate stakeholders—shareholders, consumers, employees—were embraced by New Deal regulatory regimes; issues related to corporate governance continued under the benign regulation of states; and management became a "semi-public" activity.

Subsequently, in the 1970s and 1980s, management of large firms undermined the rationale for flexible corporate governance and management autonomy by opposing federal regulatory expansion and attempting to limit the impact of the market on corporate control. In Chapter 11, the authors test their arguments about management collective action on issues of corporate political legitimacy and managerial autonomy using contributions by political action committees in the 1980s. They find cohesion on such issues, in contrast to fragmentation on firm- or industry-specific positions. In a brief, final chapter, the authors argue for increased stakeholder participation and greater alignment of management collective identity with the American democratic heritage.

Managers versus Owners addresses an important topic in a thought-provoking manner. It is not an easy book to read, however. It is obviously a collaboration, and the acknowledgments make it apparent that it has undergone several revisions with more than one publisher. The authors' statement that "our narrative may have wandered rather widely" is, unfortunately, correct. Also, it is regrettable that a book in an important series, by a notable press, should contain many typographical errors in the text and notes and lack a bibliography.

WILLIAM M. McCLENAHAN, JR.
University of Maryland
College Park

OTHER BOOKS

AGUERO, FELIPE. *Soldiers, Civilians, Democracy: Post-Franco Spain in Comparative Perspective*. Pp. xii, 316. Baltimore, MD: Johns Hopkins University Press, 1995. $48.50.

BECKER, THEODORE L. and RICHARD A. COUTO. *Teaching Democracy by Being Democratic*. Pp. viii, 184. Westport, CT: Praeger, 1996. $59.95.

BEST, JUDITH A. *The Choice of the People? Debating the Electoral College*. Pp. xxv, 163. Lanham, MD: Rowman & Littlefield, 1996. $48.50. Paperbound, $16.95.

CAMPBELL, JAMES E. *Cheap Seats: The Democratic Party's Advantage in United States House Elections*. Pp. xxiv, 336. Columbus: Ohio State University Press, 1996. $60.00. Paperbound, $22.00.

ESPING-ANDERSEN, GOSTA, ed. *Welfare States in Transition: National Adaptations in Global Economies*. Pp. xii, 276. Thousand Oaks, CA: Sage, 1996. $75.00. Paperbound, $26.95.

FRAMK, CROWSON. *Bearing False Witness: An Examination of Propaganda, Its Eight Ploys—and How to Detect Them*. Pp. vii, 103. Pittsburgh, PA: Dorrance, 1996. Paperbound, $10.00.

GEOGHEGAN, VINCENT. *Ernst Bloch*. Pp. viii, 197. New York: Routledge, 1995. Paperbound, $16.95.

GREIVE, R. R. BOB. *The Blood, Sweat and Tears of Political Victory . . . and Defeat*. Pp. xiv, 631. Lanham, MD: University Press of America, 1996. Paperbound, $39.95.

HJELMAR, ULF. *The Political Practice of Environmental Organizations*. Pp. vii, 150. Brookfield, VT: Ashgate, 1996. No price.

KENNAN, GEORGE F. *At a Century's Ending: Reflections, 1982-1995*. Pp. 351. New York: Norton, 1996. $27.50.

KOOPMAN, DOUGLAS L. *Hostile Takeover: The House Republican Party, 1980-1995*. Pp. viii, 181. Lanham, MD: Rowman & Littlefield, 1996. Paperbound, no price.

LUND, MICHAEL S. *Preventing Violent Conflicts: A Strategy for Preventive Diplomacy*. Pp. xvi, 220. Washington, DC: United States Institute of Peace Press, 1996. Paperbound, $14.95.

NASH, GEORGE H. *The Conservative Intellectual Movement in America*. Pp. xvii, 467. Wilmington, DE: Intercollegiate Studies Institute, 1996. $24.95.

PETRINOVICH, LEWIS. *Living and Dying Well*. Pp. xi, 362. New York: Plenum Press, 1996. No price.

ROSENBLOOM, DAVID H. and ROSEMARY O'LEARY. *Public Administration and Law*. 2d ed. Pp. xiv, 344. Monticello, NY: Marcel Dekker, 1996. $150.00.

SHAH, A. M., B. S. BAVISKAR, and E. A. RAMASWAMY, eds. *Social Structure and Change: Women in Indian Society*. Vol. 2. Pp. 214. Thousand Oaks, CA: Sage, 1996. $27.50.

SNOW, DONALD M. and EUGENE BROWN. *Beyond the Water's Edge*. Pp. ix, 406. New York: St. Martin's Press, 1996. $35.00.

STIEHM, JUDITH HICKS, ed. *It's Our Military, Too! Women and the United States Military*. Pp. x, 309. Philadelphia: Temple University Press, 1996. $59.95. Paperbound, $19.95.

WEEKS, WILLIAM EARL. *Building the Continental Empire: American Expansion from the Revolution to the Civil War*. Pp. x, 177. Chicago: Ivan R. Dee, 1996. $22.50.

WORTMAN, RICHARD S. *Scenarios of Power: Myth and Ceremony in Russian Monarchy*. Vol. 1. Pp. xiii, 469. Princeton, NJ: Princeton University Press, 1995. No price.

INDEX

American Behavioral Scientist

Community-Oriented Research
Grassroots Issues versus National Policy Agendas

Edited by Greg Andranovich, *California State University, Los Angeles*
and **Nicholas P. Lovich, Jr.** *Washington State University*

The borders between community issues, national politics, and the global economy are becoming progressively blurred. Formidable international forces, such as the globalization of the economy, post-fordist production, and the advent of an information society linked evermore tightly by advanced telecommunications technologies — as well as a host of seemingly disassociated post-Cold War political instabilities — combine with demographic shifts to shape the condition of community life and contemporary public affairs.

Contributors to *Community-Oriented Research: Grassroots Issues Versus National Policy Agendas* provide empirical evidence of the forces changing the face of America's communities, and illustrate how communities are addressing these challenges.

Topics covered include:
- the role of community in economic development
- how one community took a proactive stance towards its collective future
- community-oriented policing
- how non-profits are responding to state tax policies
- the relationship between the community and the reinvention of government
- the introduction of distance technology to healthcare treatment
- the need to include global variables in community level analysis

Although the articles in this issue of **American Behavioral Scientist** vary in terms of topic, what they all make clear is that community empowerment is not evolutionary, but is volitional in character. *Community-Oriented Research* promotes the idea that it is grassroots determination that will develop sustainable communities — neighborhood by individual neighborhood.

Contents: Editors' Introduction: Community-Oriented Research / From Enterprise Zones to Empowerment Zones: The Community Context of Urban Economic Development / Community Collaboration and Public Policy Making: Examining the Long-Term Utility of Training in Conflict Management / Community-Oriented Research in an Era of Community-Oriented Policing Exploring Challenges to Non-Profit Status: Issues of Definition and Access in / Community-Based Research / Telepsychiatry in Appalachia / Checking Perceptions and Reality in Small-Town Innovation Research / Epilogue: Cities and Communities in the Global Economy: Rethinking Our Concepts

American Behavioral Scientist
Volume 39, Number 5 / March 1996
Individual: $11 / Institution $37

Subscribe Today!			
Sage Customer Service: 805-499-9774 • **Sage FaxLine:** 805-499-0871			
	1 Year	*2 Years*	*3 Years*
Individual	$70	$140	$210
Institutional	$248	$496	$744

SAGE PUBLICATIONS, INC. SAGE PUBLICATIONS LTD
2455 Teller Road 6 Bonhill Street
Thousand Oaks, CA 91320 London EC2A 4PU, England
SAGE PUBLICATIONS INDIA PVT. LTD
M-32 Market, Greater Kailash I
New Delhi 110 048, India

Initiating Change:
Theory and Practice

Edited by Louise K. Comfort,
University of Pittsburgh

As the twentieth century comes to its end, perhaps its most significant characteristic is change. Change which is universal, rapid, and unpredictable in its social, political, and economic impact.

Initiating Change: Theory and Practice explores the challenges facing the public policy and public administration community. These include how to anticipate, respond to, and, indeed, how to initiate change that maintains and enhances the goals and values of American society as defined through our democratic and political process.

This Special Issue of **American Behavioral Scientist** contributors speak from careers in academia and the public service, with their positions then debated by responding authors. Discussion includes how change should take place in health care, economic development, environmental protection, and world peace. It debates citizens' cognitive impairment, our ability to estimate the boundaries of our ignorance, the discrepancies between reason and action, organizational learning, the moral basis for change, the balance of good policy with good politics, the spatial dimension of public policy, and information technology in a complex social system.

This Special Issue of **American Behavioral Scientist** is a valuable contribution to the theory, teaching, and practice of initiating and implementing change, and will be of great interest to those who work, teach, or study in the areas of public policy, public administration, and the dynamics of social change.

Order Today!
Sage Customer Service: 805-499-9774 ■ **Sage FaxLine:** 805-499-0871

American Behavioral Scientist
Volume 40, Number 3 / January 1997
Individual: $11.00 / Institution: $37.00

SAGE PUBLICATIONS, INC.
2455 Teller Road
Thousand Oaks, CA 91320

SAGE PUBLICATIONS LTD
6 Bonhill Street
London EC2A 4PU, England

SAGE PUBLICATIONS INDIA PVT. LTD
M-32 Market, Greater Kailash I
New Delhi 110 048, India

American Behavioral Scientist

LITTER CONTROL AND RECYCLING

"The by-products of humanity have begun to directly affect most of our lives, and we have all but exhausted most of the easiest solutions."
— Editor

Edited by John G. Cope, *East Carolina University*

Americans produce garbage at an estimated rate of 160 million tons per year, which is about twice that of other countries. Individual behaviors that in themselves appear insignificant, multiply into a collective problem that ultimately affects everyone–landfills are reaching capacity. Communities respond to the trash problem with a mix of three basic solutions: bury it, burn it, or recycle it.

The articles in this Special Issue of **Environment & Behavior** explore attempts to advance studies involving recycling and litter control to the next level. Among the topics covered are recycling behaviors, the problems of reducing the amount of material entering into the waste stream, the need for interventions that foster long-term behavior changes, and the formation of the unique Shelby County Environmental Court, which works to develop an effective penalty system for controlling environmental problems in a urban setting. This court has become a model for communities throughout the United States. The litter control challenge remains to change large-scale normative behavior and implement new government policies.

Contents: George Jetson and the Tragedy of the Commons: Applying Behavior Analysis to the Problem of Waste Management / Solid Waste Recovery: A Review of Behavioral Programs to Increase Recycling / Litter Reduction: A Review and Integration of the Literature / Actively Caring for the Environment: An Integration of Behaviorism and Humanism / Encouraging Proenvironmental Behavior: The Environmental Court as Contingency Manager / The Effect of Commitment on Adoption and Diffusion of Grass Cycling / The Effects of Public Commitment and Group Feedback on Curbside Recycling

Environment & Behavior
Volume 27, Number 2 / March 1995 / 144 pages
Individual $15 / Institution $44

Subscribe Today!
Sage Customer Service: 805-499-9774 • **Sage FaxLine:** 805-499-0871

SAGE PUBLICATIONS, INC.
2455 Teller Road
Thousand Oaks, CA 91320

SAGE PUBLICATIONS LTD
6 Bonhill Street
London EC2A 4PU, England

SAGE PUBLICATIONS INDIA PVT. LTD
M-32 Market, Greater Kailash I
New Delhi 110 048, India

The Environment and the City

Editors: **Christine Meisner Rosen,** *University of California, Berkeley*
and **Joel Arthur Tarr,** *Carnegie Mellon University*

It is in "...the places where man's activities are most densely
concentrated — his settlements — that the environmental impact
is greatest and the risks of environmental damage most acute."
— United Nations, 1974

The distinguished articles in this Special Issue explore the city's impact on the natural environment. For thousands of years cities have placed demands on their sites and on the surrounding countryside for food, water, fuel, building materials, and places for waste disposal. As a result, the earth's natural environment has been altered in many profound ways.

A true perspective is gained on the interaction of urban development and its effects on the natural environment, through
a study of how the market system, government institutions, politics, technology, and culture have shaped the interaction.

Urban historians, as well as researchers, students and policymakers, will appreciate the comprehensive, four-dimensional approach taken by the authors in this volume:

- Effects of cities on the natural environment
- Impact of the natural environment on cities
- Societal response to impacts and efforts to alleviate
  environmental problems
- Examination of the built environment and its role and
  place as part of the physical context in which society evolves.

Contents: The Importance of an Urban Perspective in Environmental History /
Environmental Sensibility in Edinburgh, 1839-1840: The "Fetid Irrigation"
Controversy / Creating ecological Wastelands: Oil Pollution in New York City
1870-1900 / Sanitary Services and Decision Making in Houston 1876-1945 /
Building on the Land: Toward an Environmental History of Residential Development
in American Cities and Suburbs, 1870-1990.

Order Today!
Sage Customer Service: 805-499-9774 ■ **Sage FaxLine:** 805-499-0871

Journal of Urban History
Volume 20, Number 3 / May 1994 / 144 pages
Individual **$13** / Institution **$42**

SAGE PUBLICATIONS, INC.   SAGE PUBLICATIONS LTD
2455 Teller Road   6 Bonhill Street
Thousand Oaks, CA 91320   London EC2A 4PU, England

SAGE PUBLICATIONS INDIA PVT. LTD
M-32 Market, Greater Kailash I
New Delhi 110 048, India

The New African American Urban History

Guest Editors: **Kenneth W. Goings** and **Raymond A. Mohl**
both at Florida Atlantic University

In the 1990's there has been a virtual explosion of newly published research on the black urban experience. This outpouring of recent work is evidence of great vitality in the field and is collectively representing a "new African American urban history."

In studying the urbanization of the black population, scholars exploring 20th century African American history, are discovering internal kinship and communal networks, class and culture, and a diversity and complexity in black communities. The articles in this Special Issue of **Journal of Urban History** focus on the African American urban experience in Richmond, Memphis, Norfolk and Miami.

The diversity and creative vitality of the work in this Special Issue of **Journal of Urban History** illutrates the convergence of many new lines of investigation as researchers work to create a more accurate African American urban history.

Contents/Part 1: Toward a New African American Urban History / Mapping the Terrain of Black Richmond / Connecting Memory, Self, and the Power of Place in African American Urban History / "Unhidden" Transcripts of Resistance: Memphis and African American Agency, 1862-1920 / Making the Second Ghetto in Metropolitan Miami, 1940 - 1960

Contents/Part 2: The Shifting Historiography of African American Urban History / African Americans in the City: The Industrial Era, 1900-1950 / African Americans in the City Since World War II: From the Industrial to the Post-Industrial Era / Emancipation in New York and Philadelphia / On the Waterfront: Race, Class, and Politics in Post-Reconstruction New Orleans / God and Man in Harlem / Point of Conflict: Twentieth-Century Black Migration and Urbanization / The Truly Segregated?: Exploring the Urban Underclass

---

Order Today!
Sage Customer Service: 805-499-9774 • **Sage FaxLine:** 805-499-0871

Journal of Urban History
Part 1: Volume 21, Number 3 / March 1995
Part 2: Volume 21, Number 4 / May 1995
Individual $13 / Institution $42

SAGE PUBLICATIONS, INC.   SAGE PUBLICATIONS LTD
2455 Teller Road   6 Bonhill Street
Thousand Oaks, CA 91320   London EC2A 4PU, England

SAGE PUBLICATIONS INDIA PVT. LTD
M-32 Market, Greater Kailash I
New Delhi 110 048, India

Sage Urban Studies Abstracts

An International Information Service

Sage Urban Studies Abstracts keeps you up-to-date on the most recent — and important — literature available on urban studies. . . from publishers, research institutions, legislative groups, universities and information sources around the world.

An invaluable research journal, **Sage Urban Studies Abstracts** allows you to pinpoint the most recent urban-related materials and sources vital to your professional work, research, testing, and studies. . . easily, inexpensively, and quickly.

Carefully organized. . . easy to use for maximum ease and efficiency!

- Indexed by author
- Cross-indexed by subject
- Concise summary of over 1,000 books, articles and reports
- Comprehensive source list
- Citations from over 150 professional periodicals
- Cumulative annual author subject index

Sage Urban Studies Abstracts includes such important topics as:

- urbanization
- urban growth and development
- environment
- urban history
- city planning
- criminal justice
- urban economics
- transportation

These features comprise a timely, useful reference that will save you time and money — two commodities you can't afford to waste.

Quarterly: February, May, August, November

	1 Year	2 Years	3 Years
Subscribe Today!			
Sage Customer Service: 805-499-9774 • Sage FaxLine: 805-499-0871			
Individual	$110	$220	$330
Institutional	$345	$690	$1,035

SAGE PUBLICATIONS, INC.
2455 Teller Road
Thousand Oaks, CA 91320

SAGE PUBLICATIONS LTD
6 Bonhill Street
London EC2A 4PU, England

SAGE PUBLICATIONS INDIA PVT. LTD
M-32 Market, Greater Kailash I
New Delhi 110 048, India

The ANNALS of the American Academy of Political and Social Science

Local Governance Around the World

Editor: Henry Teune, *University of Pennsylvania*

This issue of **The ANNALS** explores the impact of democratization on local government and politics.

Local Governance Around the World looks at local and global linkages that are impacting local politics in countries throughout Europe and Asia.

The articles combine theoretical perspectives on change with empirical data from local political leaders. The central theme is that local politics must be examined not only simply as local-national relations, but in the context of global changes that are now directly impacting localities.

Local Governance Around the World will be of interest to anyone concerned with the future, structure, and strength of local politics. As the political landscape around the world continually transforms, the study of politics and governance outside of national capitols is essential for understanding the practical problems of change—especially in light of the fact that these changes are once again focusing on the grass roots of democracy and issues of local autonomy.

Order Today!
Sage Customer Service: 805-499-9774 • **Sage FaxLine:** 805-499-0871

The **ANNALS** of the American Academy of
Political and Social Science
Volume 540 / July 1995
Softcover: Individual $19.00 / Institution $39.00
Hardcover: Individual $29.00 / Institution $45.00

SAGE PUBLICATIONS, INC.
2455 Teller Road
Thousand Oaks, CA 91320

SAGE PUBLICATIONS LTD
6 Bonhill Street
London EC2A 4PU, England

SAGE PUBLICATIONS INDIA PVT. LTD
M-32 Market, Greater Kailash I
New Delhi 110 048, India